Checks and Balances?

Dilemmas in American Politics

Series Editor   **L. Sandy Maisel,** *Colby College*

Dilemmas in American Politics offers teachers and students a series of quality books on timely topics and key institutions in American government. Each text will examine a "real world" dilemma and will be structured to cover the historical, theoretical, policy relevant, and future dimensions of its subject.

BOOKS IN THIS SERIES

Checks and Balances?

How a Parliamentary System Could Change American Politics

Paul Christopher Manuel
Saint Anselm College

Anne Marie Cammisa
Suffolk University

Westview
PRESS

A Member of the Perseus Books Group

Dilemmas in American Politics

Copyright © 1999 by Westview Press, A Member of the Perseus Books Group

Published in 1999 in the United States of America by Westview Press, 5500 Central Avenue, Boulder,
Colorado 80301-2877, and in the United Kingdom by Westview Press, 12 Hid's Copse Road, Cumnor
Hill, Oxford OX2 9JJ

Library of Congress Cataloging-in-Publication Data
Manuel, Paul Christopher.
   Checks and balances? : how a parliamentary system could change
American politics / Paul Christopher Manuel, Anne Marie Cammisa.
      p.   cm.—(Dilemmas in American politics)
   Includes bibliographical references (p.   ) and index.
   ISBN 0-8133-3026-2 (hardcover). — ISBN 0-8133-3027-0(pbk.)
   1. Representative government and representation—United States.
2. Cabinet system—Great Britain.   3. Comparative government.
I. Cammisa, Anne Marie.   II. Title.   III. Series.
JK271.M2755   1999
324.6'3'0973—dc21   98-27075
                                                                              CIP

PERSEUS
POD
ON DEMAND   10   9   8   7   6   5   4

In loving memory of
Guido F. Cammisa
b. 11 June 1915
d. 5 January 1998

P75731

Contents

1 Introduction to the Dilemma   1

2 Why American Government Operates Under Checks and Balances, and British Government Does Not: A Brief Comparative History   41

3 Welcome to the World of Checks and Balances: A Legislative History of the 1994 Republican Contract with America   77

4 What If American Democracy Functioned Without Checks and Balances? 115

5 Some Ideas for the Reform of American Democracy 143

Tables and Illustrations

Tables

Figures

Photos

Preface and Acknowledgments

THIS BOOK STARTED as a discussion between two professors. One of us teaches comparative politics and government at Saint Anselm College in Manchester, New Hampshire; the other teaches American politics and government at Suffolk University in Boston, Massachusetts. Both of us have found that our students in some ways lacked a context when discussing American democracy. And both of us—the comparativist and the Americanist—found that we often drew comparisons between the British parliamentary system and the American presidential system in order to provide a context for our students—a framework within which they could expand their concept of democracy and their understanding of various political systems. In discussions with each other, we wondered what the United States would be like if it had a parliamentary system. And since we are married to each other, the discussions continued on a daily basis, and the idea for this book was eventually formulated.

One of the debates in the field of political science concerns the advantages of a parliamentary system versus a presidential system. This book applies that broad debate to the case of the United States and asks students to consider whether it is better for a democracy to function under a British-style parliamentary system (which may enable a legislative majority to dominate politics and facilitate rapid change) or an American-style presidential system (which may provide for a complex balancing of powers and incremental change). In the face of a parliamentary alternative to the American presidential system, *Checks and Balances? How a Parliamentary System Could Change American Politics* illustrates how the constitutional system of checks and balances functions. Throughout, the text explains how the institutional dimension of the political equation—sometimes overlooked by politicians and scholars alike—is of vital importance to a proper understanding of American politics. We hope this book will help American students better understand their own form of government, while expanding their knowledge of other governments.

There are many people who made this book possible. First, our thanks go to series editor Sandy Maisel, who did not dismiss our idea for this book as preposterous. Former Westview editor Jennifer Knerr also played an important role in the formation of the book. Present editor Leo Wiegman and assistant editors Adina

Preface and Acknowledgments

Popescu and Kwon Chong have provided support and valuable advice. Copy editor David Toole did an excellent job of teasing out the subtleties of our sometimes confused thought processes and sentence structures. Project editor Kristin Milavec was exceptionally efficient and professional. An earlier version of Chapter 4 was presented at the 1996 fall meeting of the Northeastern Political Science Association in Boston. We would like to thank all of the participants on the panel "History and Structure of Party Systems" for their very constructive commentary, particularly Eileen McDonagh, Arthur Paulson, and John Berg. We are grateful to the very useful comments made by the anonymous reviewers on both the original proposal and the subsequent manuscript. At Saint Anselm College and Suffolk University, we had the able assistance of several students, including Aaron Frei, Eliza Brown, Janice Camara, Michael Guilfoyle, Noelle Michaud, Michele O'Connor, Laurie Silverio, Jennifer LaPierre, and Caryn Eggeraat. The staff at both Saint Anselm College's Geisel Library and Suffolk University's Sawyer Library were quite helpful in finding obscure documents through interlibrary loan. A 1996 summer research grant from Suffolk University provided support for the research. Additional research for the book was carried out at Harvard University's Widener Library, Georgetown University's Lauinger Library, and at the Library of Congress in Washington, D.C. Needed nourishment during the final stage of this project was provided by the Montrose Spa neighborhood store on Massachusetts Avenue in Cambridge, Massachusetts.

Finally, we would like to thank our families for their unwavering support throughout all of our research projects. In particular, Paul's maternal grandmother, Elvira Assunta Lagomarsino, has nourished us with great Genovese food and old school values, and our parents, Barbara and Joaquim Manuel and Mary Ida and Guido Cammisa, have always been ready and willing to help us in any way necessary.

Sadly, Anne Marie's father, Guido, passed away during the final stages of the preparation of this manuscript. A Waterbury, Connecticut, native, he was a kind and loving man, who was very proud of his family and his Italian heritage, loved life, and lived every day to the fullest. He was particularly interested in this work and in our careers. We will miss him very much. *We dedicate this book to him.*

Paul Christopher Manuel and
Anne Marie Cammisa
Cambridge, Massachusetts

1

Introduction to
the Dilemma

The United States of America may be said to be the only
country in the world founded in explicit opposition to
Machiavellian principles.

—Leo Strauss

Why Does American Government Appear So Unresponsive?

THE 1994 MIDTERM LEGISLATIVE ELECTIONS marked a watershed event in American political history. Running on a ten-point legislative agenda known as the "Contract with America," the Republican Party gained control of both the House of Representatives and the Senate for the first time since 1954. When the 104th Congress convened in January 1995, all eyes turned to the new Speaker of the House, Newt Gingrich, who had played a leading role in the design of the contract. In a flurry of activity over the congressional session's first one hundred days, Gingrich's leadership resulted in the House's approval of nine of the contract's ten proposals. In spite of this rapid legislative work, however, most of the contract's legislative initiatives had not been enacted into federal law when Congress adjourned for summer recess. Why not? What was going on in Washington? Why did the American political system appear to be so unresponsive?

One answer to these questions may be located in the Framers' institutional design for the American republic. Fearful of the tyranny of a despotic ruler, or of a majority of the citizens, the Framers designed a system of government characterized by complex **checks and balances** and divided power arrangements. These institutions were designed to protect the rights of the minority of citizens and, as such, to thwart the ability of any elected government to quickly implement sweeping changes. Hence, the institutional constraints that the Framers placed on governmental activity played a big role in the stalling of the 1994 Republican Contract with America.

To illustrate the impact of American government's institutional design, consider what could have happened during the 104th Congress if the United States functioned under British-style parliamentary rules. The British Parliament is composed of two legislative houses: the House of Commons and the House of Lords. The rules of this system accord the legislative majority in the House of Commons the necessary tools for effective and responsive governance and enable the House of Commons to dominate the House of Lords on most legislative matters. Further, in this parliamentary system, the majority party in the legislature selects the prime minister. So, if the United States functioned under British-style parliamentary rules, legislative and executive powers would be combined in the powerful House of Commons (the British equivalent to the House of Representatives). The 1994 legislative election would have resulted in Republican domination of that body. When it came time to elect the political executive (i.e., the prime minister), the Republican majority in this fictional American House of Commons would have selected its leader, the conservative Republican Newt Gingrich of Georgia, to be prime minister. In that capacity, Gingrich would have had the power not only to steer the Contract with America quickly through parliament but also to immediately implement it as the law of the land. Since the chief executive is chosen by the parliamentary majority, and not elected separately, Gingrich would not have had to deal with a Democratic president who had two years of office remaining from his 1992 election. Rather, he would have been free to reform the system in even more profound ways. Of course, Gingrich also would have faced a perilous danger, since at any moment he could have lost a parliamentary **vote of confidence**, which would have toppled his government.

The possibility of American politics functioning under a parliamentary system in which a governmental majority would be able to dominate the political system is ripe with promises, challenges, and perils. At least initially, many Republicans would have been happy to have had Newt Gingrich as their prime minister, shepherding conservative solutions to America's problems through Congress. On the other hand, most Democrats (and probably some Republicans) would have shuddered at the thought of Gingrich having that much power. Democrats perhaps would relish the thought of giving the authority of a prime minister to some of their favorite congressional leaders—former House Speaker Thomas P. (Tip) O'Neill, a Massachusetts Democrat, comes to mind. Of course, Republicans would see a "Prime Minister O'Neill" as an unmitigated disaster. In short, neither side would be particularly enthralled with a parliamentary system during that time when their political opponents formed the legislative majority.

The Dilemma: Majority Rule Versus Minority Rights

The question of how American politics would function under a British-style parliamentary system reveals an inherent dilemma of American democracy, dating back to the formation of the nation: How can we provide for the effective rule of the majority and still protect the rights of the minority? Just as the nature of the American separated system made it difficult for the 104th Congress to implement quickly the Republican contract into law, previous Congresses have been unable to pass many items supported by a majority of Americans, including health care reform, gun control, campaign finance reform, and term limits. Many good explanations—including the power of lobbying groups, insider corruption, and the insulation of politicians from the voters—have been offered to account for the failure of the government to respond quickly in these areas.[1]

Although we acknowledge the wisdom of these other explanations, this book offers an institutional reason for what we perceive as the dilemma of majority rule versus minority rights. In our view, an understanding of the institutional design of American government is of vital importance to a full and proper understanding of American politics: The way we frame our political debate and representative institutions just may be of central importance to legislative and public policy outcomes. For instance, one of the reasons Congress appears to take so long to enact and implement legislation may be found in the Constitution itself. The Framers designed an institutional structure that, in order to block majority tyranny, impedes majority rule. As we will discuss later in this chapter, the American system of checks and balances allows for the possibility that a minority in Congress can hold up or block passage of legislation, even if it is supported by a majority in the full Congress or among the population. The Framers specifically thwarted the rule of the majority, reasoning that impassioned public opinion should be tempered by deliberative processes.

Specifically, this book—drawing on the insights offered by R. Kent Weaver and Bert Rockman, among others—asks whether the current American institutional framework continues to be useful as we approach the twenty-first century.[2] As indicated in Figure 1.1, Weaver and Rockman have suggested that since an analysis of the relative impact of various institutions in politics can become quite complex and unwieldy, it is useful to focus the analysis on three tiers of explanation. The first tier of explanation involves a broad comparison of presidential and parliamentary systems. Presidential systems rely on a **separation of powers** (that is, executive, legislative, and judicial powers are placed in separate institutions), whereas parliamentary systems rely on fused power arrangements. The second tier highlights specific variations within the two systems, that is, within different types of presidential models and different types of parliamentary models. The third tier focuses on secondary institutional characteristics that may affect either a presidential or a parliamentary system in a given country; these characteristics include whether a country is federal (divided into a central government and other subdivisions, such as states) or unitary, the role of the judiciary, and other relevant social, cultural, and historical factors. This work is interested in all three tiers, but will focus its explanation on the first.

Is it time to consider a parliamentary alternative for American government? If the political structures in the United States were modified according to a British-

FIGURE 1.1   Tiers of Explanations of Differences in Government Capabilities

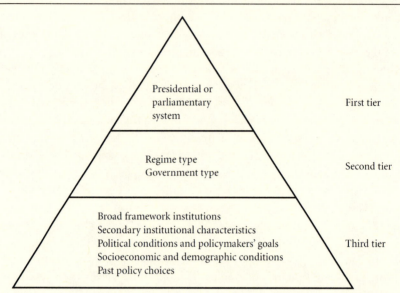

Presidential or
parliamentary
system   First tier

Regime type
Government type   Second tier

Broad framework institutions
Secondary institutional characteristics
Political conditions and policymakers' goals   Third tier
Socioeconomic and demographic conditions
Past policy choices

SOURCE: *Do Institutions Matter? Government Capabilities in the United States and Abroad,* ed.
R. Kent Weaver and Bert A. Rockman (Washington D.C.: The Brookings Institution, 1993), 10.

style parliamentary system, would American government become more responsive to its citizens? Alternatively, would a parliamentary system in Washington be
less respectful of minority rights than the current system? In this chapter we in-
troduce the dilemma of majority rule versus minority rights. We will look at the
problem of gridlock, examine the thoughts of Bagehot and Wilson, discuss six
common misperceptions about democracy, and then revisit the dilemma.

Is American Government Really Unresponsive?

It is not uncommon to hear people refer to the legislative body as a do-nothing
Congress or to describe the president in even more negative terms. Many Americans are frustrated that Congress has been slow to pass legislation supported by a
majority of the people. Although understandable, their frustration also indicates
a troubling unfamiliarity with the complex system of checks and balances in
American government. Since American government has been designed to be
more concerned with protecting the minority out of power than with facilitating
the rule of the majority in power, the very institutional design of American gov-

ernment may be seen as partly responsible for a perception among American citizens that the political system is sluggish, unresponsive, and distant.

The Framers realized that one of the greatest threats to democracy came from its very reliance on the people. In general, majority rule is viewed positively by proponents of democracy. It does, however, have its drawbacks. The Framers were primarily concerned with mob rule or what Madison termed the "tyranny of the majority." An impassioned mob might call for governmental action that in the long run would be detrimental to the public good. The majority might have selfish or irrational motives for its espousal of particular policies and might overlook the interests of the minority. The Framers believed that one role of government was to protect the interests of the minority against the passions of the majority. To do so, the Framers put in place a series of brakes on majority power. Thus American democracy is indirect (elected representatives debate and pass public policy); there are two houses in Congress (either of which may check the other); power is separated into three branches at the national level; and the system of federalism divides power between the state and federal governments. The power of the majority is dispersed and therefore muted. These brakes on majority rule also serve to slow down the policymaking process, leading to criticism of government as ineffective or inactive.

Much of that criticism has focused on **divided government** in Washington, which has been a pronounced feature of American government in the postwar period.[3] It occurs when there is a president of a different party than the majority party in the legislative branch. Although the Framers of the Constitution could not have predicted the evolution of the party system, they might have approved of divided government, in that it conforms with their desire to disperse power. If the president is of one party and the majority in Congress of another, then each branch has strong incentive to act as a "check" on the other. On the other hand, divided government has been held responsible by critics for a myriad of governmental problems, including obstructing the government's ability to get legislation passed.

In particular, critics have argued that divided government inextricably leads to **gridlock**, which may be defined as a stalemate in government over legislative priorities. Gridlock may function at many levels—including between the president and Congress, between the Senate and the House, or between the two parties within Congress—and prevents Congress from moving on legislative programs. Critics have argued that the net result of gridlock has been governmental movement without significant legislative accomplishments. Like a caged gerbil on an exercise spinning wheel, governmental gridlock generates a lot of motion without any forward progress.

In Defense of Gridlock

Not everyone thinks that either divided government or gridlock is antagonistic to good government. To the contrary, several observers have argued that divided government itself has resulted in the stability and longevity of the constitutional system. Seymour Martin Lipset, for example, has recently suggested that governmental gridlock is the very definition of responsive government, in that it exists because the people, by splitting the ticket in the voting booth, have in effect voted for gridlock. In his view, American voters since 1946 have used the midterm elections as a means to signal displeasure with certain policies of a sitting president but have still been ready to reelect him two years later.[4] Hence, gridlock has resulted in greater systemic stability because it enabled voters to express their displeasure with the sitting administration without challenging its fundamental stability. Similarly, former Congressman Bill Frenzel (R–MN) has lavishly praised the system of separated powers for its ability to filter out the temporary passions of the public from good public policy:

> . . . There are some of us who think gridlock is the best thing since indoor plumbing. Gridlock is a natural gift the Framers of our Constitution gave us so that the country would not be subjected to policy swings resulting from the whimsy of the public. And the competition—whether multi-branch, multi-level, or multi-house—is important to those checks and balances and to our ongoing kind of centrist government. Thank heaven we do not have a government that nationalizes this year and privatizes next year, and so on ad infinitum.[5]

Further, David Mayhew convincingly demonstrated that a divided government is not necessarily an unresponsive one. In a rigorous study of congressional legislative production from 1947 to 1990, he found that there were no significant differences regarding legislative policy outputs under periods of divided or unified government. Mayhew disputes the very notion that divided government and the American separated system produce either gridlock or an undesirable form of government; he argues that unified and divided governments do equally well in terms of getting important legislation passed.[6]

The Problem with Gridlock

So why do so many people think that gridlock is such a bad thing? How can an electoral mechanism that simultaneously enables citizens to signal displeasure with a sitting administration and protects the government from the temporary passions of the electorate possibly be considered in negative terms?

James Sundquist sheds some light on this question. Noting that even though Mayhew's research correctly shows that legislative output can be equally productive during periods of divided or unified rule, Sundquist contends that gridlock produces a poorer quality of legislation without much governmental accountability.[7] In his view, it is extremely difficult to hold a particular political leader or party accountable for his or her actions during a period of divided powers and competing legislative agendas. Indeed, if there is more than one center of power it becomes quite easy for a particular elected official to place the blame for failure somewhere else when a popular bill fails. The president can always blame Congress, even if his administration did a poor job. Alternatively, even if Congress had previously denied the president the requisite tools to do the job well, congressional leaders can always blame the president for poor preparation, poor leadership, and obstruction, among other things. The problem with divided government, then, is that citizens are unable to pinpoint one branch of government as the source of the problem. Neither the president nor the Congress is completely accountable to the public, and yet each has the other as an easy scapegoat. In a system of separated powers such as the American system (where the legislative power is in Congress and the executive power rests with the president), divided government is a real and serious problem.[8]

A Case of the Lack of Accountability
Under Divided Government

Consider, for example, the case of the national deficit increase in the 1980s under a divided government. Although all sides have acknowledged that the national debt rapidly increased during the Reagan presidency, they differ strongly over whose fault it is. Republican Ronald Reagan defeated the incumbent Democratic president, Jimmy Carter, in the 1980 election on a campaign that promised to accomplish five legislative goals: to build up America's defenses, to cut taxes, to cut the bureaucracy, to cut social spending, and to balance the federal budget by 1983. In the 1980 congressional elections, the Republican Party also won control of the Senate, which supported the president's legislative agenda. The Democrats, on the other hand, retained control of the House of Representatives and were opposed to the president's program. As Reagan started his first day at the job, the new president faced a hostile and confrontational House of Representatives, and the problem of divided government became the source of intense legislative battles.

Tip O'Neill, the liberal Democratic Speaker of the House, did not support the president's legislative package. However, after several meetings with Reagan, O'Neill agreed not to block the president's legislative program to increase defense spending and to support a tax cut, as long as Reagan agreed not to veto the Democratic budget, which maintained spending increases for some social programs, including social security. A bargain was reached, and a budget was passed that both cut taxes and increased spending. The net result of this deal between the president and the House of Representatives was that the federal government started to take in less money and to spend more in the early 1980s. Revenues went down at the same time that spending was going up. As one might surmise, when President Reagan left office in 1988 (he had been reelected in 1984), the national debt had significantly increased, despite the use of budgeting "tricks" to make the debt look smaller.[9]

So, who was at fault for the increased debt? The Democrats blame President Reagan, and point out that the president violated his 1980 campaign promise to balance the budget by 1983. In addition, they contend that the tax cuts and increases in defense spending that took place under his administration swelled the national debt, and they fault him for never having submitted a balanced budget. The Republicans, on the other hand, blame the Democratic-controlled House of Representatives for the increase in the national debt. They point out that since the Constitution grants Congress the power of the purse, the legislative branch is ultimately responsible for every federal dollar spent. Further, Republicans point to the record of House-approved bills in the 1980s as one that simultaneously increased social and defense spending and decreased taxes. Republicans claim that Speaker O'Neill and the House acted irresponsibly and that the House Democrats are to blame for the debt predicament. The Democrats, according to Republicans, took the easy way out by both approving President Reagan's tax decreases—which were very popular with the public—and insisting on increases in social spending, also popular with the public.[10]

In fact, even though *both* the executive and legislative branches had a hand in the increase in the national debt, neither side accepted responsibility, and both could plausibly deny their role. Each branch had ample evidence to blame the other for the rise in the national debt. R. Kent Weaver and Bert Rockman have argued that this type of poor policymaking and lack of accountability are inherent problems in the institutional design of American government. According to former Treasury Secretary C. Douglas Dillon, "the president blames the Congress, the Congress blames the president, and the public remains confused and disgusted with government in Washington."[11]

Critics of the separated powers system point to this lack of governmental accountability as a significant problem for American government. The system should be reformed, they say, in order to correct this problem, which impairs the government's very ability to govern. For example, Theodore Lowi has observed that although there is nothing necessarily sinister about a democratic government needing to run up a big deficit now and then, there is a serious problem when governmental spending outpaces revenue over a period of years, regardless of economic conditions. Lowi suggests that a constitutional system of divided powers leads directly to an institutionalized incapacity to govern. Such a system prevents elected officials from taking charge and, simultaneously, accords them with the means to deny any responsibility for government action.[12] In Lowi's view, presidential democracy in the United States is currently in "a pathological condition we must seek to heal."[13] Is Lowi correct? Has divided government led to an institutionalized incapacity to govern in the United States? What solutions are available to address these problems?

A Solution to the Dilemma? Enabling Majority Rule

The Englishman Walter Bagehot, writing in the nineteenth century, found fault with this problematic constitutional relationship between the legislative and executive branches. In his 1867 work entitled *The English Constitution*, Bagehot argues for a fusion of executive and legislative powers. Placing executive and legislative powers in the same branch, according to Bagehot, avoids altogether the problems of divided government. The government will never be divided if the legislature chooses the executive. The American system, in which both members of Congress and the president are chosen by popular election, creates the possibility that the majority in Congress will be at odds with the executive branch. In addition, Bagehot argues that the separation of powers makes it more difficult to pass legislation, since it must be approved not only by two houses of Congress, but also by a separately elected president.

Bagehot castigates the American system for its fixed and inelastic nature, which, in his view, imperils its citizens. The long and protracted procedures necessary to pass legislation make it difficult, according to Bagehot, for the United States to respond quickly to any unforeseen crises. Further, he contends that the division of legislative and executive powers leads to the problems of stalemate and lack of accountability: "The executive is crippled by not getting the law it needs, and the legislature is spoiled by having to act without responsibility: the executive becomes unfit for its name, since it cannot execute what it decides on; the legislature is demoralized by liberty, by taking decisions of which others [and not itself] will suffer the effects."[14]

Bagehot argues in favor of a parliamentary arrangement in which the elected representatives select the national leader. In contrast to the citizens in a system of divided powers, citizens in a parliamentary system are able to hold their leaders accountable for governmental action, in that the prime minister and the cabinet (both chosen from the legislature) are exclusively charged with the responsibility to govern. If they are found to be incompetent before their term is over, they can be forced from office: A vote of no confidence in parliament can bring down a government, and new elections can be quickly arranged. This characteristic flexibility of a parliamentary system enables the government to rule authoritatively and effectively and to adapt to the changing times.

Writing a few years later, and before he entered the political arena, Woodrow Wilson found himself to be in essential agreement with Bagehot's analysis. Wilson, who was elected president in 1912 and reelected in 1916, was the only American president to hold a Ph.D. in political science. Wilson argued in 1879 that the changing times at the end of the nineteenth century favored a more centralized form of government.[15] The national government faced a host of problems related to the industrial revolution: from how to protect workers to how to deal with a rapidly expanding economy. The national government, now called on to regulate new and changing areas of the national economy, was designed to function when the United States was still quite agricultural. Although he acknowledged that the system worked reasonably well in the eighteenth century and for most of the nineteenth century, Wilson insisted that the demands of the late nineteenth and early twentieth centuries required that American institutions be redesigned. In his view, the constitutional system of separated powers devised by the Framers was no longer useful precisely because it enfeebled the national administration, generating a leaderless government and a weak executive:

> Why is it that this leaderless character of our government did not disclose itself to an earlier generation as it has disclosed itself to us? The government has the same formal structure now that it always has had: why has its weakness been so long concealed? Why can it not serve the new time as well as it served the old? Because the new time is not like the old—for us or for any nation. . . . For one thing—and this can be no news to any man—the industrial revolution separates us from the times [before].[16]

Pointing out the many changes to American society brought about by the Civil War and industrialization, Wilson suggests that a form of parliamentary government should replace what he saw as an antiquated system of government. In particular, he criticized the committee system in Congress, where most of the work was done out of the public view. He preferred a parliamentary system, in which the cabinet, rather than congressional committees, would be dominant:

> I ask you to put this question to yourselves: Should we not draw the Executive and the Legislature closer together? Should we not, on the one hand, give the individual leaders of opinion in Congress a better chance to have an intimate party in determining who should be President, and the President, on the other hand, a better chance to

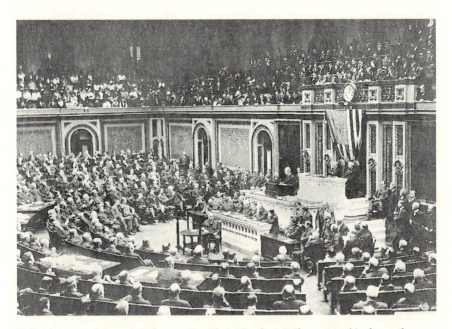

Before he entered the political arena, President Woodrow Wilson argued in favor of a parliamentary system for the United States. He is pictured here addressing Congress. Photo courtesy of Corbis-Bettmann.

approve himself a statesman, and his advisors capable men of affairs, in the guidance of Congress? [17]

An executive-driven cabinet government would be preferable to a legislative-steered committee government, according to Wilson. It could better concentrate political power, address the nation's problems, and be held accountable by the citizenry. In his view, American government needed to be able both to cope authoritatively with the many new challenges posed by industrialization and to be held accountable directly for its actions by the electorate. The best way to do this would be to centralize, rather than separate, powers.

Misperceptions About Democracy

Although the critiques of the American **presidential system** offered by Bagehot and Wilson ring true to some observers today, many people do not have a proper context to evaluate these views. For that matter, many people do not even have a clear idea of what democracy really is. In the United States, the public is so used to a presidential system, that many people often mistakenly believe that it is the only form of government a democracy can take. Further, it is ironic that many Americans today are prone to think almost piously of the Constitution and ignore the fact that like any other legislative outcome in a democracy, it was the result of political settlements among various factions at the Constitutional Convention. Such misperceptions impede any thoughtful consideration of proposals advocating the reform or even the replacement of the American presidential system with some form of a parliamentary regime. Very schematically, we can identify six broad areas of mistaken impressions:

- Misperception 1: The American Constitution defines modern democracy.
- Misperception 2: Democracies must always function in a federal system.
- Misperception 3: A democracy requires a national bicameral legislature.
- Misperception 4: The chief executive must be both the head of state and the head of government.
- Misperception 5: There can be only one winner in an election and only one representative per electoral district.
- Misperception 6: The American constitutional system would work anywhere.

Let us now examine each one of these misperceptions in turn.

Misperception 1:
The American Constitution Defines Modern Democracy

Many Americans associate the political structure of government created by the Constitution with the very definition of modern democracy. That is, many consider the separation of powers of the government into executive, legislative, and judicial branches; the checks and balances among and between these three branches; and judicial oversight (the power of the courts to invalidate actions of the other two branches) to be necessary and sufficient conditions for a democratic regime. The truth is, however, that the American Constitution has created only one form of democracy, and these three features are not present in all of the world's democracies.

To begin, let us define **democracy**. Joseph Schumpeter provides us with a useful starting point. According to Schumpeter, any political regime may be called a democracy if it meets at least the following three fundamental conditions. First, there must be broad and authentic competition among individuals, organized political groups, or political parties for all effective positions of power in the government, including the position of chief executive. Second, a high level of citizen participation is required, so that no major adult groups are excluded from the political process. Finally, basic civil and political liberties, such as the freedom of competition for political office, of assembly, of speech, and of movement, must be guaranteed. If all three of these components are present in a political system, it may be considered to be a functioning democracy. This definition builds upon the very simple premise that although a democratic regime does not involve a particular concoction of institutions, it is founded upon a basic respect for civil and human rights. Philippe Schmitter and Terry Lynn Karl remind us that democracies are not necessarily more economically successful, administratively efficient, or even more stable than nondemocratic regimes. Rather, in their view, democracy is properly understood as an ongoing process in which the representatives of the people peacefully settle disputes and establish public policy objectives.[18] As long as these conditions are met by a political regime, we can safely call it democratic.

Having defined democracy, let us now examine the three main institutional forms that it may take: presidential, parliamentary, and semi-presidential. The three characteristics of democracy and its three institutional forms are summarized in Table 1.1.

Presidential democracy is the system currently operating in the United States. Giovanni Sartori has identified three characteristics of the modern presidential system.[19] First, a president must be elected by a form of direct popular election for a term of office usually ranging from four to eight years. Remember that this is a necessary but not a sufficient condition for a presidential regime. Even though a country may hold national and direct elections for president, that does not necessarily imply that the president has real power. Second, in a presidential system the chief executive may be neither appointed nor dismissed by a legislative vote—executive power derives from a popular mandate, not from the legislative branch.[20] Third, the president is in exclusive charge of the executive branch and faces no competition from senior policymakers or from cabinet officials.[21]

Further, Juan Linz has observed that one of the most important features of a presidential system is the concept of **dual-democratic legitimacy** for the executive and legislative branches of government; that is, under the rules of presidential democracy both the executive and the legislature are elected independently by the people and therefore enjoy separate bases of legitimacy. This leads to a certain inflexibility of the system, because no matter how effective or incompetent a president may be, the legislative branch does not have the right to remove the presi-

TABLE 1.1   Key Characteristics and Variations of Democratic Regimes

Key Characteristics of Democracy
- Competition for office
- A high level of citizen participation
- Guarantee of basic civil and political liberties

Key Variations of Democracy
- Presidential system
- Parliamentary system
- Dual-executive (semi-presidential) system

Key Characteristics of a Presidential System of Democracy
- Separation of legislative (congressional) and executive (presidential) powers
- Direct popular election of the president
- The chief executive may be neither appointed nor dismissed by a legislative vote
- The president is in exclusive charge of the executive branch
- Separate elections (and separate bases of legitimacy) for the president and Congress

Key Characteristics of a Parliamentary System of Democracy (Westminster model)
- Legislative and executive functions are fused
- Prime minister is also head of the majority party of the Parliament
- Cabinet members are chosen by the prime minister from members of the majority party in the legislature
- As long as the legislative majority is maintained, the prime minister can expect to have all of his or her party's legislation passed without any revisions from the opposition

Key Characteristics of a Dual-Executive System (or Semi-Presidential System) of Democracy
- Powers are both fused and separated
- Directly elected president with constitutional powers
- Prime minister chosen from majority party in parliament

dent unless the president has committed a criminal act.[22] Indeed, impeachment is one way a presidential system might eliminate a president who has broken the law, although it is a difficult and lengthy process.

In addition, under a presidential system executive and legislative branches of government compete with each other over legislation. The legislative branch subdivides its membership into several committees and charges each with gathering relevant information on the issue over which it has jurisdiction. Once obtained, that information will enable the legislature to vie with the president over legislative items and priorities. This can lead to the problem of gridlock discussed earlier.

Parliamentary democracy stands in contrast to presidential democracy. Although there are several variations of this system in the world, the parliamentary system used in Great Britain is the world's most renowned form. Arend Lijphart has referred to the British system as the majoritarian-confrontational system;[23] it is also known as the **Westminster parliamentary model** (named for the county in which the British Parliament is located).[24] As we shall discuss in Chapter 2, this system provides for a close connection between the executive and legislative branches. Further, the British prime minister, who is the political executive, is also the head of the majority party in the House of Commons.[25] The prime minister chooses a cabinet from members of the majority party in the legislature, and the cabinet is collectively responsible to the House of Commons. As long as the legislative majority is maintained, the prime minister can expect to have all of his party's legislation passed without any revisions from the opposition. The prime minister is responsible to Parliament and must maintain the support of the governing party. Variations of the Westminster parliamentary system are used in many countries, including Greece and Ireland.[26]

The **dual-executive or semi-presidential regime** is an amalgamation of presidential and parliamentary systems. It features *both* a president and a prime minister. Concocted by French leader Charles de Gaulle, it was first introduced in the 1958 Fifth Republic Constitution. De Gaulle sought to create a strong presidency capable of responding to major threats to national security. At that time the institutional problem for France was, in de Gaulle's estimation, a weak chief executive: The parliamentary French Third Republic (1870–1939) simply collapsed when the Germans invaded, and for a variety of reasons, the parliamentary French Fourth Republic (1947–1958) disintegrated when Algeria demanded independence from French colonial rule. De Gaulle argued that a strong executive was necessary to lead the country though these types of crises. But he also understood the need for the legislature to continue to function under the parliamentary rules that it had more or less followed since 1870. The 1958 Constitution provides for a parliamentary legislature and grants the president a number of important emergency powers to deal with a crisis.

The French dual-executive system created a unique mélange of the American and English systems, in that executive and legislative powers are *separated and fused at the same time:* Analogous to the United States, there is an elected president with constitutional powers; similar to the United Kingdom, there is a prime minister who is both the chief executive and the head of the legislative chamber. Following a parliamentary system, the prime minister is selected by the majority party in the legislature, and following a presidential system, the president is directly elected by the citizens, according to the constitutional referendum of 1963.

Critics have pointed to a number of dangers created by a system that has institutionalized executive rivals and that has thus created the possibility of a battle between the president and the prime minister for control of the government. Under a

France operates under a dual-executive arrangement. In this photo, taken during the period known as co-habitation, French Prime Minister Jacques Chirac (at left) smiles as French President François Mitterrand answers a question at a 27 June 1986 press conference. Photo courtesy of Reuters/Corbis-Bettmann.

dual-executive system, divided government is called **co-habitation:** that situation when the president is of a different party than the prime minister. In France, co-habitation first occurred from 1986 to 1988, when the socialist president, François Mitterrand, had to deal with a rightist Gaullist majority, led by Prime Minister Jacques Chirac, in the National Assembly. The system worked well for a number of reasons, notably because President Mitterrand sought only to criticize the prime minister, not to obstruct his government and force a constitutional crisis.

There is a presidential-parliamentarian crossbreed in Portugal as well. In contrast to the French case, the Portuguese dual-executive model is more of a parliamentary system with a president. Although the president has independent authority and legitimacy outside of the National Assembly, the law-making function rests with the prime minister and the National Assembly. Further, the president is expected to monitor the activities of the government, and he or she may veto legislation. In the event of a stalemate in the National Assembly, the president has the power to dismiss the prime minister, appoint a new prime minister, or call for new elections. This moderating role has been very important for Portugal during its recent transition to, and consolidation of, a democratic regime after forty-

The Portuguese constitution provides for a dual-executive democratic system. Here President-elect Mario Soares (at right) places his hand over the Portuguese constitution as he takes the oath of office on 9 March 1986, while outgoing President Ramalho Eanes (at left) listens. Administering the oath of office is Parliament President Fernando Amaral. Photo courtesy of Reuters/Corbis-Bettmann.

eight years of dictatorial rule. The president is elected by universal suffrage to a five-year term, and no president may serve more than two consecutive terms.[27]

The institutional structures of France and Portugal have attempted to find an appropriate fit between the presidential and parliamentary models of democratic government in terms of each country's particular historical development and national characteristics. In each case, the net result has led to lengthy and enduring periods of democratic stability.

As the above review of presidential, parliamentary, and semi-presidential systems clearly indicates, there is not one set institutional pattern for contemporary democracies. As Table 1.2 shows, there are many different types of institutional arrangements operating in contemporary democracies. Some parliamentary systems fuse, rather than separate, the executive and legislative branches. In some cases the legislative branch is even sovereign over the judicial branch. In short, there are political systems elsewhere in the world that significantly deviate from the American constitutional system but are nonetheless democratic.

TABLE 1.2   A Sample of Contemporary Democracies Using Different Constitutional
Arrangements

	Separation of Powers	Judicial Review	Presidential or Parliamentary
Brazil	Yes	Yes	Presidential
Canada	Yes	Yes	Parliamentary
France	Yes	Yes	Semi-Presidential
Germany	No	Yes	Parliamentary
India	Yes	Yes	Parliamentary
Israel	No	Yes	Parliamentary
Italy	Yes	Yes	Parliamentary
Japan	No	Yes	Parliamentary
Portugal	Yes	Yes	Semi-Presidential
Spain	No	Yes	Parliamentary
United Kingdom	No	No	Parliamentary
United States	Yes	Yes	Presidential

SOURCE: *The World Almanac and Book of Facts, 1998* (Mahwah, N.J.: Reference Books, 1997), and
from Thomas E. Patterson, *We the People,* 2d ed. (New York: McGraw-Hill Publishing, 1998), 79.

Misperception 2: Democracies Must Function in a Federal System

The Framers of the American Constitution devised the system of intergovern-
mental relations known as **federalism,** in which powers are divided between the
national and state governments. Some students incorrectly extend this American
feature to other countries and assume that all democracies must function under
federalism. It may surprise you to learn that not only are there many forms of federalism, but some democracies do not use a federal arrangement at all.

First, let us define federalism. William Riker has defined federalism as "a political organization in which the activities of government are divided between regional governments and a central government in such a way that each kind of
government has some activities on which it makes final decision."[28] In the United
States, both the federal government and the fifty state governments have rights
under the Constitution. When conflicts arise between a state and the federal government, or between two or more states, the Constitution charges the Supreme
Court with the responsibility of settling those disputes. The system of federalism
was invented by the Framers of the Constitution as a way both to ensure that the
national government would be strong enough to function effectively and to allow
the states autonomy in local affairs.

The strength of the American federal system lies in the fact that the relationship between the national and state governments is somewhat ill defined. For example, the Tenth Amendment (part of the Bill of Rights) states that "the powers not delegated to the United States by the Constitution, nor prohibited by it to the States, are reserved to the States respectively, or to the people." In contrast, Article VI asserts that the Constitution and all federal laws made under it "shall be the supreme law of the land," regardless of any "laws of any state to the contrary." Although Article VI gives the balance of power to the federal government, the Tenth Amendment shifts that balance toward the states. The Framers, fearful of a repeat of the weak government under the Articles of Confederation, shored up the powers of the new national government. But the states would not ratify the Constitution unless there were some guarantees of their autonomy.

Throughout American history, the federal government has increased its power and authority as the country has grown larger, the economy has expanded, and the issues that the national government deals with have become more complex. Periodically, the states have made attempts to increase their power vis-à-vis the federal government, with increasing success as the twentieth century draws to a close. The unique feature of American federalism is that it recognizes a sort of dual citizenship: Individuals are citizens of the state in which they reside as well as of the nation as a whole. Although the distinction may not seem obvious, it is nonetheless important. One of the major problems under the Articles of Confederation was that the federal government was a loose confederation of *states*. Individuals were citizens of the state in which they resided; and states were members of the confederation. Under the Constitution, it is not the states that have formed the government, but the people themselves. This lends the federal government legitimacy in a democracy, which relies on popular consent. Although states were granted rights under the Constitution, in practice the federal government has had the upper hand. In recent decades, states have reasserted their rights to make autonomous decisions, and the federal government has devolved some of the powers it has taken on, giving them back to the states. Welfare is just one example of a government program that had been increasingly centralized after World War II, but has recently been decentralized, giving more power back to the states.

Although invented in the United States, federalism today exists in many variations throughout the world. Spain, for example, adopted a quasi-federal structure in 1978, in which the central government shares powers with each of seventeen autonomous communities. Article II of the 1978 Spanish Constitution states that "the Constitution is based on the indissoluble unity of the Spanish nation, the common and indivisible motherland of all Spaniards, and recognizes and guarantees the right to autonomy of the nationalities and regions of which it is composed and the common links which bind them together." The 1978 Spanish Constitution recognizes both the important unifying role of the central government and the need for some local control. Or, as Kerstin Hamann has aptly observed, "even if Spain is not a 'pure' federal state according to some definitions, it has been and still is undergoing a process of federalization—that is, moving from a unitary state to a federal state."[29] Spain adopted this quasi-federal system after the 1975 death of the dictator General Francisco Franco (who had favored a unitary system) for two main reasons: First, it was a reaction against some thirty-five years of over-centralization under Franco; and second, it was a response to many regional demands that the new democracy devise an arrangement that would find an appropriate fit between an effective national government and regional autonomy.[30]

In contrast, other contemporary democracies function under a **unitary political system:** one in which the central government exercises authority over the regional or local governments. Even though there may be elected city governments or elected regional governments under a unitary system, ultimate power rests with the central government. For example, in Great Britain, which uses a unitary system, Parliament may grant more power, or may take power away, from local officials.[31] The central government retains ultimate sovereignty over all of the regions and faces little competing sources of power.

In recent years, many central governments that use a unitary system have transferred some of their powers to local authorities. Known as devolution or regionalization, this process is similar to what has occurred in the United States. The national government decentralizes its own power by giving authority back to the subnational units; that is, devolution involves the transfer of some central powers back to the regions. This process has come about due to demands by inhabitants for more say on political decisions that affect their towns and communities. In Great Britain, regional assemblies have been instituted in response to demands by an overwhelming majority of the citizens in Wales and Scotland. The future implications of devolution for unitary systems are unclear, as Michael Curtis has recently observed:

> For comparison the distinction between federal and unitary systems is helpful, but modern trends in government have sometimes blurred the distinction. In many federal systems, such as the United States, the central institutions have grown stronger, while in some unitary states, such as Britain and France, some decentralization of power has occurred to regions and local authorities.[32]

In general, legislatures functioning under a federal system have more limited powers than those under a unitary system. One of the most convincing explanations for this phenomenon is that federal systems force national legislatures to contend with the legitimate authority of, and competing claims from, state or local governments. Central governments in a unitary framework face no such challenges for power and authority.[33]

Finally, a confederal system may be defined as a union of separate states that retain their autonomy but cooperate in certain common areas. From 1781 to 1787 the United States functioned under a confederal system. Under the Articles of Confederation, each individual state retained its own power and autonomy; the states were connected to each other by a weak national government. The American confederation was not an effective system. The national government did not have the power to tax, which meant that it did not have the power to raise funds either to pay debts left over from the War of Independence or to properly provide a national defense. The system enabled local interests to dominate, even at the expense of the national good. As we shall see in Chapter 2, the American Constitutional Convention in 1787 was originally called to find solutions to the problems inherent in the confederal system. There are no nations currently operating under a confederal system, and the closest modern day example of a confederal system may be the United Nations. Under the United Nations Charter, certain legal guarantees have generally allowed member states to protect their sovereignty from the world government (this is especially true for those nations who sit on the powerful United Nations Security Council).

Table 1.3 demonstrates the wide variety of federal and unitary systems currently used by contemporary democracies.

TABLE 1.3   A Sample of Contemporary Democracies Using Federal or Unitary Arrangements

	Federal or Unitary
Brazil	Federal
Canada	Federal
France	Unitary
Germany	Federal
India	Federal
Italy	Federal
Japan	Unitary
Portugal	Unitary
Spain	Federal
Sweden	Unitary
United Kingdom	Unitary
United States	Federal

SOURCE: *The World Almanac and Book of Facts, 1998* (Mahwah, N.J.: Reference Books, 1997), and from Thomas E. Patterson, *We the People,* 2d Ed. (New York: McGraw-Hill Publishing, 1998), 38.

Misperception 3:
There Must Be a National Bicameral Legislature

American government in Washington, D.C., is characterized by three branches of government (i.e., the executive, legislative, and judicial). The legislature is further divided into two houses: the House of Representatives and the Senate. Given this structure, some Americans have come to the mistaken conclusion that any democracy must have a national **bicameral legislature** as well. The truth is, however, that although some democratic countries do have two legislative chambers as does the United States, other countries only have one legislative chamber, or a **unicameral legislature**. There is no simple formula to account for why some countries have a single chamber and others have two: The decision characteristically reflects a country's size, as well as its political, historical, and cultural choices and experiences.

Whether unicameral or bicameral, the legislature in any democratic country is primarily charged with a law-making function: the process of preparing, debating, and passing laws. Its members consider and debate bills, which are proposals for legislative action. The discussion among legislators over bills occurs during legislative debate, which takes place on the floor of the legislature. Throughout the legislative debate, the political party in the minority plays the important function of criticizing the actions of the majority and of offering the public an alternative vision and alternative policies.

Different legislatures are governed by various types of rules. Some rules, including those governing the United Kingdom, are designed to give the majority party more control, and others, such as the rules in the United States, enable the minority to slow down the initiatives of the majority. As we shall demonstrate in Chapter 2, the Parliament actually has a minimal role in formulating proposals of law in the United Kingdom, because the prime minister's cabinet sends legislation that is already in advanced form to the floor for consideration. This procedure holds true for many Westminster-style parliamentary democracies. The American Congress, on the other hand, is a legislature that actually formulates policy, subject to executive approval.

In bicameral legislatures, the two chambers have historically been referred to as the upper and lower chambers or houses. Gregory Mahler has noted that the terms were developed in the United Kingdom. Originally, the House of Lords represented the upper segment of the population, and was considered a more prestigious body, whereas the House of Commons represented the lower strata of society. In the period since the democratic revolutions of the seventeenth and eighteenth centuries, however, the lower chamber has become the dominant chamber in the United Kingdom and elsewhere. Today the lower house in a legislature is representative of the entire population, whereas, the upper house may represent one of several possible constituencies in a country, depending upon the case: either the former aristocratic element in a society, such as the House of Lords in the United Kingdom, or the geographical interests of a region or a state, such as the Senate in the United States and the *Bundesrat* in Germany.[34]

Both chambers do not have equal power in every bicameral country. In Germany, for example, the lower chamber (the *Bundestag*) represents the national population as expressed in electoral results, whereas the upper chamber (the *Bundesrat*) represents the interests of the states or *Laander*. Although both chambers are of roughly equal power when it comes to state issues, the lower chamber in Germany is more able to dominate the upper one on other matters. In the United Kingdom, the lower chamber has more power than the upper as well.

Some contemporary democracies function with a unicameral legislature: a legislature with only one chamber. In general, small countries are more likely to function with a unicameral legislature than are large countries. There may be little need for an upper chamber to represent the territorial interests of states or regions in a country with a small territory.

Finally, Jean Blondel has found that whereas the vast majority of federal regimes in the world function with bicameral legislatures, there is no clear pattern with unitary regimes. Some unitary regimes, including France and Britain, function with a bicameral legislature. Others, such as Portugal, have a unicameral legislature.[35] Table 1.4 indicates some of the legislative institutional variation in democratic countries.

Misperception 4:
The Chief Executive Must Be Both the Head of State and the Head of Government

Given the fact that the American president is both the head of government and the head of state, there is a misperception that only one executive will always perform both of these roles under a democratic setting. However, that does not occur in all contemporary democracies. For instance, these two executive roles are divided in England, where the prime minister is the head of government and the monarch is the head of state.

By way of definition, the **head of government** is charged with effective national administration, whereas the **head of state** is asked to carry out symbolic functions, such as representing the country at the Olympics or appearing in public

TABLE 1.4   A Sample of Contemporary Democracies Using Different Legislative Arrangements

	One House or Two	If Two Houses, Which One Has More Power?
Brazil	Two	Roughly equal powers between two houses
Canada	Two	Lower house dominates
France	Two	Lower house dominates
Germany	Two	Lower house dominates
India	Two	Lower house dominates
Italy	Two	Roughly equal powers between two houses
Japan	Two	Lower house dominates
Portugal	One	Only one house
Spain	Two	Lower house dominates
Sweden	One	Only one house
United Kingdom	Two	Lower house dominates
United States	Two	Roughly equal powers between two houses

SOURCE: *The World Almanac and Book of Facts, 1998* (Mahwah, N.J.: Reference Books, 1997); Gregory S. Mahler, *Comparative Politics: An Institutional and Cross-National Approach*, 2d Ed. (Englewood Cliffs, N.J.: Prentice-Hall, 1995); Gabriel Almond and G. Bingham Powell, Jr., *Comparative Politics Today*, 6th Ed. (New York: HarperCollins, 1996).

during national holidays. These are two distinct executive roles but may be performed by the same person in some countries. In other countries these two roles are performed by two people.

In general, the head of government—given various names, such as prime minister, premier, or chancellor—is directly elected to office by the people or by the majority party in the legislature. On the other hand, the head of state—known as king, emperor, or president—may be elected to office, assume office by tradition, or be appointed. In addition, it is important to keep in mind that although some democratic systems have elected presidents, these systems do not necessarily operate under a presidential regime. In dual-executive countries, for example, elected presidents perform the head of state role, whereas their respective prime ministers carry out the head of government function. As Table 1.5 shows, the head of state is played by a variety of political actors, depending on the country.

Misperception 5: There Can Be Only One Winner in an Election and Only One Representative per Electoral District

Those who think that there can be only one winner in an election and only one representative per electoral district are incorrectly correlating the system used for

Executives from around the world. Posing for their formal picture at the 1985 Western Economic Summit are, from the right, Canadian Prime Minister Brian Mulroney, Japanese Prime Minister Yashiro Nakasone, American President Ronald Reagan, West German Chancellor Helmut Kohl, British Prime Minister Margaret Thatcher, French President François Mitterrand, Italian Prime Minister Bettino Craxi, and the President of the Commission of the European Communities, Jacques Delors. Photo courtesy of Reuters/Corbis-Bettmann.

the election of representatives to the American Congress with the very nature of democratic elections. In fact, that system is not the only, or even the most representative, system available to democracies. To clear up this misperception, let us examine two of the major electoral systems used in contemporary democracies: the single-member district plurality system and the multimember district **proportional representation system.**

The American electoral system, also known as the **single-member district plurality voting system,** is rather straightforward and easy to understand. Under the rules of this system, elections take place within specific electoral districts of approximately the same population. There is only one winner per district: the one candidate who has received the greatest amount (a plurality) of votes. In England this system is referred to as **first-past-the-post.** That term uses the imagery of a horse race, in that the first candidate who passes the finish line wins the race. The margin of victory makes no difference to the outcome. If there are only two can-

TABLE 1.5   A Sample of Contemporary Democracies Using Different Executive Arrangements

	Head of Government	Head of State
Brazil	President	President
Canada	Prime Minister	Governor-General
France	Prime Minister and President	President
Germany	Chancellor	President
India	Prime Minister	President
Ireland	Prime Minister	President
Israel	Prime Minister	President
Italy	Prime Minister	President
Japan	Prime Minister	Monarch
Portugal	Prime Minister and President	President
Russia	President	President
Spain	Prime Minister	Monarch
Sweden	Prime Minister	Monarch
United Kingdom	Prime Minister	Monarch
United States	President	President

SOURCE: *The World Almanac and Book of Facts, 1998* (Mahwah, N.J.: Reference Books, 1997); Gregory S. Mahler, *Comparative Politics: An Institutional and Cross-National Approach,* 2d Ed. (Englewood Cliffs, N.J.: Prentice-Hall, 1995); Gabriel Almond and G. Bingham Powell Jr., *Comparative Politics Today,* 6th Ed. (New York: HarperCollins, 1996).

didates, and one receives 50.1 percent of the vote, and the other receives 49.9 percent of the vote, the candidate with the larger share wins the seat. If there are three candidates—receiving 35 percent, 33 percent, and 32 percent of the vote, respectively—the one with 35 percent wins, even though he or she has not received a majority (more than 50 percent) of the votes cast. In this case, the person has received a plurality, the greatest amount of votes among the candidates.

This electoral system awards those large political parties that are able to run a comprehensive and unified campaign and thus gives incentives to smaller interests to join with a larger organization. Therefore the countries that use this system tend to have only two, or possibly three, major political parties. This system tends to produce legislative majorities and foster close relations between the representative and his or her district. This system is used by both presidential and parliamentary countries, including the United States, the United Kingdom, and Canada.

Critics of the single-member district plurality voting system have argued that it can actually distort the will of the people, because it is possible that the winning candidate will have received less than half of the total votes. Remember that in 1992, Bill Clinton won the presidency with only 43 percent of the vote (compared to George Bush's 37.4 percent and Ross Perot's 18.9 percent). Since this electoral system allows candidates to win even if a majority of the people have voted against them, some have urged for the adoption of a proportional representation system.[36]

The multimember district proportional representation voting system is the key alternative to the single-member plurality system available to contemporary democracies. Simply put, the proportional system allocates legislative seats in proportion to the votes received by each party, providing for a more accurate measurement of the will of the electorate than other electoral systems. Frank Wilson observes that "the idea [of proportional representation] is to make the legislature reflect as accurately as possible the division of political views in the electorate."[37]

A Hypothetical Case of an Election Under Proportional Representation Rules

The following example of a hypothetical election operating in a fictional country that uses straightforward proportional electoral rules will demonstrate the idea governing the proportional representation electoral system.

Let us assume that there are four political parties contending for one hundred legislative seats. Unlike the single-member plurality arrangement, this proportional electoral system divides the legislative seats into large, multimember electoral districts. Each of the political parties (Party A, B, C, and D) puts forth a rank-ordered list of candidates to the public. These lists are also referred to as closed lists, because the various political parties, and not the voters, decide the names and the order of the candidates appearing on the list. In general, the top-ranking names on each of the candidate lists either represent those party members with the most seniority or are the names of distinguished citizens and are intended to attract electoral support. Each party runs one candidate for each of the available seats in each of the districts.

Once in the voting booth, the people must vote for one of these party lists—not for a particular candidate. The voters, of course, are aware of the contenders running for office, as each party is required to publish their candidate list prior to the election. They cannot pick and choose among the candidates from the various lists. They must vote for a party list. In our hypothetical case, the following results were rendered from these elections:

Party A won 40 percent of the vote.
Party B won 30 percent of the vote.

Party C won 20 percent of the vote.
Party D won 10 percent of the vote.

If the one hundred legislative seats in our hypothetical parliament were allo-cated in *direct proportion to these percentages,* they would be allocated to the four parties as follows: The first forty names on Party A's candidate list would be awarded forty legislative seats; the first thirty names on Party B's list would be al-located thirty seats; the first twenty names on Party C's list would be allocated twenty seats; and the first ten names on Party D's list would be allocated ten seats. As such, the legislative makeup would be as follows:

Party A holds 40 seats.
Party B holds 30 seats.
Party C holds 20 seats.
Party D holds 10 seats.

This hypothetical case demonstrates the basic mechanics of the proportional electoral system: Representatives are elected from multimember electoral districts in proportion to their party's share of the vote.

Proportional representation systems also favor the formation of coalition gov-ernments drawn from among the various political parties. When there are four or five parties with representatives in parliament, governing can become very com-plex. This is especially true if no one party enjoys an absolute majority of seats. The coalition among political parties is a solution to this problem; it may be de-fined as the agreement among two or more parties to work together on a legisla-tive program. Usually the terms of a coalition bargain involve the parties splitting the important cabinet ministries among them. Ordinarily, the leader of the party with the larger share of the vote becomes prime minister; the leader of the coali-tion party becomes deputy prime minister; and the other ministries are allocated in a like manner.

The advantages of a coalition government are clear: It can create a strong par-liamentary majority, which can, in turn, govern effectively. Consider again the hy-pothetical case: If a coalition were formed between Party A and Party B, their sev-enty combined seats could form a powerful and effective ruling majority. Alternatively, if Parties B, C, and D wanted to block Party A, they could form a majority with their combined sixty seats. The possibilities for coalition are seem-ingly endless. Certainly, if no coalition at all were formed, our fictional nation could face a period of governmental turmoil.

A Hypothetical Case of an Election Under Plurality Rules

In contrast, imagine a one-hundred-member legislature under a single-member district plurality system, such as the one in the United States. Imagine that there are one hundred districts and, for purposes of simplicity, that all districts vote in the same proportion as the entire nation did under the proportional system. Remember that each election is for an individual candidate, not for the party itself. Let us also assume that the electoral results in each of the one hundred single-member districts are the same as the results under our proportional representation example:

Candidate representing Party A won 40 percent of the vote.
Candidate representing Party B won 30 percent of the vote.
Candidate representing Party C won 20 percent of the vote.
Candidate representing Party D won 10 percent of the vote.

Under these electoral rules, Party A would win every seat in the legislature, because in each district the candidate representing that party won a plurality of the vote. Conversely, there would be no representatives from the other three parties. As such, the composition of the legislature would be as follows:

Party A holds 100 seats.
Party B holds 0 seats.
Party C holds 0 seats.
Party D holds 0 seats.

The single-member plurality electoral system rewards seats on the basis of which political party wins the election. Under this system it does not matter for the allocation of seats whether the winning party secured an absolute majority or only managed a plurality of the votes. On the other hand, a proportional representation system allocates seats to political parties on the basis of the percentage won by each party. Obviously, and as our two hypothetical cases demonstrate, the legislative makeup may vary greatly, depending on which electoral system a country uses.

Two Key Forms of Proportional Representation Electoral Systems

In reality, there are several forms of proportional representation electoral systems. Let us examine two of the more common ones, the d'Hondt system and the single-transferable vote system.

Invented by Victor d'Hondt of Belgium, the **d'Hondt system**, also referred to as the highest average system, is one of the most used versions of proportional representation. Under the rules of this system, political parties present a closed list of candidates to the voters. As was true in our hypothetical case, voters are required to vote for one of these party lists, and not for a particular candidate. The voters, of course, are aware of the contenders running for office, as each party is required to publish their candidate list prior to the election. The d'Hondt system does not allow people to pick and choose among the candidates from the various lists; rather, they must vote for a party list.

Once all the votes are counted, the d'Hondt system weighs the amount of votes each party received on the basis of a formula to determine the highest average of votes cast per party. The precise calculations used to determine the allocation of legislative seats from the vote totals vary somewhat from country to country. Suffice it to say that, in general, the party with the highest average of votes cast places the most candidates from its list in the legislature and, conversely, the party with the lowest average places the fewest. Under this system it is safe to assume that those candidates at the top of each of the party's lists are elected, and those at the bottom of the lists do not receive a seat, unless the winning party has completely dominated the elections. In general, the d'Hondt method of allocating seats in a legislature tends to favor larger parties, and the countries that use it usually do not have more than three or four major parties. Variations of this system are used in many countries, including Austria, Belgium, Finland, Portugal, and Spain.

The single transferable vote (stv) system is a form of proportional representation that does not use party lists. Developed in the nineteenth century by Englishman Thomas Hare, it is also appropriately referred to as the Hare system. According to the rules of this version of proportional representation, political parties present candidates in multimember districts. In the ballot booth, voters rank their preferred candidates, not their preferred party, in order of preference on the ballot (first-preference, second-preference, third-preference). Once the ballots are tabulated, those candidates who have received the necessary quota of first-preference votes win a seat. The actual quota is based on the size of the district. Surplus votes beyond this quota are transferred to the candidates with second-preference votes, and each of those who then are able to garnish enough support are also awarded a seat. This process continues until all seats are allocated in a constituency. This system is used in several countries, including Ireland.[38]

Critics have argued that the multimember districts used by the various forms of proportional representation are too large and impersonal. This leads to the re-

TABLE 1.6   A Sample of Contemporary Democracies Using Various Electoral Systems

	Type	*Districts*
Austria	PR-list system	Multimember
Belgium	PR-list system	Multimember
Canada	Plurality	Single-member
Finland	PR-list system	Multimember
France	Mixed PR/Plurality	Single-member
Germany	Mixed PR/Plurality	Mixed single-member/multimember
Ireland	PR-stv system	Multimember
Italy	Mixed PR/Plurality	Mixed single-member/multimember
Portugal	PR-list system	Multimember
Spain	PR-list system	Multimember
United Kingdom	Plurality	Single-member
United States	Plurality	Single-member

SOURCE: *The World Almanac and Book of Facts, 1998* (Mahwah, N.J.: Reference Books, 1997); Gregory S. Mahler, *Comparative Politics: An Institutional and Cross-National Approach,* 2d Ed. (Englewood Cliffs, N.J.: Prentice-Hall, 1995); Gabriel Almond and G. Bingham Powell Jr., *Comparative Politics Today,* 6th Ed. (New York: HarperCollins, 1996).

lated problem that the voters never are able to develop a relationship with their representative, and no single representative has the electoral incentive to learn about the needs of his or her district. The internal politics of drawing up closed candidate lists can also be very negative for the various political parties. In addition, whereas with a presidential system people know who will be president immediately after the electoral results are announced, with a Hare system the prime minister may not be known until the various political parties negotiate the terms of their coalition government under parliamentary rules.[39] Supporters of proportional representation elections hold, however, that even if this system has flaws, it remains the most representative electoral system currently available to democratic regimes.

There are a number of other innovative types of electoral systems currently in use as well. France, for instance, uses a two-ballot system based on single-member districts. If no candidate wins over 50 percent of the vote on the first ballot, a second ballot is held the following week. A simple plurality is sufficient for a candidate to win in the second ballot. Germany has come up with its own rather complicated version as well: Half of its national representatives are elected by plurality and the other half by proportional representation.[40] Table 1.6 offers a sample of this great variety in electoral systems.

TABLE 1.7   A Sample of Different Regime-Types in American Democracies

	Current Regime Type	*Date of Independence*	*Colonial "Mother" Country*
Argentina	Presidential	9 July 1816	Spain
Bolivia	Presidential	2 February 1825	Spain
Brazil	Presidential	7 September 1822	Portugal
Canada	Parliamentary	1 January 1867	England
Chile	Presidential	18 September 1810	Spain
Colombia	Presidential	20 July 1810	Spain
Ecuador	Presidential	24 May 1822	Spain
El Salvador	Presidential	15 September 1821	Spain
Haiti	Presidential	1 January 1804	France
Honduras	Presidential	15 September 1821	Spain
Mexico	Presidential	16 September 1810	Spain
Nicaragua	Presidential	28 September 1821	Spain
Peru	Presidential	28 July 1821	Spain
United States	Presidential	4 July 1776	England
Venezuela	Presidential	5 July 1821	Spain

SOURCE: *The World Almanac and Book of Facts, 1998* (Mahwah, N.J.: Reference Books, 1997); Juan J. Linz and Arturo Valenzuela, eds., *The Failure of Presidential Democracy: The Case of Latin America,* vol. 2 (Baltimore: Johns Hopkins University Press, 1994).

Misperception 6:
The American Constitutional System Would Work Anywhere

Some might think that if only a country would adopt the institutions, rules, and procedures set out in the American Constitution, it could have a successful presidential-style democracy as well. The truth is, however, that even if a particular institutional arrangement can result in a long-lasting democratic regime in one country, there is no guarantee that it will have similar results elsewhere. In that regard, adaptations of the American Constitution to other countries have not worked out very well. The experience of Latin America is illustrative.

Upon winning their independence from Spain, many Latin America countries patterned their political structures on the American presidential system and incorporated the separation of powers doctrine into their own constitutional frameworks. Table 1.7 indicates the wide adoption of presidential arrangements in Latin American countries, which has prompted some political scientists to dub Latin America the "continent of presidentialism."[41] And yet, for a variety of reasons, all of these countries have suffered through periods of political turmoil, coups d'état, and regime breakdown.

Why has presidentialism had such a tumultuous history in Latin America and worked so peacefully in the United States? Many valuable explanations have been offered to account for this discrepancy, including the role of a political culture hostile to liberal democracy and the undue influence and power of the military establishment in Latin American politics.[42] Although we certainly recognize the insights of these explanations, we will focus—in line with this book's general argument—on the institutional explanation of why presidentialism has not worked very well in Latin America.

Political scientists favoring an institutional explanation have pointed to the problematic relationship between the executive and legislative branches under presidential rules. This relationship, they argue, has negatively impacted most Latin American democracies. Whereas critics of American government point to divided government, gridlock, and the lack of accountability as troublesome features of presidentialism, these very factors have contributed to *the collapse* of many Latin America presidential regimes over the past forty years. Indeed, in some cases the executive branch has even refused to accept the legitimacy of the legislature's participation in governing the country.

Catherine Conaghan, for example, notes that "the contemporary political history of Ecuador provides ample evidence . . . concerning the hazards of presidentialism for democratic regimes in Latin America."[43] In the time since 1979, Ecuador has experienced several political crises associated with the problems of the institutional design of a presidential rule. At one point the executive-legislative deadlock became so antagonistic that the president arranged to teargas the National Assembly. In Ecuador, presidents have often ignored or bypassed the legislature altogether in order to authoritatively address pressing economic problems.[44] The history of presidentialism in Colombia is characterized by legislative-executive deadlock as well. Jonathan Hartlyn has noted that it has not been uncommon for a president to issue executive decrees to break strikes, to stop unrest, to bypass congress, to legislate, or simply to govern.[45] Similar problems with the presidential institutional arrangement have occurred in almost every Latin American country, prompting claims by many scholars that a move to a parliamentary form of government is now necessary.[46]

Whether because of an antidemocratic political culture or the power of the military establishment or the problematic institutional structure of a presidential regime (or a combination of these three factors), the adoption of the American Constitution in Latin America has not resulted in a happy and long-lasting experience with democracy. One cannot simply export the American Constitution to another country and wait for democracy to set roots and grow. Unfortunately perhaps, politics, is much more complicated than that.

Conclusion: The Misperceptions Reconsidered in the Light of the Dilemma

As the preceding discussion clearly indicates, the American Constitution has established only one of many possible institutional structures available to contemporary democracies. There are a variety of ways available to devotees of democracy to organize a legislature, to design the executive branch, to structure the government, and to hold elections: separated or fused executive and legislative chambers, unicameral or bicameral legislative bodies, single-member or multi-member districts, federal or unitary systems, and so on.

Among the world's democracies, the United States has perhaps been the most self-conscious about preventing majority tyranny. The Framer's solution to the dilemma of majority rule versus minority rights was to hazard executive-legislative deadlock rather than risk majority tyranny, leaving us with an institutional structure thoroughly antagonistic to majority rule. If it is true that this institutional design is currently responsible for a perception among citizens that their political system is not responsive to them, perhaps a move to a parliamentary system is the answer for what ails contemporary America.

Woodrow Wilson suggested almost one hundred years ago that if the United States functioned under a British-style parliamentary system, change could conceivably take place very quickly, enabling governmental leaders to rapidly adopt new laws and adapt the government to the changing times. Was President Wilson correct? Is the British parliamentary system the answer to the dilemma of majority rule versus minority rights in the United States? What would American government look like under Westminster parliamentary rules? Is American government really unresponsive? And if so, what are we to do? We will consider these questions in the following chapters.

Structure of the Remainder of the Book

This book illustrates how the American constitutional system of checks and balances functions in comparative perspective. Chapter 2 contrasts and compares the historical development and institutional structure of the executive and legislative branches in the United States with the Westminster system in the United Kingdom. Chapter 3 presents a legislative history of the Republican Contract with America, which dominated the first one hundred days of the 104th Congress, and highlights several features of the American institutional framework, including the separation of powers, the system of checks and balances. Chapter 4 considers what politics in the United States might look like if it had adopted a version of the British parliamentary model two hundred years ago. Chapter 5 suggests some ideas for the reform of the American presidential system. This book does not argue that the American government should adopt a British-style parliamentary system. Rather, it seeks to challenge the reader to consider how institutional frameworks influence both a country's politics and its public policies.

Notes

1. See David Burnham, *Above the Law: Secret Deals, Political Fixes, and Other Misadventures of the U.S. Department of Justice* (New York: Scribner, 1996); Martin L. Gross, *A Call for Revolution: How Government Is Strangling America—and How to Stop It* (New York: Ballantine, 1993); Amatai Etzioni, *Capital Corruption: The New Attack on American Democracy*, 2d ed. (New Brunswick, N.J.: Transaction Books, 1988); Joseph S. Nye, Jr., Philip D. Zelikow, and David C. King, eds., *Why People Don't Trust Government* (Cambridge, Mass.: Harvard University Press, 1997); Drew Pearson, *The Case Against Congress: A Compelling Indictment of Corruption on Capitol Hill* (New York: Pocket Books, 1969); Kevin P. Phillips, *Arrogant Capital: Washington, Wall Street, and the Frustration of American Politics* (Boston: Little Brown and Company, 1994).

2. R. Kent Weaver and Bert A. Rockman, *Do Institutions Matter? Government Capabilities in the United States and Abroad* (Washington, D.C.: Brookings Institution, 1993), 10–11.

3. The sitting president has faced a hostile majority in at least one of the legislative chambers for thirty of the fifty years from 1946 through 1996. See Leon D. Epstein, "Changing Perceptions of the British System," *Political Science Quarterly* 109, no. 3 (1994): 494.

4. Seymour Martin Lipset, *American Exceptionalism: A Double-Edged Sword* (New York: W. W. Norton, 1996).

5. Bill Frenzel, "The System Is Self-Correcting," in *Back to Gridlock? Governance in the Clinton Years*, ed. James L. Sundquist (Washington D.C.: Brookings Institution, 1995), 105–108.

6. David R. Mayhew, *Divided We Govern: Party Control, Lawmaking, and Investigations, 1946–1990* (New Haven: Yale University Press, 1991). Also see David R. Mayhew, "Divided Party Control: Does It Make a Difference?" *PS: Political Science and Politics* 24, no. 4 (1991): 637.

7. A government may be said to be accountable when the electorate is given the opportunity to clearly and intelligently evaluate the achievements of a sitting government on the basis of it legislative record. Did the economy improve? Were social problems ameliorated? Or simply, did the government do what it promised it would do? All of these factors, and perhaps more, may go into a citizen's calculations before he or she decides to vote for that particular political party again.

8. See James L. Sundquist, *Constitutional Reform and Effective Government*, rev. ed. (Washington, D.C.: The Brookings Institution, 1992).

9. See Timothy J. Penny and Steven E. Schier, *Payment Due: A Nation in Debt, A Generation in Trouble* (Boulder, Colo.: Westview Press, 1996) and G. Calvin Mackenzie and Saranna Thornton, *Bucking the Deficit: Economic Policymaking in America* (Boulder, Colo.: Westview Press, 1996). For a description of the budgetary process during the Reagan years, see Allen Schick, *The Capacity to Budget* (Washington, D.C.: The Urban Institute Press, 1990).

10. Leon Epstein has pointed out that every year the federal deficit exceeded 3 percent of the gross national product was a year in which the government was divided. See Epstein, "Changing Perceptions," 495.

11. Weaver and Rockman, *Do Institutions Matter?* 2–3. C. Douglas Dillon's quote originally appeared in "The Challenge of Modern Government," in *Reforming American Government: The Bicentennial Papers of the Committee on the Constitutional System,* ed. Donald L. Robinson (Westview Press, 1985), 26; Weaver and Rockman have argued that "institutions alone do not deter responses to the problems, but they can make it harder to find solutions. . . . America's institutions do not make it easy to lead." See Weaver and Rockman, *Do Institutions Matter?*, 481.

12. Theodore Lowi, "Presidential and Parliamentary Democracies: Which Work Best? *Political Science Quarterly* 104, no. 3 (1994): 414. Lowi is dissatisfied with the use of the term gridlock, "which may imply that there is a single, definable obstruction, which once removed, would permit the flow to resume." See pages 414–415.

13. Theodore J. Lowi, "Presidential Democracy in America: Toward the Homogenized Regime," *Political Science Quarterly* 109, no. 3 (1994): 401.

14. Walter Bagehot, *The English Constitution* (1867; reprint, London: Fontana, 1993), 70.

15. Woodrow Wilson, "Cabinet Government in the United States," *International Review* 7 (August 1879): 146–163.

16. Woodrow Wilson, *The Politics of Woodrow Wilson, Selections from his Speeches and Writings,* ed. August Heckscher (New York: Harper and Brothers, 1956), 41–48.

17. Wilson, *Selections,* 41–48.

18. Philippe C. Schmitter and Terry Lynn Karl, "What Democracy Is . . . and Is Not," *Journal of Democracy* 2, no. 1, (1991): 75–89.

19. Giovanni Sartori, *Comparative Constitutional Engineering: An Inquiry into Structures, Incentives and Outcomes* (New York: New York University Press, 1994), 83–94.

20. Of course, an important exception to this is the process of impeachment spelled out in the U.S. Constitution. The Framers decided on the impeachment process as a way to remove a president from office on the basis of criminal charges, not on the basis of political reasons. The president may be removed from office by the Senate if he is impeached (formally charged with a crime) by the House of Representatives, which has the sole power of impeachment (Article I, section 2). Impeachment does not guarantee removal from office. The Senate must vote to convict the president, and the vote requires a two-thirds majority (Article I, section 3). Grounds for impeachment are treason, bribery, and "other high crimes and misdemeanors" (Article II, section 4). Only one president, Andrew Johnson, has ever been impeached; the Senate failed to convict him, and so he remained in office.

21. Although it is certainly true that presidential systems can be responsive, and that parliamentary systems can be stable, the dominant traits and tensions among them allows for an approximate comparative typology. As Juan Linz has observed, "All presidential and parliamentary systems have a common core that allows their differentiation and some systemic comparisons." See Juan Linz, "Presidential or Parliamentary Democracy: Does It Make a Difference?" in *The Failure of Presidential Democracy: Comparative Perspectives*, vol. 1, eds. Juan Linz and Arturo Valenzuela (Baltimore: Johns Hopkins University Press, 1994), 3-74. The above quotation is from page 5.

22. Linz and Valenzuela, *The Failure of Presidential Democracy*, 5–22.

23. Arend Lijphart, *Democracies: Patterns of Majoritarian and Consensus Government in Twenty-One Countries* (New Haven: Yale University Press, 1984), 216.

24. Lijphart, *Democracies*, 216. The consensual parliamentary system is another important form of parliamentary democracy. Arend Lijphart notes that this model—the name comes from the word consensus (to get along)—is designed so that all of the members of parliament can discover broad-based agreement on legislation. Whereas the rules of the Westminster system tend to pit winners against losers, this arrangement encourages the majority party to seek input on legislative bills from opposition parties. Often, rigorous legislative debate takes place on the floor of the parliament, and the opposition leadership, as well as lower-ranking government members, has opportunities to suggest amendments. Hence, the open and flexible nature of the consensual parliamentary model encourages increased participation from all sides. Belgium, for example, has used this system to guarantee that its two major nationality groups will cooperate in governmental policymaking, no matter which party wins the elections.

25. This is not to be confused with the speaker in the American House of Representatives, who performs a leadership function.

26. See Sartori, *Comparative Constitutional Engineering*, 101.

27. See *Constituição da República Portuguesa: As Três Versões Após 25 de Abril 1989/1982/1976* (Lisbon: Porto Editora, 1990), 228–231; David Corkill, "The Political System and the Consolidation of Democracy in Portugal," *Parliamentary Affairs* 46, no. 4 (1993): 517–532; Paul C. Manuel, *The Challenges of Democratic Consolidation in Portugal, 1976–1991: Political, Economic and Military Issues* (Westport, Conn.: Praeger, 1996).

28. William H. Riker, "Federalism," in *Handbook of Political Science: Governmental Institutions and Processes*, eds. Fred I. Greenstein and Nelson W. Polsby (Reading, Mass.: Addison-Wesley, 1975), 5:101.

29. Kerstin Hamann, "The Creation of Regional Identities and Voting Behavior in Spain," (paper presented to the Iberian Study Group, Center of European Studies, Harvard University, 17 February 1998), 5.

30. Peter J. Donaghy and Michael T. Newton, *Spain: A Guide to Political and Economic Institutions* (Cambridge, U.K.: Cambridge University Press, 1987), 100–101.

31. It is important to note that the national legislatures in both Great Britain and France, although dominate, do face some local challenges. New "country" parliaments are

being developed in Great Britain; and regional assemblies in France exercise some delegated powers.

32. Michael Curtis, *Introduction to Comparative Government,* 4th ed. (New York: Longman, 1997), 22.

33. Frank L. Wilson, *Concepts and Issues in Comparative Politics,* 4th ed. (Upper Saddle River, N.J.: Prentice-Hall, 1996), 161.

34. See Gregory S. Mahler, *Comparative Government: An Institutional and Cross-National Approach,* 2d ed. (Englewood Cliffs, N.J.: Prentice-Hall, 1995), 75.

35. Jean Blondel, *Comparative Legislatures* (Englewood Cliffs, N.J.: Prentice-Hall, 1973), 144–153.

36. See the useful discussion by Philip Laundy, *Parliaments in the Modern World* (Brookfield, Vt.: Gower Publications, 1989), 15–16.

37. F. Wilson, *Concepts and Issues,* 66.

38. Laundy, *Parliaments,* 15–16.

39. Wilson, *Concepts and Issues,* 66–67.

40. See William Safran, *The French Polity,* 4th ed. (New York: Longman, 1995) and David Conradt, *The German Polity,* 6th ed. (New York: Longman, 1996).

41. Juan Linz and Arturo Valenzuela, *The Failure of Presidentialism: The Case of Latin America,* vol. 2 (Baltimore: Johns Hopkins University Press, 1994), x.

42. See the discussion of these various approaches in James A. Bill and Robert L. Hardgrave, Jr., *Comparative Politics: The Quest for Theory* (Landover, Md.: University Press of America, 1981). Also see Howard J. Wiarda and Harvey F. Kline, *Latin American Politics and Development* (Boulder, Colo.: Westview Press, 1985); Alain Rouquie, *The Military and the State in Latin America,* trans. Paul Sigmund (Berkeley: University of California Press, 1987); and Alfred Stepan, *Rethinking Military Politics* (Baltimore: Johns Hopkins University Press, 1988).

43. Catherine M. Conaghan, "Loose Parties, Floating Politicians, and Institutional Stress: Presidentialism in Ecuador, 1979–1988," in Linz and Valenzuela, *The Failure of Presidentialism*, 2:254-285.

44. Conaghan made these comments at a conference held at Georgetown University in Washington, D.C., entitled "Presidential or Parliamentary Democracy: Does it Make a Difference: A Research Symposium on Stable Democracy" and organized by Juan Linz and Arturo Valenzuela, 14–16 May 1989.

45. Hartlyn made these comments at a conference held at Georgetown University in Washington, D.C., entitled "Presidential or Parliamentary Democracy: Does it Make a Difference: A Research Symposium on Stable Democracy" and organized by Juan Linz and Arturo Valenzuela, 14–16 May 1989. Also see Jonathan Hartlyn "Presidentialism and Colombian Politics," in Linz and Valenzuela, *The Failure of Presidentialism* (Baltimore: Johns Hopkins University Press, 1994), 2:220–253.

46. See Linz, "Presidential or Parliamentary Democracy."

2

....

Why American Government Operates Under Checks and Balances, and British Government Does Not

A Brief Comparative History

The United States came within a hair's breadth of adopting a kind of parliamentary system.

—Robert Dahl

T ODAY, PRESIDENTIAL AND PARLIAMENTARY SYSTEMS are the two principle forms of democratic organization. Although there are many variations of these two systems among the democratic countries in the world, Great Britain is commonly considered the archetype of a parliamentary system, whereas the most famous example of a presidential system is the United States.

How did these two great democracies adopt their present institutional forms? Why does the United States function under a complex constitutional arrangement of checks and balances, whereas Great Britain does not? What factors are responsible for this discrepancy? How does it affect the practice of democracy in each country today? To answer these questions, this chapter will compare and contrast political development in the United States and in Great Britain. In so doing, it will illustrate how each nation's political history influenced the development of its present form of democracy.

Comparing Political Development in Great Britain and the United States

Both the United States and Great Britain faced very different obstacles and challenges in the history of their political development. In his work *Political Order in Changing Societies*, Samuel Huntington argues that disparate patterns of political development in the two countries resulted in very different institutional structures.[1] The Framers of the American republic did not have to dislodge a domestic monarchy, an aristocracy, or a clergy from a privileged place in society in order to implement their new constitutional order. Therefore, the Constitution was afforded the luxury of setting its own roots and developing over time into preeminent governmental authority. In contrast, the end of the feudal order was a tortuous and divisive process in Great Britain, as democratic forces seized power from the entrenched establishment of the monarchy, the church, and the landed aristocracy. Over the centuries-long process of British political development, Parliament managed to establish itself as that country's preeminent political authority. Currently, Great Britain's parliamentary legislation has become sovereign, taking on the status that the United States accords its Constitution.[2]

One effect of these divergent patterns has been the development of very different concepts of "the Constitution" in the United States and in Great Britain. The word itself comes from the verb "to constitute," which means to compose or create. A constitution creates a government. American government was created by a written document. The Framers basically started from scratch and wrote down what the government could do, what it could not do, and how political power would be divided. The very flexibility of the document, which contains general principles and provisions for amendment, meant that constitutional government in the United States was given a chance to flourish as well as change. The Constitution is a relatively short document that gives the outline of government; it is left up to future generations to fill in that outline. However, the general principles in the Constitution are expected to be immutable. In the United States, the Constitution is the "supreme law of the land," superseding both laws written by Congress or the states and actions taken by the president. Obviously, eighteenth-century America did not have as long of a history of government as did nations in Europe at that time, so the Framers had the benefit of making a fresh start and of learning from the past mistakes of other nations. To illustrate the differences between the formation of government in the United States and Great Britain, let us take a brief look at the history of each country's political system, starting with England.

The Evolution of the British Parliament

Political development in the United Kingdom is distinctive. Unlike other European countries, the United Kingdom evolved relatively peacefully over several centuries,[3] which is not to imply that the United Kingdom did not confront long periods of violence and political instability. Rather, in the long sweep of British history, the country confronted the challenges of political modernization slowly, sequentially, and successfully.[4] For the sake of brevity, we will focus our inquiry on some of the key stages in the evolution of the Parliament:

- the adoption of the Magna Carta and the origins of Parliament in the thirteenth century,
- the expansion of parliamentary power in the sixteenth and seventeenth centuries,
- the emergence of the working class as a potent parliamentary political force in the nineteenth and twentieth centuries, and
- the ascension of the House of Commons as England's most powerful governing body.

The houses of Parliament on the River Thames, London—the birthplace of parliamentary democracy. The tower on the left is the House of Lords, and the clock tower is, of course, Big Ben. Photo courtesy of Corbis-Bettmann.

The Origins of Parliament

The origins of the British Parliament may be traced to the battle between a nascent governing council and the monarch over the **Magna Carta** in 1215 (a copy of the Magna Carta is included in Appendix A). At that time, absolute political power and legitimacy in Great Britain were in the hands of the monarch, according to the terms of the political and religious doctrine known as the **divine right of kings**. That doctrine, employed by monarchs throughout Europe, held that the king's power and authority flowed to him directly and absolutely from God. Further, as God's custodian on earth, the monarch should be given the same solemn respect and unquestioning obedience a person would offer to God. This doctrine granted monarchs a great deal of political legitimacy and authority: If the people in a country believed that God had chosen a particular person to rule over a nation, who would be in a position to contest God's will? The doctrine of the divine right of kings helped to maintain political stability and a hierarchical social order in continental Europe and, to a lesser extent, in Great Britain for centuries. And the emperor in Japan effectively used this claim to political legitimacy until the end of World War II.

No monarch, however, could tend to all aspects of governance on his own. Even in the thirteenth century, the demands on a political leader were great. So a practice developed in Great Britain by which the monarch would consult with a so-called Great Council—composed of earls, barons, and members of the church hierarchy—prior to the introduction of new rules or new taxes. These consultations were not an invitation to the Great Council to struggle with the monarch over policy issues, but rather served to help the monarch implement decisions he himself had already made. Although the advisors could offer opinions, it was up to the monarch to decide if any suggestions proposed by the Great Council were to be incorporated into law.[5] The Great Council served as an advisory board to the monarch, but it held very little power of its own.

This system of governance was challenged by Great Britain's leading barons in 1215, when they submitted the Magna Carta, or "Great Charter," to King John I for his approval. Predicated on the principle that Great Britain should be ruled by law, the Magna Carta placed express boundaries on the arbitrary power of the king. Among the provisions outlined in the Magna Carta were guarantees that the established feudal rights of the privileged class of landowners existed beyond the control of the monarch, that freemen, merchants, and clerks were protected from arbitrary arrest, and that all free men had the right to trial and judgment in accordance with the due process of law. Most importantly, the Magna Carta limited the powers of the monarch, especially in matters concerning justice and finance.

Not unexpectedly, the reaction of King John I was negative. He repudiated the Magna Carta, insisting that he had the right to rule absolutely. After an arduous period in which armies loyal to the monarch took up arms against those loyal to the barons, the monarch was defeated and was forced to accept the Magna Carta. Finally adopted in 1225, the Magna Carta remains as part of British law today.[6]

The question of why the barons composed, submitted, and fought over the Magna Carta is an interesting one. Perhaps the best explanation involves the claim that the experience they gained by helping the monarch govern as members of the Great Council led many barons to believe that the country should be governed by a set of laws, not just by the whims of a monarch. It is easy to imagine how difficult it would be for barons and church officials, powerful men in their own right, to be prohibited from incorporating their ideas into the king's proposals. These individuals came together with a singular purpose: to propose a document that would be accepted as the law of the land.[7]

To be sure, the adoption of the Magna Carta placed Great Britain on a very different political trajectory from the rest of Europe, which remained under the doctrine of the divine right of kings for centuries to come. The Magna Carta established the framework for what would become the British Parliament.

The Expansion of Parliamentary Power

The resolution of the battle over the Magna Carta changed British political history, but it did not resolve the relationship between the monarch and what eventually became the Parliament. Many questions still remained. What ramifications would it have for the rule of the monarch? What powers did the Parliament actually have? Who, finally, would actually govern Great Britain? These, and many similar questions, were at the crux of a power struggle between the monarch and the Parliament over the next several centuries.

We start in the sixteenth century with a series of events surrounding Henry VIII's quest for power. He wanted a male heir to the throne, but he and his Spanish queen, Catherine of Aragon, had only female offspring. Frustrated, Henry demanded a divorce from Catherine in the hope that a new wife might have a son. The pope, however, refused Henry's request for a divorce. Because Britain was then a Catholic country, the British king was subject to decisions made by the pope on religious issues. Furious, Henry sought to find a way around the pope's decision. But the pope, for both moral reasons (divorce was against Catholic canon law) and political reasons (he did not want to offend the powerful Catholic nation of Spain), was unrelenting: As a Catholic king of a Catholic country, Henry had to stay married to Catherine. So Henry decided to find another way.

Beginning around 1529 he mobilized anticlerical elements in the Parliament. Parliamentary leader Thomas Cromwell supported King Henry VIII's break with Rome; he understood well the potential political gains for Parliament. After gaining the support of key parliamentarians with Cromwell's assistance, King Henry VIII announced his decision to break relations with the Roman Catholic Church. In its stead, he created the Church of England, placed himself in charge, and approved his own request for a divorce from Catherine.

After the king made the break official, Cromwell pushed through a number of religious reform measures in Parliament. These included the dissolution of all monasteries and the transfer of the property-wealth of the Roman Catholic Church to Parliament. In the end, the king got his divorce from Catherine, and the Roman Catholic Church lost its privileged position in England. Further, under Thomas Cromwell's leadership, the Parliament filled the void left by the dissolution of the Roman Catholic Church, thereby dramatically expanding its power and authority. Matters previously left to the church were now under the purview of the Parliament. In sum, this series of events reinforced the development of parliamentary power in Great Britain, continuing a political trajectory originally started some three hundred years earlier with the adoption of the Magna Carta.

Let us fast-forward to the first half of the seventeenth century. At this time, the rulers of Great Britain, the **Stuart monarchs**, wanted to return Roman Catholicism to Great Britain against the wishes of the Parliament. The Stuarts hoped to follow the example of the absolute monarchs in continental Europe, particularly in France. At that time political modernization was occurring in France under the concept of the divine right of kings, which served to justify modern centralization under the traditional authority symbols of God and the church. Centralization was located in the monarch, and the bureaucracy developed specialized departments to carry out his edicts. There was no provision for popular political participation: The only act required of the citizens was to pay homage to the king in the form of taxes. By asserting its absolute power as the nation's unifying force, the monarchy was able to centralize national institutions and rapidly create modern armies and navies. Samuel Huntington refers to this process as the continental European model of political modernization, well illustrated by the cases of France, Spain, and Portugal.[8] Indeed, both the imperial power of Portugal and Spain in the fifteenth and sixteen centuries and the military and economic power of France in the seventeenth and eighteenth centuries generated widespread aristocratic support for this absolutist model of political development on the European continent. Consequently, the Stuart monarchs felt that the return of monarchical absolutism was the best way for Great Britain to modernize and to stay competitive with its neighbors. Yet, since the adoption of the Magna Carta in the thirteenth century, and since Henry VIII's break with the Roman Catholic Church in the sixteenth century, England was on a different trajectory from the rest of Europe. The Stuarts wanted to change that.

As you might expect, Parliament reacted strongly against the plans of Stuart King James I, who was succeeded by Charles I in 1625. Parliament passed the Petition of Right in 1628, which set limits on the king's power. The idea behind this legislation was to prevent the monarch from inviting the Roman Catholic Church back and, thus, to preserve the independence and authority of the Parliament. This parliamentary challenge to royal authority did not sit well with Charles I. As tensions heated up, both the king and the Parliament appealed to their respective followers, and each ordered the outfitting of armies. With all peaceful resolutions exhausted, those armies loyal to Charles I engaged the armies loyal to the Parliament in 1642, leading to a bloody civil war. This conflict eventually ended with the victory of the parliamentary forces, who quickly consolidated their power. They ordered the beheading of King Charles I—which took place in 1649—abolished the monarchy, and declared England to be a commonwealth. A Council of State, led by Oliver Cromwell, was appointed to rule in the place of the monarch.[9]

These events bring us to the last half of the seventeenth century. One might think that having won the civil war, the Parliament would be enjoying its newfound authority. The reality in 1660, however, was that the Parliament's experiment in government *sans roi* was a disaster. Cromwell turned out to be a despotic ruler, and his death in 1660 left the Parliament with few options. Incredibly, the Parliament decided to restore the Stuart monarchy. Charles II, son of Charles I, became king in 1660 and was in turn succeeded by James II in 1685. This new generation of Stuart kings wanted the return of Roman Catholicism to England and continued to fight with the Parliament. After almost thirty more years of monarch-parliamentary conflict, the sides took up arms against one another once again. This time, however, a civil war was avoided, as Leonard Freedman points out:

> There was one more impasse between king and Parliament. Again an army took the field against the incumbent monarch, James II, whom Parliament accused of scheming to bring back Catholicism. This time the insurgents were an invading force led by William of Orange, who had been invited by parliamentary leaders to take over the throne. But this time there was no civil war. James, with his army defecting, remembered what happened to Charles I, and fled into exile without a struggle. Thenceforth the British spoke of the "Glorious Revolution" of 1688, so named because it was successful, popular and bloodless.[10]

The Glorious Revolution of 1688 resolved the religious question and constructed the monarchy on a new basis: William of Orange and his wife, Mary, owed their very position as the new British monarchs to Parliament. This new relationship was codified in the **British Bill of Rights** approved by the Parliament, which provided that the Parliament had authority over the monarch to raise taxes and pass laws. This bill specified that the monarch had the power neither to promulgate nor to rescind a law. Later, the **Act of Settlement of 1701** further placed the monarchy under the power of the Parliament and established new succession rules to the crown.[11] In total, these provisions clearly established the preeminent position of Parliament in British politics and society—a remarkable development, especially when considering that the French Revolution would not happen until 1789!

A Democratizing Parliament

Although parliamentary domination and autonomy eroded the authority and power of the monarch in the seventeenth and eighteenth centuries, it remained an undemocratic body in the eighteenth century. At this time the Parliament's upper house, the House of Lords (which, as you will recall, evolved from the king's Great Council), dominated the Parliament and was composed of the nobility, the landowners, and the Church of England. The lower body, known as the House of

Commons, was also not representative of the general population. Its representation was tilted to favor the less populated rural areas and was dominated by rural landowners. They maintained their position by the use of **rotten boroughs**—a corrupt system of representation that enabled a small group of rural electors to dominate parliamentary districts.[12]

Simultaneously, a larger economic and social event was gradually gaining steam: the industrial revolution. Once it took root, the industrial revolution dramatically changed British society, as well as the nature and internal operation of Parliament, and caused much social and political instability.[13] There were social dislocations, as many peasants flocked to the cities from the countryside for work, creating great pockets of poverty in the cities. As vividly depicted in the novels by Charles Dickens, including *Oliver Twist* and *A Christmas Carol*, conditions in the eighteenth and nineteenth century for working-class people in London, Manchester, and elsewhere in England were abysmal. And yet, as mentioned above, the aristocrats and rural landlords controlling Parliament prevented this developing, urban working class from participating in the political life of the country.

At this time two major parliamentary political groups, the **Tories** and the **Whigs**—considered to be the forerunners of modern political parties—argued over reform measures that would remedy these new social problems caused by industrialization. The Tories, who were mostly conservative and rural aristocrats, dominated Parliament in the early part of the eighteenth century and resisted dramatic change. The Whigs, a group of the new entrepreneurial elite, believed in free trade and argued that the Tory conservative leadership was depriving the country of business opportunities. They took particular aim at the rotten borough system, which, they claimed, was manipulated by the Tories to maintain a parliamentary majority.[14] The Whigs, taking advantage of elite concerns that the societal unrest among the working class could develop into a violent class revolution, gained power in the 1830 parliamentary elections. Once in power, the Whigs initiated a process of reform aimed at restoring social order and improving the business climate. In particular, the 1832 Reform Act eliminated the rotten borough system, expanded the electorate, and added electoral districts in urban areas. More reforms followed throughout the nineteenth and twentieth centuries, including the 1867 Reform Act, which enfranchised the urban working class. In their totality, the various reform acts not only expanded the franchise but also led to the democratization of the internal workings of Parliament. Indeed, the parliamentary acts of 1911 and 1949 completed the democratization process by restricting the power and authority of the undemocratic House of Lords and by placing ultimate governing authority squarely with the democratic House of Commons.[15]

TABLE 2.1   Important Events in the Formation and Evolution of British Democracy

I. The Origins of Parliament	
1215–1225	The Great Council of Barons wins passage of the Magna Carta
II. The Expansion of Parliamentary Power	
1534	Parliament passes Act of Settlement during reign of Henry VIII
1642	Civil War between Parliament and Stuart kings
1649	Parliament wins civil war. Charles I beheaded and the Parliament installs Oliver Cromwell as England's new leader
1660	Cromwell, who proves to be a despotic leader, dies. Parliament restores Charles II to the British throne
1688	The Glorious Revolution brings William and Mary to the British throne Parliament passes the Bill of Rights, which provided that it had authority over the monarch to raise taxes and pass laws
1701	Parliament passes the Act of Settlement, which established new succession rules for the British crown
III. A Democratizing Parliament	
1832	Parliament passes reform act that enfranchises middle class
1867	Parliament passes reform act that enfranchises the urban working class
1911	Parliament passes reform act that limits power of House of Lords
1949	Parliament passes reform act that provides for the domination of the House of Commons over the House of Lords

The Long Sweep of British History

The cumulative effect of British political development has been the construction of a democratic and parliamentary government under a symbolic monarch. Of note, two significant landmarks were realized over the centuries-long evolution of parliamentary power. First, centralized authority came to be located in the law-making machine, the Parliament.[16] Second, rejecting the notion of a fixed and fundamental set of laws, the country adopted the idea of a flexible and sovereign legislative body. As James Q. Wilson has pointed out, "in Great Britain . . . the Parliament can do almost anything that it believes the voters will accept."[17] This approach to government holds that it is better to accord the legislative body the authority to enact laws in response to the societal needs of the time than to be limited by a set of checks and balances detailed in a written constitution.

Key Institutional Features of British Democracy

The British Constitution

The **British Constitution** is referred to as an "unwritten constitution" because the rules and procedures that orient British political life were not devised and set

down on paper at one particular moment in time. Rather, these rules and procedures are contained in a series of documents and precedent-setting laws. Technically, then, the British Constitution is written, in that it consists of existing documents; it is unwritten in the sense that governmental principles are not drawn
together into one concise document written for the specific purpose of forming a
government. In order not to confuse it with the American Constitution, it is perhaps better to think of the so-called British Constitution as a constitutional
framework that has evolved over the past several hundred years and that loosely
directs political life in Britain. It is not a single written document, nor does it
specify the component parts of government and the powers of each branch. This
"unwritten" constitution derives from five distinct sources:

- statute law
- common law
- conventions
- authoritative works
- external agreements[18]

Statute law, the first basis of the British constitutional framework, is made up
of certain parliamentary acts that have defined the institutional relationship between the monarchy and the Parliament. As we have just seen, the Magna Carta of
1215, the Bill of Rights of 1689 and the parliamentary acts of 1911 and 1949
helped to define those institutional relationships and are examples of statute law.

Common law, a second source of the British constitutional framework, takes
one of two forms: **executive prerogative power** and the judicial interpretation of
statute law. The first of these, executive prerogative power, technically belongs to
the crown, although in practice is utilized by the prime minister and the government. As we shall see later in this chapter, the British monarch no longer has any
real power, and all executive decisions are now made by the prime minister. These
decisions include the appointment of ministers, the negotiation of treaties, and
the declaration of war. The second form of common law, judicial interpretation of
statute law, establishes that once a court upholds a statute law as part of common
law a precedent is created that is to be followed by other courts.

Convention is the third basis of the British constitutional framework. Convention typically embodies the terms of a resolution of a past generalized social and
political crisis and, as such, carries authority. For example, although there are no
specific rules governing the parliamentary motion of confidence, *by convention* a
sitting government must resign if it loses a vote of confidence. This happens in
spite of the fact that no lawful, authoritative document sets forth these rules, and

there are no criminal penalties if they are disobeyed.[19] Philip Norton points out that conventions are followed by political actors because they fear that the British constitutional system is unworkable without them:

> [Conventions] are complied with because of the recognition of what would happen if they were not complied with. For the Queen to refuse her assent to a measure passed by the two Houses of Parliament would draw her into the realms of political controversy, hence jeopardizing the claim of the monarch to be "above politics." A government that sought to remain in office after losing a vote of confidence in the House of Commons would find its position politically untenable: it would lack the political authority to govern.[20]

Significant and authoritative *scholarly works* represent the Constitution's fourth source of power. These works have been authored by British scholars throughout history and have influenced policymakers' understanding of how the organs of government should be organized, of how they should function, and of how they should relate to each other. These scholarly works include the writings by A. V. Dicey and Walter Bagehot, among others.[21] A. V. Dicey, for example, is credited with emphasizing the supremacy of Parliament in British politics, a supremacy that makes the government accountable to the Parliament. In addition, and as we saw in Chapter 1, Walter Bagehot's 1867 work entitled *The English Constitution* strongly argues for the need of fused executive and legislative powers to avoid the problems intrinsic to a divided power arrangement.[22]

Finally, a number of recent *international agreements* have had bearing upon the British constitutional framework. These agreements include the European Convention of Human Rights of 1951, the European Communities Act of 1972, and the European Communities (Amendment) Act of 1986. These **external agreements** provide that European community laws might take precedence over British law; and their long-term implications indicate that there may be a shift of power from the British Parliament to some sort European parliament. The full implications, of course, are not yet known.[23]

Taken as a whole, these five distinct sources have contributed to the development and evolution of the British constitutional framework today.

The Westminster Parliamentary System

Technically, the British Parliament is composed of the monarch, the House of Lords, and the House of Commons. All three continue to have a role to play in the law-making function of the Parliament. In fact, the House of Commons—the only democratically elected institution of the three—controls all legislative initiatives.

As we learned in Chapter 1, there are two executives in the British parliamentary system: the head of government and the head of state. The British head of government is the prime minister, and the British head of state is the monarch (the king or the queen). By convention, the monarch performs a symbolic legislative function. If you look at a popular magazine or newspaper in Britain, you will immediately see the difference: The British prime minister is often pictured speaking about legislation at his official residence of 10 Downing Street, whereas members of the royal family, such as Queen Elizabeth and Prince Charles, are pictured representing Great Britain at various events, such as the Olympics or the opening of an art gallery or the symphony season.

Furthermore, after every parliamentary election, the monarch sends for the leader of the new majority. And at the opening of each session of Parliament the monarch reads the government's proposals for the upcoming legislative session. This text is prepared by the leadership of the majority party in Parliament, and the monarch must read whatever is put before him or her. The monarch also must sign any statute passed by Parliament. Ironically, even if Parliament were to pass a law that abolished the monarchy, the queen would be required to sign it. Hence, the monarch remains involved in British politics but is no longer an active player.[24]

The recent death of Diana, Princess of Wales, may serve as an illustration of the monarchy as a symbol of British culture and government. Although Princess Diana's status was diminished by her divorce from Prince Charles, the public in Britain and abroad clearly viewed her as an embodiment of British society and culture: The public accorded her status as a symbol of Britain. When the public perceived the funeral preparations by Queen Elizabeth and Prince Charles to be a slight to Diana, the monarchy was shaken to its core. The monarchy's power as head of state derives from its symbolic nature. If the symbol is tarnished, as it appeared to be when Charles and Elizabeth seemed less distraught over the Princess's death than the rest of the world, its power is diminished.

Like the monarch, the upper house in the legislature, known as the **House of Lords**, is not a democratic body: *None* of its over 1,200 members have been elected to serve. As was the case in the eighteenth century, the House of Lords continues to be composed of the elite segments of British society. Today there are several ways to get into the House of Lords: The monarch may appoint you, if you have attained a prominent position in British society; you may have a birthright, if you are born into a noble family; or you may serve if you are part of the hierarchy of the Church of England. The House of Lords has very restricted powers but may play a constructive role as a debating society on the important issues of the day. It is possible for the government to appoint new members as lifetime peers to the House of Lords.

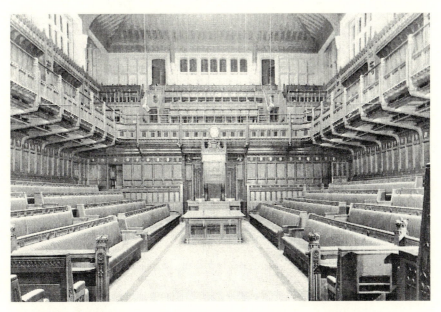

The Chamber of the British House of Commons in London—the center of British parliamentary democracy. Photo courtesy of Corbis-Bettmann.

The majority party in the lower legislative body, the **House of Commons**, controls British politics. That party selects the head of government, known as the **prime minister**, to be the executive and to direct the legislative branch. To help govern, the prime minister designates a cabinet from among the ranks of the majority party in the legislature. The British cabinet differs from the American cabinet in two main ways. First, British law allows cabinet members to continue to serve out their term as representatives. In the United States, cabinet secretaries can be selected from outside of Congress, and members of Congress who serve on the cabinet are required to resign from their elected position. Second, in Britain the government is distinct from the Parliament; it is composed of the prime minister and his or her cabinet, and it has exclusive responsibility for the administration of the country.

The Westminster system allows the prime minister to dominate the parliament as long as he or she can maintain a legislative majority. Unlike a U.S. president, who faces reelection after four years and cannot serve more than two terms, the British prime minister has no fixed term and no term limits on his or her office. In addition, the prime minister can expect to have all of his or her legislation passed without any revisions from the loyal opposition.

At present, there are 651 members in the democratic House of Commons. Each member of Parliament, known as an **M.P.**, is elected to represent a single-member constituency under a first-past-the-post electoral system (explained in Chapter 1). Parliamentary elections must be held no later than five years after the last ones. The government can usually decide when to schedule the next parliamentary elections, which gives it enormous advantage over the opposition: At any point within five years of the last election, the government can call for new elections. That decision is frequently controlled based on poll numbers. When the poll numbers are favorable, the incumbent government can call for new elections with a reasonable expectation of winning and of thereby extending its term of office. In recent years, the Conservative Party used this strategy to maintain a legislative majority that lasted for almost eighteen years—first from 1979 until 1991, under the skillful leadership of Margaret Thatcher, and then from 1991 until 1997, under John Major. In 1997 the Labour Party, led by Tony Blair, finally regained power. If Blair proves to be an able prime minister, there is every reason to expect him to remain in that position for some time to come.[25]

The government and the opposition sit facing across from each other in the House of Commons. The leaders of the majority party, the government, sit on the front benches across from the leaders of the minority party. The minority party is also called the **loyal opposition**, which is a term from British history. It signifies that even if a political party disagrees with the policies of the majority party, it remains loyal to the crown and to the country.

As you can see in the photograph of the House of Commons, the government sits on the left-hand side, and the opposition sits on the right-hand side (viewed from the public sitting area). The leaders of the government and opposition sit across from each other on the front benches. Hence, those in a leadership capacity are known as **front-benchers.** Further, the opposition leadership is referred to as the shadow cabinet because they sit across from the government's ministers, in a sense shadowing their counterparts.

Junior-ranking members of Parliament from both sides sit on the benches behind their respective leaders and, as such, have come to be known as **back-benchers.** Independent M.P.s represent a specific region or issue and are not officially allied with either the government or the opposition. They are known as **cross-benchers**.

The **British speaker,** chosen from the ranks of the Parliament, performs an arbiter role. The speaker does not have to be a member of the majority party. For example, Betty Boothroyd, the present speaker, was a Labour M.P. elected to the position when the Conservative Party held a majority in the House. The speaker sits in the so-called speaker's chair, located at the far end of the building.[26]

The job of the government is to present, pass, and implement a legislative package; the opposition tries to block these legislative initiatives. Unlike the opposition in the American system of checks and balances, the parliamentary opposition in Great Britain has little chance to amend or challenge legislation prepared by the government; for the most part it is limited to criticizing the legislation in the hope that it might prevail in the next elections. If, however, a government proves to be incompetent and has lost sufficient legislative support from among the ranks of the majority party, it may be possible for the opposition to successfully request that the government face a vote of confidence. If the government loses such a motion, it will have to resign, and new elections will almost certainly be held.

One of the most entertaining British political events in the House of Commons is **question-time:** when government ministers, including the prime minister, are subjected to questions from the opposition leadership, the opposition back-benchers, and the government back-benchers. Whereas the questions asked by government back-benchers tend to be tame and respectful of the government, opposition questions from both the leadership and the back-benchers have been known to be rather abusive. If London is not in your immediate travel plans, C-SPAN regularly broadcasts taped sessions of question-time. It is worth tuning in!

Finally, it is important to note that although there are no constitutional checks and balances on the actions of Parliament, there are some general limitations on parliamentary action. The rights of free speech and assembly, for example, are important elements of British convention and tend to frame the legislative activities of the Parliament. In addition, mindful that the public will hold the government accountable for its actions in the next elections, prime ministers have been, on the whole, careful to respect and safeguard democratic liberties.[27] One can safely state today that after some eight hundred years of evolution, Great Britain is presently a fully democratic nation operating under a parliamentary institutional structure without a formal set of checks and balances.

The Creation of the American Presidential System

Originally a British colony, the United States became an independent nation in the last half of the eighteenth century. As we have shown, by the time the United States was established, Britain's governmental system had already gone through a great deal of change. The government in place in Britain in 1787 was the result of *evolution*; the Americans were creating a new system as the result of a *revolution*. Therefore, the Americans could both dispense with elements of the British system they found oppressive and hold onto elements that they felt furthered their notions of the proper role of government: "With few exceptions, the leaders of the American Revolution respected the British constitutional system. Indeed, many of them saw the Revolution as a fight to secure the rights they had assumed to be theirs as Englishmen. Therefore, when the time came to devise their own system of government, the framers relied heavily on the British constitutional tradition."[28] Indeed, because it was based on British constitutional principles, the American Constitution can be considered another step in the evolution of British government.

However, the American Constitution was also a clear rejection of at least some British constitutional principles. And as the American Constitution has evolved over time, it has departed from its British predecessor. It is important to remember that the American government was not, like the British government, created in response to a feudal and monarchical history. The Framers of the American Constitution, using democratic principles, created a system of checks and balances as a reaction to their experience as colonists. They were more concerned with limiting government than with creating a responsive government.

In a sense, the writing of the American Constitution established a second trajectory for the development of British constitutional principles. While the Parliament was consolidating power in itself, the Framers centralized power in the Constitution and explicitly rejected monarchical absolutism. In this regard, James Q. Wilson has noted: "The American revolt against British rule, culminating in 1775 in the War of Independence, led many colonists to conclude that political power should never again be entrusted to rulers whose authority was based on tradition and other unwritten understandings. The central idea behind a written constitution was to limit and define political authority."[29]

The following sections of this chapter will focus on the development of the American political system: its philosophical influences, its roots in the colonists' experiences as subjects of the British crown, and its evolution over time. In particular, we will address the following four issues:

- the origins of American democracy, especially the Articles of Confederation, the Declaration of Independence, the Constitutional Convention, and the Virginia plan (perhaps the world's first plan for a modern parliamentary system);
- the concerns of the Framers of the Constitution, including both their fears of excessive executive power and of the tyranny of the majority, and their attempts to avoid both;
- the key institutional features of the new government, especially the system of checks and balances; and

• the subsequent development and expansion of democracy in the United States.

The Origins of American Democracy

The United States began as thirteen colonies subject to the British crown. Each of the colonies had some amount of self-governance, and each was in many ways independent of the others. Although Britain had ultimate political authority over the colonies, for many years that control did not have an effect on the everyday lives of colonists. In the late 1700s, however, that began to change. Britain passed a series of legislative initiatives that the colonists found oppressive: the Sugar Act of 1764, the Stamp Act in 1765, the Townsend Duties in 1767, and the Tea Act in 1773. Each of these acts was an attempt by Britain to gain revenues by taxing the American colonists. British lawmakers saw these acts as reasonable: The nation had a sizable debt, due in large part to its assistance to the colonies in the French and Indian War. The colonists saw it differently, and "no taxation without representation" became a rallying cry. Radical revolutionaries led by Samuel Adams organized the Boston Tea Party as a protest against the Tea Act. The revolutionaries had two purposes: to galvanize opposition against Britain, and to make British lawmakers so angry that they would pass punitive measures, further encouraging rebellion.[30]

The Declaration of Independence from Great Britain

In 1774, the First Continental Congress was called to consider action against the British government. It did not go beyond a call for a boycott of British goods. By 1776, however, the seeds of independence had been sown, and the Second Continental Congress, convened in that year, asked Thomas Jefferson to write what became the Declaration of Independence (a copy of it is included in Appendix B). The Declaration gave voice to the frustrations of the colonists. It claimed that the king's actions were unfair, that he had violated the colonists rights, and that such unjust actions were sufficient to warrant the rejection of one form of government and the creation of another. The Declaration also set out the Enlightenment ideals of the consent of the governed and of natural rights, including life, liberty, and "the pursuit of happiness." The Declaration of Independence contained fighting words. Its purpose was not only to let the king know, in no uncertain terms, the extent of colonial anger against his actions; it also was to draw foreign attention to the colonists' plight, in the hopes of raising funds and armies for the inevitable conflict. Finally, and perhaps most importantly, the document was written in the hopes of mobilizing public opinion in the colonies in favor of rebellion. Thus it contained a list of grievances against the king, in addition to its statement of principles.

The Declaration of Independence is a powerful document that sets out America's philosophy of government: individual rights, equality, and the consent of the governed. What the Declaration did not do was actually create the form that the government should take. Another document was necessary to constitute a government, and the Articles of Confederation, adopted in 1781, served as the earliest constitution of the fledgling American government. Ratified even as the War for Independence was being waged, the Articles of Confederation specified the form of national government under which the newly independent colonies would operate. Unfortunately, as we shall see, that form proved unworkable, and a second, more long-lasting form of government was finally established with the ratification of the Constitution in 1789.

The Articles of Confederation

As we saw in Chapter 1, the United States under the Articles of Confederation (a copy of it is included in Appendix C) functioned under what is known as a confederal system. In this system, each individual state retains its own power and autonomy: The states are loosely associated under a weak national government. Individuals are citizens of the state in which they reside, and the federal government has no real authority over individual citizens. The states, not their citizens, make up the confederation. The confederation, called a "league of friendship," was similar to the United Nations today, in which each individual nation retains its sovereign status. As a form of government for a single nation, however, the confederation proved to be unworkable.

The biggest problem was that the national government was too weak to function effectively. The confederation had no separate executive branch (although there was a plural executive controlled by Congress and with limited power); there was no judicial branch; and Congress was unicameral. Each state had only one delegate, and those delegates were chosen not by popular election but by the state legislatures. Further, the confederation had no power to levy taxes or regulate commerce. Since the new federal government did not have the power to tax, it did not have the power to pay war debts or to properly provide a national defense. Without the power to regulate commerce, it also had no real means of coordinating activities among the states. By 1787 it became clear that this system could not last. "The consequences of an overly weak authority were clear: public disorder, economic chaos, and inadequate defense."[31] The American Constitutional Convention, which eventually devised the balance of powers system and federalism, was originally convened to find solutions to the problems inherent in the confederal system.

Constitutional Convention

Having found the Articles of Confederation to be unsuccessful, the new nation felt it had to return to the drawing board. In 1787, delegates from twelve of the thirteen states (Rhode Island chose not to send a representative) gathered in Philadelphia to discuss amending and revising the Articles. Because there were no other viable functioning democratic models in the world to emulate, their deliberations were both inventive and original. There was general agreement that the Articles had created a central government that did not have enough power; but beyond that, there was little agreement about what should be done to strengthen it or even how strong it should be.

Indeed, delegates to the Constitutional Convention strongly disagreed over many questions. For example, Alexander Hamilton favored a hereditary executive. Delegates quarreled over the form of representation to the new national legislative body as well. The Framers debated every aspect of the form and shape of their new democratic government at the Constitutional Convention in Philadelphia. The first ten amendments to the Constitution, which are known as the Bill of Rights and which have been so important to American political life and development over the past two hundred years, were also the subject of great debate. They were adopted because many of the delegates were concerned that the new national government might threaten individual liberty or states rights.

Virginia Plan: The First Design of a Parliamentary System?

You may already be familiar with some of the great controversies of the Constitutional Convention: whether representation should be based on population or given equally to states, whether slavery should be allowed, and how to account for slaves in determining population. What you may not know is that the Framers of the Constitution very nearly decided to establish a parliamentary rather than a presidential system. Although the concept of a parliamentary government as we know it today was still evolving, England had, by the late 1700s, established one very important characteristic of its parliamentary system: that the executive would be selected from the legislature.[32] Following the British example (as well as the example of most of the original thirteen states, which then required that the governor be chosen by the state legislature), the delegates to the Constitutional Convention originally voted to have Congress select the "national executive."

While the delegates to the Convention were still considering ways to amend the Articles of Confederation, the Virginia delegation quickly took control by submitting a proposal that would scrap the Articles altogether. The **Virginia plan** created a strong national government and established a bicameral legislature, with representation based on population. In addition, the Virginia plan proposed that "a National Executive be instituted; *to be chosen by the National Legislature*" (emphasis added). Several elements of the Virginia plan created controversy; most remember the plan for its reliance on population in determining representation. The Great Compromise (also known as the Connecticut compromise) accepted the bicameral legislature from the Virginia plan and gave the lower house popular representation. The compromise allowed for the upper house to have each state represented equally, as suggested by the New Jersey plan (although the New Jersey plan had proposed a unicameral, or one-house, legislature).

But representation was not the only problem delegates had with the Virginia plan. There was much discussion about whether the single executive proposed by the Virginia delegation was appropriate and, once that was decided, about the best method for the selection of the executive. Although the presidency is in many ways the defining feature of American democracy, it is important to remember that this office represented completely unknown territory to the Framers. The only real example they had of a national executive was a monarch—and they had fought a war to end the tyranny that monarchy imposed. In 1787, no other country had a president, or even a prime minister in the modern sense (at the time in Britain, the prime minister was an agent of the king). The authors of the Constitution were charting new territory in the creation of the national executive. "In 1787, the problem was far more baffling than it would be today, because the democratic executive was all but unknown. A popularly elected President was a novelty; the chief alternative solution, a prime minister chosen by the parliament, had not yet emerged in its modern democratic form even in Britain."[33]

The problem in creating the national executive revolved around how much power the office should hold. If the president were selected by the Congress, then the office would be relatively weak, subject to the whims and desires of the legislature. On the other hand, a single national executive, independent of Congress, might concentrate power too narrowly, thus creating the possibility for tyranny in the executive branch. Tyranny in the hands of one individual was to be avoided at all costs, given the experience of the colonists with the British monarchy. One way to limit the concentration of power in the presidency had already been tried and found wanting: having a plural executive. The Articles of Confederation had created an executive committee, which ultimately proved to be unwieldy. A single executive would create more energy in the office, eliminating the possibility of stalemate, which might occur if the members of a plural executive could not come to agreement on an issue. The delegates knew they wanted a single executive, but they did not know how to guarantee its autonomy from Congress. The Framers were not sure what to do. As a matter of fact, they voted in favor of the executive being chosen by the legislature a total of three times.

Delegates ended up with two choices: Either the legislature would chose the executive, as proposed under the Virginia plan, or selection would be made by an electoral college, as suggested by the New Jersey plan. After a great deal of discussion, the convention sent the matter to committee for consideration. The committee both decided that an electoral college would choose the executive and resolved another related issue, the term of office, by deciding that the president would be elected for a four-year term and would be eligible for reelection. The committee's decision was sent back to the full convention, which eventually voted in favor of the revised plan. Thus was the presidency born, a new and untried institution that ultimately proved to be one of the great successes of the Constitutional Convention.[34] And thus died the possibility of sending American political development in a parliamentary direction.

The Fear of Tyranny at the Founding

One of the greatest fears of the Framers at the Constitutional Convention was that pure democracy might degenerate into a form of tyranny. The form of tyranny they feared was not only the despotism of a single individual but also the tyranny of the majority, or the potential for mob rule. To guard against the danger of the tyranny of the majority, the Framers fashioned a representative democracy that provided for individual liberty by limiting the power and authority of the majority (and which, not coincidentally, favored the interests of the propertied minority). In their thinking on this matter, the Framers borrowed ideas from two notable political philosophers:

- the concepts of individual rights and the consent of the governed from the Englishman John Locke, and
- the notion of the separation of powers from the Frenchman Baron de Montesquieu.

Let us briefly examine these influential ideas of Locke and Montesquieu.

In his work entitled *The Two Treatises of Civil Government*, published in 1689 and 1690, John Locke advanced the then controversial argument that all individuals possess natural rights given to them by God. The existing government in

Britain relied on the doctrine of the "divine right of kings," which declared that kings derived their right to rule directly from God. In contrast, Locke suggested that every person has a natural right to "life, liberty, and property." Further, Locke stated that these rights were not granted by governments, but were "natural": that is, granted to individuals by their very nature as human beings. Natural rights are God-given rights and, as such, can be neither acquired nor given away. These rights suggested by Locke are rightly understood to be negative rights: rights that cannot be legitimately taken away by a government. Since God (not government) has granted each individual rights, no government can ever have the authority to take these rights away.[35]

Locke envisioned a political order without the absolute rule of a king and suggested that the rights of life, liberty, and property were natural to mankind and existed in the original state of nature. Unlike the British political theorist Thomas Hobbes, who described life in the state of nature to be "nasty, brutish and short," with individuals locked in a perpetual conflict over scarce resources, Locke envisioned a more peaceable state of nature. In Locke's view, individuals had the right of liberty as long as they did not violate the rights of others. The problem, however, was that in an unchecked state of nature the God-given rights of individuals could become imperiled by other individuals. Consequently, Locke suggests that government emerged from the state of nature by the terms of an agreement among people to provide for the protection of their rights.

The decision by individuals to leave the state of nature and form a government brings us to one of Locke's most important concepts: the social contract. He understood social contract theory to mean that individuals agree to leave the state of nature only on the terms of a social contract: Consequently, the *people* are rightly understood as the source of government. This concept is an important departure from the "divine right of kings," in that it holds that the government does not have a divine right to rule. In Locke's view, government is a human creation, because humans *precede* government: that is, although there can be people without a government, there can never be a government without people. Government, then, is ruled by the consent of the people, or the consent of the governed.

The Framers' also borrowed liberally from the ideas of another political philosopher, the Frenchman Baron de Montesquieu. In his 1748 work entitled *On the Spirit of the Laws*, Montesquieu gave the Framers an intellectual justification for the necessity of separated and equal branches of government. Montesquieu persuasively argued that fused legislative and executive powers would naturally lead to tyranny: "When legislative power is united with executive power in a single person in a single body of the magistracy, there is no liberty, because one can fear that the same monarch or senate that makes tyrannical laws will execute them tyrannically."[36]

Montesquieu holds that the best way to prevent the tyranny of the one, or of the many, is to divide political power into three separate branches, defined as the executive, the legislative, and the judicial. He envisioned that in such a three-branch arrangement, the legislature would have the authority to enact the law, the executive would be granted the power to both execute and enforce the law, and the judicial branch would be required to punish any and all violations against the law. Montesquieu argued that once these powers were clearly separated liberty could be safeguarded, for even if a person were to advance his or her selfish interests in one of the branches, the other two branches would be able to limit his assent to absolute power.[37]

Perhaps James Madison best articulated the vision of the Framers in Federalist No. 47, where he states that the very definition of tyranny is to consolidate all powers into one central authority. Madison, in particular, agreed with Montesquieu and viewed the separation of powers as a necessary precaution against the ambitions of those holding power. He held that it was of primary importance to create a system of checks and balances among the three branches of government that would effectively balance power against power and thus avoid tyranny. He argued for shared as well as divided powers, noting that "the accumulation of all powers, legislative, executive, and judiciary, in the same hands, whether of one, a few, or many, and whether hereditary, self-appointed, or elective, may justly be pronounced the very definition of tyranny."[38]

Political philosopher Harvey Mansfield has observed that Montesquieu's insights not only influenced Madison but also pulled a majority of the Framers in the direction of divided executive, legislative, and judicial powers. Mansfield notes that the Framers, following Montesquieu, considered that the separation of powers was a needed precaution against the "encroaching" and ambitious nature of politicians.[39]

These views were evident in the Declaration of Independence in 1776. The Declaration was a statement predicated upon the Lockean principles of individual rights and the consent of the governed and upon Montesquian principles of separated powers. The very first two sentences of the 1776 preamble of the Declaration of Independence reveal this influence: "We hold these Truths to be self-evident: that all Men are created equal, that they are endowed by their Creator with certain unalienable Rights, that among these are Life, Liberty and the Pursuit of happiness—That to secure these Rights, Governments are instituted among Men, deriving their just Powers from the Consent of the Governed."

The ideas presented within this sentence clearly echo the thoughts of John Locke. In particular, Thomas Jefferson refers explicitly to Locke's concept of negative rights and designates them to be "unalienable."[40] Further, he uses Locke's phrase "consent of the governed" to legitimize the new government, and he uses the term equality in

The signing of the American Declaration of Independence. Photo courtesy of the Architect of the Capitol.

Locke's restricted sense: namely, that each individual has an equal right to the God-given gifts of life, liberty, and the pursuit of happiness. These concepts informed the central philosophy behind the design of the new American Republic at the Constitutional Convention in Philadelphia in 1787 and are the root of the contemporary dilemma of majority rule versus minority rights in the United States.

Key Institutional Features of American Democracy

The American Constitution

Enacted in 1789, the new American Constitution established separate executive, legislative, and judicial branches. In the words of Seymour Martin Lipset, the Constitution provides for "a weak and internally conflicted political system" by according each branch the necessary power to prevent the other branches from absorbing more power.[41] Or, as James Sundquist argues:

> The men who made up the Federal Convention of 1787 wavered during the course of their deliberations on most of the specific features of the constitutional structure that

evolved, but they never vacillated on its central principle. That was the doctrine that the powers of the government must be separated into independent branches—legislative, executive, and judicial. Nearly all the delegates arrived in Philadelphia clearly committed to that objective. . . . The British government was cited as the model, but not today's British government. It was the government that existed—or was understood to exist—at that time, which was a government of separated powers.[42]

As such, and paradoxically, the same Constitution that assigns the president of the United States the duty to be the commander-in-chief of what has become the world's most powerful nation simultaneously limits his ability to get Congress to pass his legislative package.

The American Constitution is the oldest written constitution still in use, and its intricate design and complex checks and balances represent a uniquely American contribution to the art of democratic governance. It sought to divide, restrict, limit, check, and balance national governmental powers, and it is predicated on five central and interrelated principles:

- The Constitution subordinates the elected political leadership to itself, as the fundamental law of the nation.
- It divides and balances powers among the legislative, executive, and judicial branches: *Legislative power* is assigned to Congress under Article I; *executive power* is delegated to the president under Article II; and *judicial power*, or the power to interpret laws, was entrusted to the Supreme Court under Article III.
- It restricts the power, authority, and activities of national government vis-à-vis individuals through the Bill of Rights.
- It limits the power of the national government by granting state governments their own legal and political power and authority by the terms of Article IV and the Tenth Amendment.
- It also contains provisions for amendment.

In these interlocking ways, the Constitution has patterned the structure and behavior of American government. Over the past two hundred years, as political and social conflicts have been settled, the resolutions of the various political and social disputes have been codified by amendments to the Constitution and have themselves become part of the fundamental law. Once part of the Constitution, these very settlements have then demarcated the contours of subsequent change.[43]

Further, the Framers feared that the House of Representatives might be more likely than the other branches of power to wrest power away from the Senate, the executive, and the judiciary. To limit this possible tendency, the Framers decided to have the three branches chosen by different means:

> It seems to have been widely assumed at the convention that the House of Representatives would be the driving force in the system; that the people's representatives would be turbulent and insistent; that they would represent majorities and would be indifferent to the rights of minorities; that the people would be the winds driving the ship of state and their representatives would be the sails, swelling with every gust.[44]

As we shall see in the next chapter the Framers were most prescient in their views of the House of Representatives; the Contract-with-America Congress is an apt illustration of the House as the "driving force in the system," with "turbulent and insistent" members.

The Framers were steadfast in their desire to put a brake on the wily House of Representatives. In order for legislation to be passed, they required that it must also be approved by the Senate. And the Framers expected the Senate to be a quite different chamber from the House. Again using Britain as an example, the Framers in some measure modeled the Senate after the House of Lords. They expected senators to be from the landed aristocracy: propertied and learned men.[45] The method of election of senators would also be different from representatives: Whereas members of the House were to be chosen by direct popular election every two years, senators would be elected in staggered six year terms and chosen by state legislatures. (This method was changed in 1913, with the adoption of the seventeenth amendment, which provided for the direct election of senators.) And, of course, senators would represent their entire state, whereas the constituencies of representatives would be districts of similar population. (Although, in the case of states entitled to only one House seat, those representatives represent their entire state as well.)

The Framers were afraid of the concentration of power, whether in the hands of one, a few, or many. So they made certain that each branch would have some measure of control over the other branches by giving each one some of the powers of the others. Thus the president may veto congressional legislation; Congress may override presidential vetoes and must approve presidential appointments; the president appoints justices to the Supreme Court (with congressional approval); and the Supreme Court may hear cases having to do with U.S. law. (This eventually evolved into the power of judicial review: the power to decide whether an action of the president or Congress is constitutional.) In this way, each branch has the power to check another branch, and power is diffused rather than concentrated.

The Framers invention of the electoral college is noteworthy. The Framers, although fearful of an executive too dependent on Congress, did not propose popu-

The United States Capitol Building in Washington, D.C. Photo courtesy of the Architect of the Capitol.

lar election of the president. Instead, they decided to have each state "appoint, in such manner as the legislature thereof may direct, a number of electors, equal to the whole number of senators and representatives to which the state may be entitled to in Congress"(U.S. Constitution, Art. II, sec. 1). Further, representatives and senators were not to be eligible to become electors. By now, all states have established popular elections as the method of selecting electors (that is, members of the electoral college). But under the Constitution, other methods of selection—for example, having the state legislature choose the electors—would also be acceptable. Indeed, some states used this method for the first fifty years or so. Although Americans think of the president as being popularly elected, in fact, when Americans go to the voting booth, they are casting their ballots not for a particular candidate but for the electors who have promised to vote for that candidate.

Judicial Review

One further restriction on government was not specifically discussed in the Constitution: the idea of judicial review. The Framers set up a separate judicial branch, which would have the power to interpret the law. Judicial power allows for judges to decide whether the law has been applied correctly in individual cases. Judicial review gives the court additional authority. In the United States, the Supreme Court can rule on whether or not congressional legislation, acts of the president, or state laws adhere to the Constitution. There is evidence that the Framers also expected the Supreme Court to exercise judicial review. The Court established judicial review in the 1802 case, *Marbury v. Madison*, giving the judicial branch a powerful check on both the president and Congress. If the Court says that a law is unconstitutional, that law becomes invalid. The Court's decision can be changed only be an amendment to the Constitution or by its own reversal. This is one reason that Supreme Court appointments are often controversial. In the 1980s, Republicans were hoping that Reagan would be able to appoint enough conservative justices to achieve a majority on the Supreme Court and overturn the *Roe v. Wade* decision, which had made abortion legal in all fifty states. *Roe v. Wade* is an important example of the use of judicial review, which, over time, has been applied more frequently to state laws than federal laws. *Roe v. Wade* invalidated *state* laws that restricted abortion.[46]

A Democratizing American Government

In the years since the ratification of the Constitution, American government has gradually become more representative of the population. Unlike the British case, where the electorate was expanded by acts of Parliament (as we saw with the 1832 and 1867 Reform Acts), the expansion of the electorate in the United States has tended to take the form of constitutional amendments.

The Constitution, which in its original form implicitly condoned slavery and did not extend rights to slaves, was significantly altered after the American Civil War (1861–1865). The addition of the Thirteenth, Fourteenth, and Fifteenth Amendments to the Constitution, the so-called Civil War amendments, ended slavery, granted citizenship to the former slaves, and granted the former slaves the right to vote. Similarly, the Nineteenth Amendment was approved in 1920—after a long struggle for suffrage—granting women the right to vote. In 1971, the Twenty-Sixth Amendment gave eighteen-year-olds the right to vote, in response to youth protests that they were eligible for the draft at eighteen and yet had to wait three years for the right to vote. These changes have been made largely within the constitutional context that the Framers left us. In 1789, for example, representation for "We the People" was restricted to white men who were at least twenty-five years old. Over time, a series of difficult and contentious events have led to a generalized awakening of the principle of liberty and have resulted in the expansion of American citizenship.

TABLE 2.2   Important Events in the Formation and Evolution of American Democracy

I. The Philosophical Influences on the Framers of American Democracy

1512	Baron de Montesquieu, and the doctrine of separated powers
1660	John Locke, and the principle of limited government

II. British Laws and Taxes that Led to the American Declaration of Independence

1764	Sugar Act (repealed by Parliament in 1766)
1765	Stamp Act (revised by Parliament in 1766)
1767	Townshend Duties (taxes on a number of imported goods, including tea)
1770	Boston Massacre
1773	Boston Tea Party
1776	Declaration of Independence
1776–1781	War of Independence
1781–1987	Articles of Confederation

III. The Constitutional Convention

1787 (May)	Representatives convene in Philadelphia
1787 (July)	Virginia plan is presented and ultimately rejected
1789	Constitution voted on, ratified by states

IV. A Democratizing American Government

1865–1870	13th, 14th, 15th Amendments to the Constitution grant citizenship to the former male slaves
1920	19th Amendment grants all women the right to vote
1964	Civil rights legislation helps African-Americans overcome local restrictions on voting
1971	26th Amendment grants eighteen-year-old Americans the right to vote

Today, the concept of "We the People" covers all Americans, including African-Americans, women, and people over the age of eighteen.

Scholars point to the flexible nature of the Constitution as one of the key reasons that American democracy has survived for two hundred years. The Framers developed a document that not only gave structure to the government but also created a structure for change. When Americans refer to constitutional rights and principles today, they have a somewhat different version in mind than the Framers did. Yet the fundamental rights—life, liberty, self-governance—remain intact. American history shows a gradual expansion of those rights to include more and varied segments of the population than the Framers originally intended.

Conclusion

This chapter has briefly compared and contrasted political development in Great Britain and in the United States to illustrate how each nation's political history influenced the evolution of its form of democracy and to explain why the United States adopted a system of checks and balances and Great Britain did not. It is important to remember that the evolution of political development in Great Britain led that country to reject the notion of a fixed and fundamental set of laws and instead to adopt the idea of a flexible and sovereign legislative body. This British approach to government holds that it is better to accord the legislative body the authority to enact laws in response to the societal needs of the time than to be limited by a set of checks and balances detailed in a written constitution. In clear contrast, the American Framers rejected the notion of legislative supremacy and sovereignty. Rather, they upheld the concept of checks and balances operating under constitutional law.

The intricate design and complex balancing of powers in the Constitution represent a uniquely American contribution to the art of democratic governance. The Framers were fearful of tyranny, whether of the one, the few, or the many. To guard against the danger of tyranny, they created a system of separated powers to avoid concentrating powers in the hands of one or a few: They instituted a representative government in order to avoid the tyranny of the majority; and they limited government and created a system of checks and balances within government in order to avoid both the tyranny of the majority and a concentration of power.

In conclusion, a core difference between the British and American system may be identified in their views of the purpose of government. Britain relies on a flexible legislative body to respond to societal needs; the United States advocates limiting government to guarantee individual freedoms and avoid tyranny. As the preceding review of their respective political histories clearly demonstrates, Great Britain was most afraid of despotic tyranny (and so concentrated power in the legislature), and the United States was not only afraid of despotic tyranny but also of any concentration of powers—even in an elected legislature. Hence, the Framers of the American Constitution separated powers in a representative system as a method of limiting government.

In the next chapter, we examine how the American constitutional system of checks and balances thwarted quick government action on the part of the Republican-controlled 104th Congress, two hundred years after the Constitution was ratified.

Notes

1. Samuel P. Huntington, *Political Order in Changing Societies* (New Haven: Yale University Press, 1968), 93–139.

2. Huntington, *Political Order*, 93-139.

3. For some background on British political history, see Betty Kemp, *King and Commons, 1600–1832* (New York: Macmillan, 1957); David Robertson, *Class and the British Electorate* (New York: Basil Blackwell, 1985); and Kenneth D. Wald, *Crosses on the Ballot: Patterns of British Voter Alignment Since 1885* (Princeton: Princeton University Press, 1983).

4. See Huntington, *Political Order*, 93–139.

5. See the useful discussion in Colin Campbell et al., eds., *Politics and Government in Europe Today* (Boston: Houghton Mifflin Company, 1995), 74–75.

6. See Gregory S. Mahler, *Comparative Politics: An Institutional and Cross-National Approach*, 2d ed. (Englewood Cliffs, N.J.: Prentice-Hall, 1995), 106–108.

7. See the discussion by Philip Norton, *The British Polity*, 3d ed. (New York: Longmans, 1994), 38. He notes that "the Great Council itself was essentially the precursor of the House of Lords. The House of Commons evolved from the summoning to council, in the latter half of the thirteenth century on a somewhat sporadic basis, of knights and burgesses as representatives of the counties and towns. At various times in the fourteenth century the Commons deliberated separately from the Lords, and there developed a formal separation of the two bodies."

8. See Huntington, *Political Order*, 93–139.

9. See Mahler, *Comparative Politics*, 107.

10. Leonard Freedman, *Politics and Policy in Britain* (New York: Longman, 1996), 35.

11. Mahler, *Comparative Politics*, 183; Norton, *British Polity*, 39.

12. Norton, *British Polity*, 40.

13. See E. P. Thompson, *The Making of the English Working Class* (New York: Pantheon Books, 1964).

14. Norton, *British Polity*, 40; Freedman, *Politics and Policy*, 35.

15. See Michael Curtis, *Introduction to Comparative Government*, 4th ed. (New York: Longman, 1997), 38–39.

16. See Herbert M. Levine, *Political Issues Debated: An Introduction to Politics*, 4th ed. (Englewood Cliffs, N.J.: Simon and Schuster, 1993).

17. James Q. Wilson, *American Government, Brief Edition*, 3d ed. (Lexington, Mass.: D. C. Heath and Company, 1994), 6.

18. Norton, *British Polity*, 73.

19. Norton, *British Polity*, 59–63; see also Gillian Peele, *Governing the UK*, 3d ed. (Oxford: Blackwell, 1995), 1–47.

20. Norton, *British Polity*, 61.

21. See A. V. Dicey, *Introduction to the Law of the Constitution*, 10th ed. (London: Macmillan, 1959); Walter Bagehot, *The English Constitution* (1867; reprint, London: Fontana, 1993); Ivor Jennings, *The British Constitution*, 5th ed. (Cambridge, U.K.: Cambridge University Press, 1966); S. A. de Smith and Rodney Brazier, *Constitutional and Administrative Law*, 7th ed. (Harmondsworth: Penguin, 1994); Geoffrey Marshall, *Constitutional Theory* (Oxford: Clarendon Press, 1971).

22. Peele, *Governing*, 24–28.

23. Curtis, *Comparative Government,* 38–39.

24. Freedman, *Politics and Policy,* 120–121.

25. See Peele, *Governing,* 145–178.

26. The British speaker in the House of Commons should not be confused with the American Speaker in the House of Representatives. The American Speaker, similar to the British prime minister, is the leader of the majority party.

27. Freedman, *Politics and Policy,* 40–41.

28. Alan R. Gitelson, Robert L. Dudly, and Melvin J. Dubnick, *American Government,* 4th ed. (Boston: Houghton Mifflin Company, 1995), 36.

29. Wilson, *American Government,* 9.

30. See Theodore Lowi and Benjamin Ginsburg, *American Government,* 2d ed. (New York: W. W. Norton, 1992), 32–35.

31. Thomas E. Patterson, *We the People,* 2d ed. (New York: McGraw-Hill, 1998), 31.

32. As Matthew Shugart and John Carey note, although the Framers considered an executive *chosen by* the Congress, they never envisioned making an executive *responsible to* the legislature. Matthew Soberg Shugart and John M. Carey, *Presidents and Assemblies: Constitutional Design and Electoral Dynamics* (Cambridge, U.K.: Cambridge University Press, 1992), 5.

33. Robert A. Dahl, *Pluralist Democracy in the United States: Conflict and Consent* (Chicago: Rand McNally and Company, 1967), 80.

34. Dahl, *Pluralist Democracy.*

35. In contrast, a positive right is something the government must give to you, such as the right to a job or to a minimum standard of living or to an education. Locke's views were especially controversial in seventeenth-century continental Europe, as kings continued to justify their rule as divinely sanctioned. It was possible to publish these ideas in England, however, as the Parliament had won the Glorious Revolution in 1688 over the Stuart monarchy, which had sought to justify its rule on the basis of the divine-right-of-kings doctrine.

36. Charles de Secondat, Baron de Montesquieu, pt. 2, bk. 11, chap. 6 of *The Spirit of the Laws,* ed. and trans. Anne M. Cohler (New York: Cambridge University Press, 1989).

37. Montesquieu, *Spirit.*

38. James Madison, "Federalist No. 47," in *The Federalist Papers,* ed. Clinton Rossiter (New York: New American Library, 1961).

39. Bradford P. Wilson and Peter W. Schramm, eds., *Separation of Powers and Good Government* (Lantham, Md.: Rowman and Littlefield Publishers, Inc., 1994); Mansfield's quote is on page 10.

40. The only modification on Locke's original formulation of rights was the insertion of the expression "pursuit of happiness" in the place of "property."

41. Lipset, *American Exceptionalism,* 39.

42. James L. Sundquist, *Constitutional Reform and Effective Government* (Washington D.C.: The Brookings Institution, 1992). Also see Norton, *British Polity,* 48. Norton notes that the situation of apparent divided powers in England influenced the framers in Philadelphia to devise a system of executive and legislative powers.

43. See the useful discussion in Lawrence S. Graham et al., *Politics and Government: A Brief Introduction to the Politics of the United States, Great Britain, France, Germany, Russia, Eastern Europe, Japan, Mexico, and the Third World* (Chatham, N.J.: Chatham House Publishers, Inc., 1994), 1–7.

44. Dahl, *Pluralist Democracy*, 111–112.

45. Sundquist, *Constitutional Reform*, 22-45.

46. See Karen O'Connor, *No Neutral Ground* (Boulder, Colo.: Westview Press, 1996).

3

Welcome to the World of Checks and Balances

A Legislative History of the 1994 Republican Contract with America

Gingrich seems to think of himself as a kind of prime minister, chosen by the House of Representatives, as a U.S. equivalent of the British Parliament. Since, under the Constitution, he cannot bring down the government, he appears ready to act as a kind of 'counter government.'

—Eugene J. McCarthy

The 104th Congress came in like a lion and went out like a lamb.

—Cokie Roberts

Introduction to the 104th Congress

SEPTEMBER 27, 1994: On a beautiful early fall day, more than 350 Republican congressional candidates lined the steps of the United States Capitol. The group included both current members of the House of Representatives (incumbents) and others trying to gain a seat in the House (challengers). There was more than a sense of optimism among the group; there was almost a sense of euphoria. These men and women had gathered in the warm fall sun to make a dramatic statement. They were trying to wrest control of the House from what they saw as its Democratic stranglehold, and they were doing so on a conservative party platform that essentially nationalized the election. The 367 Republicans who signed the contract promised that they would debate and vote on a ten-point legislative agenda within the first one hundred days of Congress. Further, they told their constituents, "If we break the contract, throw us out." In an era when elections had been criticized as too focused on local issues, the Republican candidates brought forth a national agenda. In a time when the public was fed up with gridlock in Congress, the Republicans promised swift action. And in a time when the country seemed to be moving toward the middle, the Republican contract pulled the political debate to the far right.

The sense of euphoria that was just beneath the surface on that beautiful September day emerged in full force just six weeks later, when the Republicans swept the Congress. For the first time in forty years, the Republican Party won the majority of seats in the House. They had also taken control of the Senate, bringing back the "divided government" that had been the mainstay of American politics throughout the 1970s and 1980s. Only this time, it was the Democrats who had the presidency and the Republicans who controlled Congress. For the Democrats, the election results were staggering. "When the returns were in, dozens of Democratic incumbents were swept away, while not one Republican House member, senator or governor was defeated."[1] Not only that, some of the Democrats who lost were among the most powerful players in Congress, including Speaker Thomas Foley, who was the first sitting speaker in 130 years to be voted out by his constituents. Only two years earlier, the Democrats had been filled with a similar sense of euphoria when they finally gained control of the White House for the

House Republican leader Newt Gingrich opens a ceremony in front of Capitol Hill on 27 September 1994 to present the Contract with America to the American people. It contains a ten-point reform program that a Republican majority would seek to enact in the first one hundred days of the 104th Congress. Photo courtesy of Reuters/Corbis-Bettmann.

first time in twelve years. Now they faced a weakened and relatively unpopular president and a Congress dominated by the opposing party. In Washington, it seemed as if the world had been turned upside down.

Not surprisingly, the Republicans seized the moment with vigor. Having run for reelection on a national platform that had received intense media coverage, the House Republicans were quick to claim that they had a mandate for change. In fact, "the 'Contract' proved to have far more significance after the election than before it, serving as the key organizing force for the newly minted majority."[2] Elected politicians often claim to have a "mandate" for their policies, but this time it was different. The Republicans had an actual document with specific details; their mandate was almost palpable. Conservative commentator Charles Krauthammer summed up the Republican position in 1994: "Having intentionally nationalized the campaign on this program, the Republicans have acquired the mandate to enact it."[3] The Republicans had an agenda and they had control. Nothing could stop them from making their contract into law. Right? Well, let us fast-forward for a moment to 1996, as the 104th Congress came to a close. The Republicans had had two years to enact the contract; one might think that it had become the law of the land. In fact, only three major provisions of the contract had been signed into law: the line-item veto (which was later overturned by the Supreme Court)[4], welfare reform, and the elimination of unfunded federal mandates (requirements that the federal government imposed on states without reimbursement).

Welcome to the World of Checks and Balances

What on earth happened? How could those jubilant fall days of 1994 have led to such limited legislative success? Welcome to the world of checks and balances. In fact, as we saw in Chapter 2, the Framers of the Constitution specifically set out to create a system that would thwart legislative initiatives such as the Contract with America. Obviously, they could not have had the contract in mind when they wrote the Constitution, but they were fearful of debate that was ruled by passion and instead tried to institutionalize deliberation.

What happened to the contract first was that the Senate (whose Republicans had *not* run on the contract) refused to be rushed by the flurry of activity in the House. The Framers of the Constitution required that in order for a bill to become law it must pass both chambers of Congress (the House and Senate) in identical form. Second, the president also balked at going along with everything that was coming out of the Republican Congress. And since the Constitution gives him power to veto legislation, even if the House managed to get the Senate to agree to a particular bill, there was no guarantee that the president would sign it. The Constitution also gives Congress the power to override a presidential veto but makes it more difficult than passage of legislation. For a bill to pass initially, there must be a simple majority in both houses. To override a presidential veto, the bill must receive a two-thirds majority, which is much more difficult to obtain. Despite their majority in both houses, the Republicans did not comprise two-thirds of the members of either house, meaning that they would have to convince Democrats to vote to override a veto. Many Democrats in Congress were doing everything in their power to delay or postpone consideration of items on the contract and were not about to vote for veto overrides. (You may have heard some discussion about a "veto-proof" majority. Very optimistic Republicans were hoping to gain sixty-six seats in the Senate, which would have given them a two-thirds majority and eliminated the necessity to get Democrats to vote for veto overrides.)

The Framer's Fears of the Tyranny of the Majority and the 1994 Republican Contract with America

About now you might be protesting, "But this is gridlock! Surely the Framers of the Constitution did not intend to create gridlock!" You have to think back to the concerns of the Framers. Although they did not exactly go about trying to create gridlock, they realized that legislative inaction could be part of the price of the elimination of what they thought was a greater evil: tyranny. You might be thinking, "How can the Contract with America represent tyranny when the electorate clearly voted for the Republicans?" In fact, as we discussed in Chapter 2, the Framers were as much afraid of the tyranny of the majority as they were of the tyranny of the few or of one. Let us briefly review the Framer's fear of tyranny in terms of the Republican contract.

First, James Madison, in Federalist No. 10 (reprinted in Appendix D), describes the evils of a "faction," which could lead to the tyranny of the many: "By a faction I understand a number of citizens, whether amounting to a majority or minority of the whole, who are united and actuated by some common impulse of passion, or of interest, adverse to the rights of citizens or to the permanent and aggregate interests of the community." In other words, a faction is a group united by a common interest, an interest that is in opposition to the public good. Although Republicans and Democrats can have endless debates over whether or not the contract was in fact "adverse to the rights of citizens," that is actually beside the point. In creating the general principles of government, the Framers had to establish broad protections against large-scale political movements, and they had no way to predict whether such movements would be good or bad. Madison explains in Federalist No. 10 that a minority faction would be easy to control, whereas a majority faction would create more difficulties:

> If a faction consists of less than a majority, relief is supplied by the republican principle, which enables the majority to defeat its sinister views by regular vote: It may clog the administration, it may convulse the society; but it will be unable to execute and mask its violence under the forms of the Constitution. When a majority is included in a faction, the form of popular government on the other hand enables it to sacrifice to its ruling passion or interest, both the public good and the rights of other citizens.

A majority faction, according to Madison, has great potential for harm in a democratic system. If an idea that is contrary to the public good takes hold of the majority of citizens, then the public good could be sacrificed to the will of the majority. How, then, can a majority faction be controlled? The Framers of the Constitution believed that only a "republican" form of government could do this.

They were not referring to what we know today as the Republican Party; instead the Framers meant a representative form of government. Elected representation, according to Madison, could eliminate the threats of a faction by allowing representatives "to refine and enlarge the public views, by passing them through the medium of a chosen body of citizens, whose wisdom may best discern the true interest of their country and whose patriotism and love of justice will be least likely to sacrifice it to temporary or partial considerations."

This view seems to take us back in circles. If the purpose of elected government is to "refine and enlarge" public opinion, thereby avoiding political faction, why then was the Republican Congress unable to pass the contract intact? Madison and the Framers were also afraid of tyranny within government itself, as Madison's Federalist No. 51 (reprinted in Appendix E) makes clear: "You must first enable the government to control the governed; and in the next place, oblige it to control itself. A dependence on the people is no doubt the primary control on the government; but experience has taught mankind the necessity of auxiliary precautions."

What are these auxiliary precautions? They are the very checks and balances we discussed in the previous section. In Federalist No. 51, Madison says that "the great security against a gradual concentration of the several powers in the same department, consists in giving to those who administer each department the necessary constitutional means and personal motives to resist encroachments of the others." By departments, Madison was referring to the institutions of government, thus the president can "resist encroachments" from Congress by exercising the veto; the Senate can resist encroachments from the House by refusing to pass identical legislation; and both houses can resist encroachments from the president by overriding his vetoes.

The Framers forced public opinion to be muted in two ways. First, Congress, as an elected body, would deliberate over issues that had sparked the passions of the people, and second, the system of checks and balances would create a further brake on initiatives by one part of government. Hence, the Framers knowingly made it difficult for legislation to pass and created a system that inevitably thwarted House Republicans' plans for the Contract with America. In fact, the architects of the contract were well aware of the institutional obstacles they faced in passing the legislation. That is why their campaign promise was *not* passage of the items on the contract, but merely bringing them to a vote in the House, a much more achievable goal.

The history of the Contract with America is an apt illustration of our central dilemma: that the rule of the majority is often impeded by constitutional protections of minority rights. The remainder of this chapter will examine the history of the contract, by

- exploring the background against which the contract was developed,
- examining the actual tenets of the contract itself, and
- taking a look at what actually happened in Congress as the contract was being debated.

Throughout, you will note the frustrations of both the majority and minority parties. Chapter 4 shall return to the 104th Congress and imagine what might have happened if we had a parliamentary system. For now, let us turn to the congressional system in existence.

Background: Where Did the Contract Come From?

Imagine that you are a Republican representative in 1994. You have been part of · the minority party for as long as you can remember. The last time the Republicans had the majority was in 1954, which was certainly before you were elected and possibly even before you were born. What has this minority status meant to you? Most likely it has meant immense frustration, as you have watched your legislative proposals die before even being considered and seen even your attempts at amending Democratic proposals thwarted because of Democrats' limitations on amendments to bills on the floor. You have been excluded from the decision-making process, perhaps even cut out of important meetings by Democratic representatives. From your perspective, at least, a form of the tyranny of the majority has been alive and well in the Democratic-controlled Congress for the past forty years! Your frustration is shared by your fellow Republicans, who have experienced similar setbacks in their attempts at legislating.

Aside from having your party gain control of the Congress, what would be at the top of your wish list? Probably two things: First, you would wish for a change in the way the House works. You would like to see an easing of the rules so that your voice could be heard and your proposals considered. Second, you would probably have some pet legislative ideas that you would like to see enacted, probably some conservative policies that do not have a chance in a Democratic Congress. In fact, these were the two major goals of the architects of what eventually became the Republican Contract with America.

The first goal, changing the rules, was shared by some frustrated Democrats. Congressional Scholar Roger H. Davidson notes that "agitation for changing the way Congress does its business came to a head in the 1990s. There were tensions between senior leaders and junior members, between appropriators and authorizers, between House and Senate members. Most troubling was the escalating combat in the House between an entrenched Democratic majority and a restless Republican minority."[5] During the 103rd Congress, while Democrats still held the majority, Republicans submitted a proposal to change House rules. Proposed by Gerald Solomon (R–NY), the "Mandate for Change in the People's House" listed forty-three reforms to change the way the House did business: from floor and committee procedures to relations with the president. Although many rank and file Democrats supported at least some of the changes, House leadership was obviously not pleased with the proposal, which ultimately failed. However, Democratic leaders had been persuaded to appoint a Joint Committee on the Organization of Congress, which considered the proposals and held hearings on congressional procedures. The hearings drew attention to the procedural problems in Congress and strengthened the Republicans resolve.[6]

In early 1994, as the midterm elections were drawing near, Republicans began to work on a national campaign strategy. House Republicans got together for a conference in Salisbury, Maryland, on a snowy February weekend. The purpose of the conference was to develop and refine a legislative agenda for the 104th Congress. Members of the conference defined five major goals of what they called their "vision" of America:

1. Individual liberty
2. Economic opportunity
3. Limited government
4. Personal responsibility
5. Security at home and abroad[7]

The goals of this conference eventually evolved into the contract. Representatives Newt Gingrich and Dick Armey, who stood to gain much by a Republican victory (they became Speaker and majority leader, respectively), pushed to develop a platform on which all Republicans could run. The decisions about what to include as the major planks of the platform were largely based on public opinion poll results. The Republicans chose to highlight those conservative issues that resonated with voters and avoid more controversial subjects, such as abortion and school prayer. Eleven working groups made up of Republicans in Congress put together the ten planks, which were all versions of bills that had already been proposed by Republicans but had been frozen out by the Democratic majority.[8] Somewhere along the way, Kerry Knott, executive director of the House Republican Conference, identified the ten bills as a "contract." As the contract was being drafted, a preface was added that included eight procedural reforms initially proposed in the "Mandate for Change in the People's House."

The Contract with America was not the first time Republicans had attempted to use a contract as an electoral tool. In fact, Ronald Reagan went to the Capitol in 1980 to sign a similar contract with Republican candidates for Congress as he campaigned for the presidency.[9] The main difference was that the election of 1980, which resulted in a Republican president and a Republican Senate, sent a Democratic majority back to the House of Representatives. The 1980 contract, although it spelled out Republican goals for governing, could not become the legislative tool that the 1994 contract became. Democrats in the House were able to maintain more control of the legislative agenda because of their majority status in the 97th Congress. Although Reagan was successful in defining legislative priorities, the Democratic House was able to block some of his initiatives. Republicans used the idea of a contract in subsequent elections, although the contracts did not get much press attention until 1994, when it appeared that the party might be able to take control of Congress.

There is another important caveat to remember about the Contract with America: Although it defined the activities of the 104th Congress, it did not necessarily define the election in the minds of voters. Even with as much fanfare as it received, a majority of Americans were unfamiliar with the contract in November 1994. And some Democrats believed that without the contract, the Republicans could have won even more seats in the House. The voters who were aware of the contract were, in some districts, more familiar with the Democrats' negative interpretation of it.[10] On the other hand, the contract mobilized Republican candidates; and voters, whether or not they were aware of the contract itself, were able to differentiate between Republican and Democratic views of government. Shortly after the election, the *Washington Post* noted that "surveys clearly show Americans intended to seize the reins of government from Democrats and hand them over to Republicans."[11] The contract, which may not have directly impacted voters decisions, did help to create a national identity for the Republican party: "Few would suggest that the contract itself was the most significant factor in the GOP's historic gains. But it appears to have benefited Republicans overall by providing a national agenda and offering challengers a specific program to promote if they did not already have one."[12]

The contract is particularly useful for our purposes because it provided a national platform on which one party could run, and it gave rise to a clearly identified, nationally known party leader in the person of Newt Gingrich. Both of these factors made the American congressional election of 1994 look similar to an election in the British parliamentary system, in which party is paramount, voters are shown clear differences between and among parties, and legislative leadership comes directly from party leadership. As we shall see, although the election superficially resembled a British parliamentary election, the legislative process itself remained firmly rooted in the American constitutional system.

The Contract with America

Before getting into a discussion of how the contract fared in Congress, let us step back for a few moments and examine the document itself. The Contract with America contained a preface, which stated its purpose and described some changes in the way Congress worked. It also presented ten major legislative planks, which included recommendations for change in several substantive policy areas. The document emphasized the possibility of a new Republican majority in the House with the upcoming 1994 election; this new majority would "transform the way Congress works," reduce the size of government, and "restore accountability to Congress." The preface promised that if the Republicans won the majority in the House, they would bring eight procedural reforms to a vote on the first day of the 104th Congress.[13] Following is a list of those procedural reforms:

1. Require that all laws that apply to the rest of the country apply to Congress as well. (For years, Congress had exempted itself and its employees from most workplace and nondiscrimination laws.)
2. Select an independent auditing firm to audit Congress for waste, fraud, and abuse.
3. Cut the number of House committees and cut committee staff by one-third.
4. Limit the terms of all committee chairs.
5. Ban casting of proxy votes. (Previously, the rules of the House had allowed an individual committee member to authorize another member of the committee to vote in his or her absence. "Proxy" votes are convenient for members of Congress, who often have to be in several places at the same time, but they also mean that committee meetings are sometimes sparsely attended.)
6. Require committee meetings to be open to the public.
7. Require a three-fifths majority vote to pass a tax increase. (In Congress, most bills are passed with a simple majority vote—half plus one. A three-fifths majority would make tax increases much harder to pass.)
8. Implement zero-base budgeting. (Zero-base budgeting is an accounting tool that essentially requires all budgets to start from zero funding, rather

than from last year's "base" budget, which is the usual starting-point for governmental budgets.)

Although these were by no means the only procedural changes favored by the 104th Congress, the eight reforms would have a dramatic impact on day-to-day activities in the House. By voting on them on the first day, Republicans intended to demonstrate their intention to change the way Congress works.

The substantive portion of the contract is contained in its ten major planks, which Republicans promised to bring to a vote on the floor of the House within the first one hundred days of the 104th Congress. Although listed as "acts," the ten planks do not translate into ten pieces of legislation. Several planks included what became two or more bills. Following is a list of the ten issues presented in the contract:

1. **The Fiscal Responsibility Act** had two parts, both of which entailed amendments to the Constitution: the balanced budget amendment and the line-item veto.
2. **The Taking Back Our Streets Act** was also known as the anticrime package, which eventually was divided into several bills dealing with victim restitution, the exclusionary rule, prison construction, and law enforcement.
3. **The Personal Responsibility Act** dealt with welfare reform, both giving more discretion to the states and providing restrictions on eligibility.
4. **The Family Reinforcement Act** provided tax breaks for families and the elderly, child support enforcement, and penalties for child pornography.
5. **The American Dream Restoration Act** repealed the marriage tax penalty (married couples pay more in taxes than they would if single and making two incomes) and established a tax credit for children.
6. **The National Security Restoration Act** prohibited foreign (UN) command of U.S. troops and the use of defense cuts to finance social programs; it also proposed developing an anti-ballistic missile (ABM) system.
7. **The Senior Fairness Act** raised the Social Security earnings limit (under which seniors who earn over a certain amount of money lose a percentage of their Social Security benefit) and also repealed the 1993 tax increases on Social Security benefits.
8. **The Job Creation and Wage Enhancement Act** gave incentives to small businesses, cut the capital gains tax, and eliminated "unfunded mandates" (requiring states or businesses to engage in specified activities without reimbursing them).

9. **The Common Sense Legal Reforms Act** was designed to discourage litigation. It limited punitive damages, instituted "loser pays" rules, and limited product liability.

10. **The Citizen Legislatures Act** limited the terms of both senators and representatives.

As you can see, there was some overlap among the ten planks; for example, tax breaks for the elderly are addressed in both the Family Reinforcement Act and the Senior Citizens Fairness Act. In addition, several planks contained two or more bills; for example, the Fiscal Responsibility Act consisted of both the balanced budget amendment and line-item veto, which were considered as two separate pieces of legislation. These anomalies later made scoring of the contract difficult. If the House passed the line-item veto but not the balanced budget amendment (which actually happened), would plank number one be considered a win or a loss? Nonetheless, the fact that the contract included such detailed legislative initiatives gave the newly elected Republicans a focal point in Congress. Plus, it provided a scorecard, a way to keep track of how well Congress was doing. Although the contract promised only to bring these items to a vote in the House, Republicans, Democrats, and the media all eventually used the scorecard to judge the issues based on final passage into law.

You will note that the Democrats did not have their own contract, at least not in terms of a specific, detailed agenda. Scoring for the Democrats would be simpler—they could be judged successful if they kept the Republicans from passing items on the contract. Fortunately for the Democrats, the American constitutional system makes it easier to keep the status quo than to implement sweeping changes. This also illustrates a difference between the British parliamentary system and the American congressional system. In the British parliamentary system, the opposition party (similar to what we would call the minority) is a "party-in-waiting" that develops and promotes an alternative legislative agenda and is ready to implement it at any given moment, should there be a vote of no confidence to topple the majority party. Clearly, the Democrats had an agenda they wished to pursue, should they regain the majority in the next election, which was two years away. However, their agenda was not set forth in a written document, and knowing that they had to face at least two years of a Republican Congress, their purpose was to block the majority party's legislation rather than to promote their own. Of course, their role was similar to the role the Republicans had played in the previous Congress. The minority party in the American system is put in the position of creating obstacles to the majority party, regardless of which party is in power.

The First Hundred Days of the 104th Congress

Let us now turn to the contract's fate in the legislative process. Having won the elections of 1994 in a sweep, the Republicans wasted no time in flexing their new-found muscles. "The voters gave Republicans their first Senate majority in eight years, their first majority of governors since 1960, and their first House majority since 1954, a breadth of power few if any active Republican politicians can re-call."[14] To see what happened to the Republican legislative agenda, let us take a snapshot picture of three different days during those much-discussed first hundred days: day one, or January 4, when the Republicans took over the reins of Congress for the first time in fifty years; day fifty, midway through the first hundred days; and day one hundred, the deadline the Republicans had set for themselves. For each day, we will mark the progress of the contract, the obstacles that had been set in its way, and its successes.

Day One: Let the Hundred Days Begin

On the first day of the 104th Congress, an ebullient Newt Gingrich takes over the speakership to the raucous cheers of House Republicans and observers in the gallery. After the swearing in and speeches, the House gets down to business and starts to change some of the procedural rules that the Republicans felt had bogged down the Democratic Congress. The day ended well after 2 A.M., setting the stage for the long workdays to come.

The first day of the 104th Congress began officially at noon on January 4, when the House chaplain opened the session with a prayer. All of the newly elected and reelected representatives were gathered in the House chamber on the south side of the Capitol building. Many had family members with them: husbands, wives, parents, and reflecting the relative youth of the "freshman" class of Congress, lots of babies and children. The Republicans—both freshmen and incumbents—were ecstatic at their newfound majority status; in stark contrast, Democrats' faces reflected the gloom they felt at having lost the locus of power. At about quarter to one, the vote for Speaker began. As the clerk called the roll in alphabetical order, members announced their preferences: Republicans voted for Gingrich, and most Democrats voted for Gephardt, although some voted "present" in a form of protest over a candidate they felt represented Democratic failures. At 1:17 P.M., the roll call was completed, and to no one's surprise, Newt Gingrich had been elected as Speaker of the House: the first Republican Speaker in forty years. Republicans in the House and in the visitors' gallery erupted in boisterous applause. The new Speaker received a standing ovation, which repeated itself when he had made his way through the crowded House and arrived at the Speaker's podium. In contrast, a grim minority leader, Richard Gephardt (D–MO)—who had been the Speaker under the Democratic majority—was now responsible for transferring power away from his party and to the opposition. As the applause died down, Gephardt managed to joke: "This is not a moment I've been waiting for." In testament to the system's peaceful transitions of power, Gephardt then announced, "With resignation but with resolve, I hereby end forty years of Democratic rule of this House." Handing the gavel to Gingrich, Gephardt said, "You are now my Speaker. Let the great debate begin."[15]

The great debate began almost immediately. After Gingrich completed a thirty-minute speech, he was sworn in by the "dean" of the House (Democrat John Dingell of Michigan, the House's longest-serving member). Gingrich, as the official Speaker, then administered the oath of office to the rest of the representatives, and the House got down to work. The first order of business was consideration of the rule changes specified in the preface to the contract. The contract had specified that these changes would be passed on the first day of the 104th Congress, and Republican leaders, intent on keeping that promise, prohibited amendments to the rules package. In a striking reversal of roles, Democrats loudly protested the prohibition, saying that the Republicans were locking them out of the process. Of course, when Republicans were in the minority, they had said the same thing about the consideration of Democratic bills. In fact, Republicans had vowed to allow a more open amending process when they took over Congress. But, as a news account reported, adhering to the contract was more important to Republicans than opening up the amendment process, at least on the first day:

> The Democrats began January 4 by saying the Republicans were hypocrites for bringing the package up under a procedure that prevented amendments, a practice the GOP had promised to curtail after complaining about it for years in the minority. But the Contract With America had committed the GOP to enacting its institutional measures on the first day of the session, and its leaders said they did not want to be denied by dilatory tactics or prolong debate on Democratic amendments.[16]

For their part, Democrats borrowed from Republican practices and complained that they were being held back from creating broader reform. Representative David Bonior (D–MI) proposed several amendments, including one that would impose limits on book royalties (clearly aimed at Gingrich, who had accepted a several-million-dollar advance for a book deal):

> In the sometimes acrimonious back and forth over who is more committed to reform, opening day continued a contest that has been under way for several years, only the parties have switched roles since the election. Now it is the Democrats, whose

leaders once quashed efforts to radically restructure the institution, who contend that the majority party is stifling reform in Congress; and it is the Republicans, just after taking power, who must defend their operations.[17]

Opening day was taken up by legislative activity on the rule change measures: first debate and a vote on procedural motions and then debate and a vote on actual legislation. At the end of the day, the Republican House had voted in several sweeping changes to the way it does business: It eliminated some committees; changed the jurisdiction of others; eliminated 600 (mostly Democratic) staff positions; ended proxy voting; required open committee meetings; limited individual representatives from holding committee and subcommittee chairs for more than three consecutive terms, and the speakership for more than four; required a super-majority for tax increases; and required an audit of the House's financial records. At 2:24 A.M. on Thursday, January 5, the House adjourned, after a grueling fourteen-and-one-half-hour day.

At the end of the day, the House had kept the promise made in the preface to the Contract with America. In so doing, it had reversed a years-long trend toward decentralization of power. Since 1974, when another famous freshmen class arrived in Congress (the so-called Watergate Babies, who were elected on a reform agenda in protest of the Nixon administration), power had been devolving away from the Speaker and toward committees and subcommittees. The 104th Congress ended that trend, placing more power in the hands of the Speaker and limiting the powers of committee and subcommittee chairs. Despite the somewhat acrimonious debate, the House Republicans won every vote on that first day, and for the most part, Democrats voted in favor of the Republican reforms.

One day down, ninety-nine to go.

Day Fifty: Exhaustion Sets In

Midway to the one-hundred-day mark, Republicans in the House have passed only four of the ten planks of the platform, in addition to the preface. Lawmakers are exhausted; representatives as well as their staffs complain of long days, lack of sleep, and the otherwise frenetic pace of the "contract" Congress. Now not just satisfied with voting on the contract, Republicans are beginning to focus on getting it signed into law.

As February 22 dawned—the midway point of the first one hundred days—Republicans in the House were able to claim some major legislative accomplishments, but they had a lot of work still ahead of them. After the marathon first day, Republicans had also been successful in passing a bill to end Congress's exemption from workplace laws. The hectic pace of the first day continued, as Congress abandoned the traditional break between opening day and the State of the Union Address and shortened the President's Day recess from its usual ten days to five.[18] In January and February, the House took up some of the more popular provisions in the contract: the balanced budget amendment and line-item veto (which together made up the first plank of the contract), the crime bill (which was split into six smaller bills), the national security bill, and the unfunded mandates legislation. Republican unity during consideration of these bills was extraordinary: in 73 of the first 139 roll call votes, Republicans were unanimous. On only 13 votes did more than ten Republicans defect to the other side.[19] Such statistics drew comparisons to Congress in the 1980s, when congressional Republicans were called "Reagan Robots" for showing unwavering support during votes on administration proposals. Remarkably, House Republicans in the 104th Congress were even more unified than the so-called Reagan Robots. Their majority status was clearly giving energy to the Republicans: "Republicans' unity is an illustration of a phenomenon familiar to political scientists: New majorities tend to be cohesive because the euphoria of newly acquired power is a strong unifying force."[20]

For their part, Democrats were adjusting to their minority status, which took them by surprise and for which they were completely unprepared.[21] Generally, liberal Democrats chose to work against the Republicans by offering "amendments designed to draw sharp distinctions between the parties rather than to lure Republicans to cross party lines."[22] On many votes, however, Democrats chose to cross party lines to go along with the contract legislation. Republicans defected from the leadership on only a handful of occasions, and only once did they actually kill a contract provision: On February 15, twenty-four Republicans decided to vote with Democrats to eliminate the anti-ballistic-missile defense provision. In the end, Republican leaders decided that strict adherence to the specifics of contract was less important than passage of legislation, and so they gave in on this occasion, and others, to demands for compromise from within the party's ranks.

Day fifty was a time, albeit brief, for reflection. The GOP conference held a rally in the Canon House Office Building caucus room. Speaking to that rally, Representative John Boehner (R–OH) said, "We are changing America for the better just as we promised we would."[23] Representatives and staff persons waived American flags and cheered. Although Republicans were pleased with their successes in the first fifty days, they also knew that they had been considering some of the most popular bills in the contract, the ones most likely to gain bipartisan support. The second fifty days would be filled with more acrimonious debate, as the House considered more contentious issues, such as welfare reform and term limits. Tax reduction legislation, although popular, held its own perils, because any reduction in revenues would have to be offset by a concomitant decrease in spending. Spending cuts are always infinitely more difficult to pass than tax cuts. In addition, the Senate, which is a more deliberative body, was also beginning to draw in the reins on the revolution and, in any case, was not inclined to go along easily on every House measure. Bills were already being slowed down by Senate consideration. In the first few weeks of February, House Republicans were operating at a breakneck pace, while the Senate was taking its time: "In the time House leaders have allotted for the line-item veto, several crime bills, a national security measure and regulatory reform over the next three weeks, the Senate will be debating just one thing: a constitutional amendment to balance the budget."[24]

This breakneck pace was beginning to take its toll on both members and staff. As the first fifty days were drawing to a close, House committees struggled to meet deadlines for legislation set by House leadership. Committee consideration of health, environmental, and safety regulations, for example, went into the wee hours of the morning.[25] Democrats (and some Republicans) began to complain about the cost of such a frenetic pace. According to the *Washington Post*, "critics are also beginning to notice frayed edges: sloppy legislation, uninformed debate and unseemly willingness to take on gargantuan tasks with little or no forethought."[26] The long days were immensely tiring physically as well. Staff and representatives regularly worked fourteen or fifteen hour days, getting little sleep and eating a lot of junk food. (Imagine if the intensity of exam week lasted for one hundred days, and you get an idea of how exhausted they were.) Bad health habits inevitably led to irritability, lack of concentration, and illness, as many staffers and members came down with severe colds. Even Newt Gingrich came down with the flu shortly after the halfway mark in the one hundred days was reached.

An exhausted House of Representatives looked forward to April 13, if only for a chance at a vacation.

Day One Hundred: The Reality of Checks and Balances

Week of April 3: With all but one of the contract's planks having been voted on by the House, the time is ripe for the Republicans to celebrate, and celebrate they do. Events at the Capitol include several circus elephants performing on the east plaza, a parody of Newt Gingrich performed by comedian Chris Farley, a video of the original "signing of the contract" during the 1994 election, and speeches by several leaders, including, of course, Newt Gingrich. In a final ecstatic note, on Friday, April 7, the House votes on the last plank of the contract—the tax reduction bill—and finishes up the contract legislation on day ninety-four, six days before their actual deadline. Newt

Gingrich wraps up the week by addressing the public on prime-time national television, something that no Speaker has ever done before.[27] Still exhausted but happy, Republicans vow NOT to come up with a contract for the next one hundred days. Their happiness is muted, however, by the knowledge that only one of the contract's planks has actually been signed into law.[28]

The morning of April 5 dawned bright and sunny, a spring replica of the beautiful fall day—was it only six months earlier?—that had marked the signing of the Contract with America. Now, although it was still more than a week away from April 13, the actual one-hundred-day mark, the Republicans were beginning to celebrate. Barnum and Bailey was marking its 125th anniversary, and Republicans had invited the circus to bring its elephants to the east plaza of the Capitol, where the animals performed in unison, prompting comparison to the unified front the Republicans (whose symbol is the elephant) had presented throughout the first three months. On April 7 (day ninety-four), with a last gasp of energy, the Republicans passed a tax reform measure, the last of the contract legislation. A short time later, the celebration began in earnest when the Republican National Committee sponsored a party on the steps of the Capitol, where they replayed the video of the signing of the contract.

What was the cause of all this celebration? Aside from the fact that the grueling first one hundred days were almost over (on the actual 100th day, Congress would be in recess), Republicans were pleased to report that they had kept the promise they made in September: The House had voted on every single one of the contract's ten planks. Where did this leave the contract?

Well, it was not exactly law. Only one item, restrictions on unfunded mandates, had been signed by the president.[29] And this item was only one part of plank eight, the Job Creation and Wage Enhancement Act (see above); so technically, not a single full plank was actually completed. The Senate had approved several measures, including the line-item veto, limits on child pornography, and the paperwork reduction act. The Senate had also explicitly rejected one House bill: the balanced budget amendment, which was only half of the first plank (the other half was the line-item veto). Since, then, the bills the Senate approved were only pieces of various planks, you could say that not a single plank was completed in the Senate either, depending on how you were keeping score. Finally, the House itself had explicitly rejected some parts of the contract, including the ABM proposal mentioned earlier and the congressional approval of peacekeeping missions, both parts of the national security plank.

What were the prospects for House legislation that had not yet been considered in the Senate? Bills certainly were not going to be considered as quickly by the Senate, and some faced the prospect of defeat or significant revision. And even

FIGURE 3.1 *Congressional Quarterly*'s Contract Score Card (as of April 1996)

□–Action begun
■–Action completed

	House Committee	House Floor	Senate Committee	Senate Floor	Conference/Final	President
Preface Congressional Process						
• Require that Congress end its exemptions from 11 workplace laws. (HR 1, S 2—PL 104-1)		■		■	■	■
• Revise House rules to cut committees and their staffs, impose term limits on committee chairmen, end proxy voting, require three-fifths majority for tax increases. (H Res 6)		■				
1 Balanced-Budget Amendment and Line-Item Veto						
• Send to the states a constitutional amendment requiring a balanced budget. (H J Res 1)	■	■	■	■		
• Give president line-item veto power to cancel any appropriation or targeted tax break. (HR 2, S 4)	■	■	■	■		
2 Crime						
Require restitution to victims (HR 665); modify exclusionary rule (HR 666); increase grants for prison construction (HR 667); speed deportation of criminal aliens (HR 668); create block grants to give communities flexibility in using anti-crime funds (HR 728); limit death row appeals. (HR 729)	■	■				
3 Welfare						
Convert nutrition programs into block grants to states, end payments to mothers under age 18 who have children out of wedlock, require proof of paternity to receive welfare, require work after receiving two years of welfare benefits, impose a lifetime five-year cap for most welfare benefits, end payments to most noncitizens, allow states to impose other restrictions and cap welfare spending. (HR 4)	■	■				
4 Families and Children						
• Require parental consent for children participating in surveys. (HR 1271)	■	■				
• Offer tax credits for adoptions and home care of the elderly. (part of HR 1215)	■	■				
• Increase penalties for sex crimes against children. (HR 1240)	■	■				
• Strengthen enforcement of child support orders. (part of HR 4)	■	■				

(continues)

FIGURE 3.1 *(continued)*

■–Action begun
■–Action completed

	House Committee	House Floor	Senate Committee	Senate Floor	Conference/Final	President
5 Middle-Class Tax Cut — Add $500-per-child tax credit; ease "marriage penalty" for filers of joint tax returns; expand individual retirement account savings plans. (part of HR 1215)	■	■				
6 National Security — Prohibit use of U.S. troops in UN missions under foreign command; prohibit defense cuts to finance social programs; develop a missile defense system; cut funding for UN peacekeeping missions. (HR 7)	■	■				
7 Social Security — Repeal 1993 increases in Social Security benefits subject to income tax; permit senior citizens to earn up to $30,000 a year without losing benefits; give tax incentives for long-term insurance. (part of HR 1215)	■	■				
8 Capital Gains and Regulations — • Cut capital gains tax rate; accelerate depreciation on equipment. (part of HR 1215)	■	■				
• Reduce unfunded mandates. (HR 5, S 1—PL 104-4)	■	■	■	■	■	
• Reduce federal paperwork. (HR 830, S 244)	■	■	■	■	■	
• Require federal agencies to assess risks, use cost-benefit analysis, reduce paperwork, and reimburse property owners for reductions in value due to regulations. (HR 9, S 291, S 333, S343)	■	■	■			
9 Civil Law and Product Liability — • Establish national product liability law with limits on punitive damages, other restrictions. (HR 956, S 565)	■	■				
• Make it harder for investors to sue companies. (HR 1058)	■	■				
• Apply "loser pays" rule to certain federal cases. (HR 988)	■	■				
10 Term Limits — Send to the states a constitutional amendment limiting congressional terms. (H J Res 73, S J Res 21)	■	■	■			

(continues)

98

FIGURE 3.1   *(continued)*

House Changes to Contract	Date of House Vote	Outlook (as of April 1996)
No significant changes.	Jan. 5 (HR 1)	President Clinton signed the bill Jan. 23 (PL 104-1).
Three-fifths "supermajority" limited to income tax rate changes, rather than all tax increases.	Jan. 4-5 (H Res 6)	Implemented by House on first day. Democrats say GOP is fudging on promises for open votes.
Dropped requirement for three-fifths majority vote of each chamber to increase taxes.	Jan. 26 (H J Res 1)	Senate on March 2 failed to pass H J Res 1 by 65-35, two votes short of required two-thirds majority.
No significant changes.	Feb. 6 (HR 2)	Senate passed a different version, S 4, on March 23. Conference will be difficult.
Postponed federal mandatory minimum sentences for gun crimes; block grants made more flexible; provisions added to require reimbursement to states for costs of incarcerating illegal aliens.	Feb. 7-14	Packaging the proposals in Senate could raise the stakes. Democrats will fight some "get tough" proposals such as restricting death row appeals. Controversial proposals to ease gun control laws could be added.
Food stamps exempted from nutrition block grants; more programs consolidated into block grants; federal entitlement to many welfare programs ended; some modification in restrictions on aid to unwed mothers under age 18 and noncitizens. Restrictions added to Supplemental Security Income payments for disabled children, drug addicts, and alcoholics.	March 24	Influential senators are cautious about ending welfare entitlements and giving states full power over programs. Restrictions on unwed teenage mothers and legal immigrants are controversial. Clinton wants more emphasis on helping states move welfare recipients into jobs. Might be added to budget-reconciliation bill.
Dropped some statutory mandatory minimum sentences for sex crimes in favor of directing federal sentencing commission to increase punishment guidelines.	March 23 (HR 4) April 4 (HR 1240, HR 1271) April 5 (HR 1215)	Tax breaks will be caught up in Senate's revisions of all tax-cut proposals amid concern about the deficit. Child support and sex crime provisions enjoy strong bipartisan support.
Tax cuts made contingent on Congress voting on a plan to balance the budget.	April 5	Clinton has proposed a phased-in $500-per-child tax credit covering fewer families. Senate Republicans are wary of cutting taxes while deficit is high, but IRA provision may survive.
House substantially watered down anti-missile defense provision in floor action.	Feb. 16	Clinton strongly opposes restrictions on peacekeeping missions. Senate Majority Leader Bob Dole is pushing his own less-restrictive peacekeeping bill. Other provisions may shift to defense authorization bill.

(continues)

FIGURE 3.1   *(continued)*

House Changes to Contract	Date of House Vote	Outlook (as of April 1996)
No significant changes.	April 5	Repealing tax increase will be hard in Senate because trust fund is short of money. Clinton has supported "modest" increase in earnings exemption. (p. 999)
Capital gains rate cut by a third; provision added to phase out alternative minimum tax; "freeze" added on new regulations (HR 450); property-owner reimbursement scaled back.	Feb. 1 (HR 5) Feb. 22 (HR 830) Feb. 24 (HR 450) March 3 (HR 9) April 5 (HR 1215)	Senate may well reduce most tax cuts; unfunded mandates bill signed March 22 (PL 104-4); paperwork bill cleared April 6; Senate is split on how far to go to restrict new regulations; freeze proposal changed by Senate to 45-day review period.
Added new limits on medical malpractice awards.	March 10 (HR 956) March 8 (HR 1058) March 7 (HR 988)	Senate scheduled to consider a narrower product liability bill (S 565) the week of April 24, with trial lawyers and consumer groups still adamantly opposed. Big floor fights could occur on punitive damage caps and medical malpractice awards. Investor lawsuit bill considered less likely to move to floor this year; "loser pays" faces strong opposition in Senate.
No significant changes.	Defeated March 29	Senate leaders say they will take up the issue. Supreme Court rules this year on constitutionality of state term limits.

SOURCE: *Congressional Quarterly Weekly Reports* 53, no. 14 (8 April 1996), 996–997.

those bills that survived Senate action and conference committee action might eventually receive a veto from President Clinton[30]:

> Like the welfare bill, the most important and controversial legislation that the House has approved this year faces varying degrees of trouble in the Senate. "Most of the [House contract] will be addressed in one form or another, but a lot of it may be changed," Senate Majority Whip Trent Lott (R–MS) said. Even if approved by the Senate, at least some could run into a presidential veto.[31]

One might think that actually Democrats had more cause to celebrate than Republicans. Despite the rhetoric about a Republican revolution tearing down laws that had been in place since the New Deal, there had been little real change, by the first one hundred days, in the nation's laws, other than those affecting Congress. Nevertheless, Republicans had significantly altered the national agenda, and Democrats were preparing for difficult fights in the Senate. As the one hundred days came to a close, "Republicans headed home . . . in a state of weary euphoria," while Democrats "looked at the same legislative output and saw disaster."[32]

And how was everyone going to mark the end of the one hundred days? With a three-week recess.

Constitutional Limitations on Passage of the Contract

Whatever Happened to the Senate?

With so much attention being paid to the House of Representatives for the better part of six months, one might begin to wonder about the importance of the Senate. Although the focus of activity and media coverage was clearly the House, in the American system of checks and balances, the Senate plays a critical role as a check on its companion chamber.

To begin with, the contract was not nearly as important in the Senate as it was in the House. The much ballyhooed signing ceremony in September 1994 was attended by House Republicans only. Although senators had been invited to sign the contract, they chose instead to have their own, much smaller, campaign event a week earlier, at which they introduced the Senate campaign platform. Remember "Seven more in 94"? Probably not. Republicans needed seven more seats to gain a majority in the Senate, and so they came up with a seven-point legislative agenda that was not nearly as far-reaching as the House contract. Nor did it include some of the contract's important provisions, such as unfunded mandates, tax breaks, and the line-item veto. In addition, senators did not sign their agenda, nor did they make any promises regarding scheduling or votes. Finally, although the House contract included specific legislative language, the Senate pledge dealt more in generalities.[33]

The Senate is a much different body than the House. Individual members are granted much more leeway, and one Senator can actually block legislation from coming to a vote. (Legislation is brought to the Senate floor by "unanimous consent," which means that if one person does not want that legislation considered, he or she can stop it.) Senators consider themselves to be much more individualistic than House members, and most would not want to commit to something as restrictive as a contract. Part of the reason for this is that the Senate has a much different electoral outlook than the House. In the Senate, terms are for six years, and elections are staggered so that every two years only one-third of senators are up for reelection. In the House, obviously, every Representative is up for reelection every two years. Hence, even if Republicans running for election or reelection to the Senate had chosen to sign the contract, they would have made up a very small percentage of the senators elected in 1996. On the other hand, every House Republican would have to face his or her constituents in 1996, thus giving individual representatives motive to keep the promises made in the contract. Republican senators did not face the same electoral concerns.

The Framers of the Constitution knew what they were doing in 1789. They wanted Congress to be accountable to the people, and so the House of Representatives would have to face frequent elections. But they also wanted to create a check on the passions of the public, the "tyranny of the majority" that we talked about earlier, and so they created a Senate that could have the luxury of being more deliberative and more reflective, since its membership would not have to concern itself as frequently with the vagaries of elections. Although the Framers were not specifically thinking about the contract, they clearly wanted to put obstacles in place that would limit the ability of Congress to make sweeping changes, and they gave the minority party much more power in the Senate. In keeping with the Framers' view of the Senate's role, Senate rules have evolved over the years to encourage discussion over quick action. Senators can hold up legislation by simply talking it to death: a legislative tool known as the **filibuster**. According to Senator Robert Byrd (D–WV), himself a practitioner of the filibuster, "The rules of the Senate are made for the convenience of those who wish to delay."[34] The Senate today is, indeed, a more deliberative body. And it is also more conservative, not in the strict ideological sense but in the sense of being cautious. For example, although House Republicans were prepared to push for tax cuts from the beginning of the 104th Congress, Republican senators were more hesitant to pass such legislation. Pete Domenici (R–NM), chairman of the Senate Budget Committee, urged Congress to put its energies into reducing the deficit before tackling large-scale tax cuts.[35]

When House Republicans finished their versions of contract bills, they sent them to the Senate for consideration, and often, especially in the beginning of the first one hundred days, the Senate held up those bills. Majority Leader Bob Dole (R–KS), who himself was running for president, wanted to establish clear differences between the House and Senate. He scheduled consideration of legislation based on the preferences of Senate Republicans, not on the basis of the contract. However, as the first hundred days drew to a close Dole and the House Republicans saw the electoral advantages of going along with the contract. According to Eddie Mahe, a Republican political consultant, "It may have been Newt Gingrich and the House that has the 'Contract With America,' but in the minds of the overwhelming majority of Americans who know anything about it, it's not a House Republican Contract, it's a Republican Contract."[36] Senators were wary of being accused of putting up obstacles in the way of House Republican reforms. Nevertheless, Majority Leader Dole would not make any promises about passing contract bills: "The next 100 days will belong to the Senate. We aren't setting any deadlines, and no one expects the Senate to be a rubber stamp for the House."[37]

No wonder House Republicans only promised to bring contract bills to a vote on the House floor. They knew there were no guarantees on what would happen to legislation once it left the House. What's more, they could not even guarantee passage in their own chamber, even with a Republican majority.

President: The Bills Stop Here

As you know, in order for a bill to become law, it must pass the House and Senate in identical form and be signed by the president. Although President Clinton, shortly after the 1994 elections, had been placed in the position of defending his "relevance" in the face of the Republican majority in Congress, he still had a very powerful tool: the presidential veto. Since the Senate had not even considered most of the contract legislation by the end of the first hundred days, the president had had very little opportunity to exercise the veto. As the one hundred days came to a close, Clinton began to indicate that he just might veto some of the contract bills. Clinton stated: "In the first 100 days, the mission of the House Republicans was to suggest ways in which we should change our government and our society. In the second hundred days and beyond, our mission together must be to decide which of these House proposals should be adopted, which should be modified, and which should be stopped."[38]

Although he had the ability to stop legislation with a veto, President Clinton ended up not using that tool frequently. The only contract bill that he did actually veto after the one hundred days were up was a welfare reform bill, which was eventually retooled and sent back to him and which he ultimately signed. As noted earlier, the Republicans did not have a "veto-proof" (two-thirds) majority in either chamber, so you might imagine that President Clinton would have used this tool more frequently. In fact, the Clinton administration had been pummeled by the health care debacle in 1994 and by the subsequent election of Republicans. Facing his own reelection in 1996, Clinton chose not to differentiate himself too clearly from the Republicans. Seeing the popularity of the contract among the American public, the president—with an eye to the 1996 election—made a political choice to support many of its provisions, even when they were at odds with his political inclinations.

One reason the House was able to push the contract was that Republicans perceived the president to be in a weak position. They wanted to get legislation through as quickly as possible, knowing the president would be unlikely to wield his veto weapon too fiercely during an election year. Although the power was there, it went relatively unused.

The Supreme Court

Although the judiciary would not become involved in the Contract with America until later, it is nonetheless an important player in the system of checks and balances. We have seen how division of power within Congress acts as a brake on the speedy passage of legislation and how the presidential veto may act as a further brake. Once legislation has been passed and signed into law, it sometimes faces another hurdle. The Supreme Court, under the Constitution, has the power to declare a law unconstitutional, even though that law went through the normal legislative process and was signed by the president. The line-item veto is an example of a law that faced this additional hurdle. The president used the line-item veto in 1997 to delete several programs and tax breaks in congressional spending bills. Some of the entities (including the state of New York) that faced financial injury from the cuts filed suit, and the Supreme Court, in a 6–3 decision on 25 June 1998, ruled in their favor and overturned the line-item veto. The Court relied on the constitutional separation of powers—the very checks and balances that we have been discussing—in making its decision. The line-item veto, according to the Court, was a violation of the separation of powers because it gave the president the authority to take a legislative action. In vetoing part of a bill, and not the bill in its entirety, the president was effectively amending legislation and overstepping the bounds of the executive branch. Even though Congress had agreed to such a veto, the Court still found that it was a violation of constitutional intent. According to the Court, the line-item veto can be instituted only by an amendment to the Constitution.

Thus the Supreme Court serves as an additional brake on political processes. The Framers specifically set up the three branches of government in such a way that any one branch has the ability to thwart the actions of the other two, thus limiting the tyranny of the one, the few, or the many.

Conclusion: How the Constitutional System of Checks and Balances Makes the American Congress Function Differently than the British Parliament

Despite all of the hoopla over the contract, and the comparisons made here between the election of 1994 and a parliamentary election, the legislative history of the contract actually illustrates how different the American presidential system is from the British parliamentary one. What happened during the first three months of the 104th Congress is that Republican leaders attempted to impose some characteristics of the British parliamentary system on the American congressional

The American system of checks and balances keeps any one branch from dominating the entire political system. Here, President Clinton waves as he is applauded by Vice President Al Gore (at left) and by his rival in the legislature, House Speaker Newt Gingrich (at right) and as he takes the podium for the State of the Union Address on 24 January 1995. Photo courtesy of Reuters/Corbis-Bettmann.

process: notably, a well-defined legislative agenda and party discipline. "The normal inertia of the institution gave way to a frenetic pace, with major legislation actually passing the House and occasionally the Senate. The Congress acted more like a parliament than a traditional Congress."[39] House Republicans were successful in actually imposing these characteristics on the House (albeit for a limited time); but the system itself is set up in such a way that other, outside barriers, limited policy success in ways that are unheard of in the British parliamentary system. To conclude this chapter, let us examine some of the characteristics of the American system that distinguish it from politics in Great Britain.

The Legislative Process Is More Open

One of the reasons there are so many steps to the American legislative process is to ensure that a large number of voices can be heard. For example, as bills are being considered in both chambers of Congress, there are generally committee hearings, at which outsiders (interest groups, individual citizens, even members of the administration) are invited to participate and testify. After the hearings, committees hold "**markup**" sessions in which a bill is debated and amended by committee members—both majority and minority. Usually markup is itself open, with the press and public welcome to attend. Prior to committee consideration, subcommittees have often already completed a similar process in considering the same bill. Finally, the bill is considered on the floor, where individual senators and representatives may also make amendments. Again, members of both the majority and minority parties can propose floor amendments to legislation. The process is long, convoluted, and often difficult. No wonder the old saw says that you do not want to watch either sausages or legislation being made!

In contrast, the process for creating legislation is much more streamlined in the British parliamentary system. The majority party, having run on a well-defined agenda, is truly given a mandate to implement it. Party leaders work together to develop legislative language—without the input of the minority party (or parties, as the case may be). The actual writing of legislative language occurs in what we might think of as the old-fashioned "smoke-filled back room." The government sends legislation to the floor in advanced form, and it is usually not open for amendments. Traditionally, votes are party-line, with the party in power voting for the legislation, and minority parties voting against. If party leaders cannot keep their rank and file members (known as back-benchers) in line for votes, then they know their government is headed for trouble. In addition, the executive branch is not separated from the parliament. Cabinet ministers, unlike the American system, do not have to resign their legislative seats to take their executive posts. And, of course, the British prime minister has enormous power, serving as both the chief executive (like the American president) and the head of the legislative majority party (like the American Speaker of the House). Gillian Peele has noted that Conservative Prime Minister Margaret Thatcher took full advantage of her powers:

> . . . by the end of the 1980s, Mrs. Thatcher's government had itself generated a major constitutional and political debate as her style of premiership incurred charges of authoritarianism. Moreover, the Conservative administration's policies underlined the absence of checks and balances in the British system and the enormous extent of the powers vested in an elected government, powers which, while they might be lawfully exercised, were difficult to reconcile with ideas of limited, consensual or balanced government.[40]

Such a streamlined process makes the creation of legislation much easier, but it also keeps minority parties, or even back-benchers in the majority party, from having much say. Even in the 104th Congress, which was so dominated by Republican leadership, Democrats as well as rank and file Republicans had opportunities to amend legislation; and interest groups and the public had some opportunity to comment on legislation as it was being made (although Democrats complained loudly that Republicans were trying to stifle alternative views during committee hearings and floor consideration). Where the Republican 104th Congress was similar to the British Parliament was in the creation of the contract itself. Republican leaders got together outside the traditional legislative process to propose the planks of the contract. The legislative language of the contract was written outside the public eye, without input from the opposing party, which, of course, would not be interested in working with the other side as it created its campaign document. Working only with party members and interest groups favorable to its positions, the Republican Party was able to create an unabashedly conservative document.

At first glance, it appears that the creation of such a detailed legislative platform was highly unusual for the American congressional system. It should be noted, however, that congressional parties had been doing similar sorts of manifesto electoral programs for some time. If the Republicans had lost the 1994 congressional elections, the contract would have been ignored as well. The unexpected Republican takeover of the House for the first time in forty years brought an incredible amount of publicity to the contract, and the contract become a focal point for the legislative activities of the 104th Congress.

Recent elections have been noted for their attention to individual districts and their lack of party unity. Even when the parties had more control over congressional elections, they would talk about general principles, not specific details of legislation. "The parliamentary tenor of the House in its first hundred days meant that deliberation in the classic sense—carefully thinking through alternatives, debating them, and then moving to a broader public judgment—was virtually absent in the House, either in committees or on the floor. The emphasis was on processing legislation, not on debate and discussion."[41]

The Republican contract differed from a British parliamentary legislative agenda in two important ways. First, legislation was written prior to the actual election, which would not be necessary in a parliamentary election. Second, and even more importantly, despite the fact that the Republicans had detailed legislative language ready to go as soon as they were elected, they still had to go through the steps of the legislative process discussed above. Had the Republicans been in Parliament, they could simply have brought the bills up for a largely predetermined vote. Although floor votes were largely predetermined in the 104th Congress, there was a long way to go between the introduction of a bill and the vote on the floor. Despite having a majority and a specified legislative agenda, Republi-

The executives from two of the world's great democracies, American President George Bush and British Prime Minister John Major, at the north portico of the White House on 21 December 1990. Photo courtesy of Reuters/Corbis-Bettmann.

cans were not assured of legislative success. Note the aversion of minority leader Richard Gephardt to the pace of the legislative agenda: "This hundred days is a self-imposed national emergency that made no sense. It's caused all of them to jerk stuff through the procedure much faster than it should be. There hasn't been enough committee consideration or floor consideration."[42]

Party Discipline Is Fleeting, at Best

One notable characteristic of the first one hundred days of the 104th Congress was the unity with which the Republicans voted. According to a survey of legislative votes done by *Congressional Quarterly*, most of the freshmen Republicans voted with the party on contract legislation 94 percent of the time or more. Fifty-three of the 75 freshmen had scores of 100 percent; 141 of the 230 House Republicans voted with the party 100 percent of the time. The lowest scoring Republican was Connie Morella (R–MD), with a 73 percent voting record on contract legislation.[43] These numbers are striking because they are so high for the American Congress. They are not high at all compared to a British-style parliamentary system, where party discipline is paramount. The governing party in Parliament normally expects most of its members to vote with it on legislation.

On the other hand, the Democrats in the 104th Congress show a sharp contrast to a minority party in the British Parliament: Southern Democrats, for example, voted with the contract 67 percent of the time—two Southern Democrats had 100-percent voting records and five Southern Democrats had 94-percent voting records with respect to the Republican contract.[44] Minority party members in Parliament would not be voting for the majority party legislation. Instead, they would be trying to distinguish themselves from the majority by creating an alternative legislative agenda. Back-benchers of both parties in Parliament tend not to act unilaterally or to cross party lines. As a kind of "government-in-waiting," the minority party wants to have a plan of action should the majority party lose control of the legislature.

Coalition-building—not a hallmark of the 104th Congress—is usually a characteristic of the American congressional system. Knowing that legislation has to go through an arduous process to get passed, proponents of a particular bill often try to create a bandwagon by courting members of the other party and interest groups. Compromise and bargaining are usually two characteristics of coalition-building. Coalitions in American politics generally form around an issue or cluster of issues. In contrast, a "coalition" in the British parliamentary government usually refers to two or more parties who have joined together to create a majority when no one party received a large enough percentage of votes in the parliamentary election.

Accountability Is Limited

One very positive attribute of the party discipline that exists in the British parliamentary system is the high level of accountability. Since one party is in charge of both the executive and the legislative branches, that party can and must take full responsibility for both the enactment of legislation and its implementation. And if the voters do not like what is going on in government, they know exactly whom to blame: the majority party. In the American system, with its separation of powers and its openness, it is often difficult to see who is responsible for action or inaction in government. If public opinion turns against some aspect of the contract as the laws are being implemented, governmental actors will busy themselves with playing the "blame game." Republicans will say that it is the Democratic administration's fault for not implementing the laws properly. Congressional Democrats will say it is the Republicans fault—after all, they (the Democrats) did everything they could to stop the Republican legislation from passing. Congressional Republicans might counter that Democrats in Congress weakened the bill through the amendment process. And the president can say that it is not his fault, he is just trying the best he can to implement the flawed legislation Congress sent him. The British prime minister has no such option in Parliament. He or she is responsible for the creation and implementation of legislation, and the voters will hold him or her accountable.

In the American system, on the other hand, no one can ever really be held accountable for legislation, and so it is much easier for members of both parties to distance themselves from unpopular policies when running for reelection. Since the reelection motive is so strong, it is extremely difficult to establish responsibility, much to the chagrin of the voting public.

"Policy Windows" Are Only Open for a Short Time

John Kingdon, in his book *Issues, Alternatives and Public Policies*, describes the process by which an issue reaches the top of a government's decision agenda in the U.S. Congress. According to Kingdon, a "**policy window**" opens up when politics, policy, and problems come together to create the right time for a particular piece of legislation to pass. When a problem in society exists, when there is a proposal to solve that problem, and when the political mood is right, legislation will be enacted. Otherwise, the legislation does not really have a chance. That is why large numbers of bills are proposed in Congress but only a very limited number ever make it to a floor vote, much less become enacted. Members of Congress are aware of the fleeting nature of these policy windows and rush to enact legislation when they feel a window has opened up. The 104th Congress clearly saw an open policy window during the first one hundred days of the legislative session and rushed to pass all of the Republican bills in the House. The idea for the one hundred days came from the early days of the New Deal (which the Republican contract was basically trying to undo). Because of the magnitude of the Great Depression, President Roosevelt rushed to pass legislation when he first got into office, and Congress pretty much went along with him. (The roles were reversed during the 104th Congress: Congress pushed legislation and the president went along with it.) Roosevelt was able to push a great number of bills through during his first one hundred days because of the palpable crisis the country was experiencing. The Republicans wanted to imitate that sense of urgency and immediacy during their first one hundred days as the majority party, although the nation certainly was not facing a crisis as immediate as the Great Depression had been. However, the idea of the one hundred days did create a window of opportunity—a policy window—through which the Republicans could control the legislative process.

The concept of a policy window, and the idea of rushing to pass legislation, is antithetical to the way the British parliamentary system works. The policy window opens up as soon as a party wins the majority and remains open until the next election. The majority party often has enough power and enough votes to pass any bill it would like, and so there is usually no sense in hurrying legislation through. The party in power may as well take as much time as it likes to develop legislation. There are some exceptions to this, of course. If there is an immediate crisis, such as a war or a depression, then the party will probably be in a rush to pass bills. In Britain, after the 1979 victory of the Conservative Party and through the early 1980s, Prime Minister Thatcher rushed through legislation to take apart the welfare state that she had campaigned against. This was not so much because of a national crisis but because she wanted to powerfully demonstrate the new direction in which she would take the country. In this regard Gillian Peele notes:

> The experience of [British] government after 1979 underlined how . . . few barriers there were to restrain a radical government determined to press forward its programme even against opposition from local authorities, the courts and the House of Commons. It also underlined how ambiguous was the idea that government ought to consult affected interests, a requirement which constitutional writers such as Ivor Jennings had once emphasized strongly. Indeed, it was part of the Conservative government's strategy to ensure that organized interests should not be allowed to shape public policy.[45]

In contrast, House Republicans felt that quick passage of the contract was necessary not only as a powerful symbolic move but also because they knew the policy window might not stay open for long.

Thus the complicated American legislative process results in more openness, allows for minority voices to be heard, encourages compromise and bargaining, and favors deliberative processes. The British parliamentary system is less open but allows the majority party to get its work done in a less encumbered fashion. The 104th Congress illustrates the strengths and weaknesses of the American system: On one hand, it was an anomaly, since the Republicans had a defined legislative agenda, kept party unity, and the House acted quickly on legislation. On the other hand, it was characteristic of the way Congress works, since the outcome of contract legislation was not foreordained, (particularly when you take into account the Senate, the president, and the judiciary) and Republicans had to work within a policy window.

Plus ça change, plus ç'est la même chose.

Notes

1. Juliana Gruenwald, "Shallow Tactics or Deep Issues: Fathoming the GOP Contract," *Congressional Quarterly Weekly Reports*, 19 November 1994.

2. Norman J. Ornstein and Amy L. Schenkenberg, "The 1995 Congress: The First Hundred Days and Beyond," *Political Science Quarterly* 110, no. 2 (1995): 194.

3. Charles Krauthammer, "Republican Mandate," *Washington Post*, 11 November 1994, sec. A, p. 31.

4. The Supreme Court overturned the line-item veto with a 6–3 vote on 25 June 1998. The Court said that the veto violated the constitutional separation of powers by giving the president legislative powers. In a concurring opinion, Justice Anthony M. Kennedy said that "Liberty is always at stake when one or more of the branches seeks to transgress the separation of powers." (Quoted in Robert Pear, "Spending at Issue," *New York Times*, 26 June 1998, sec A, p. 16.) Note that one branch (the Supreme Court) stepped in when another branch (the presidency) was usurping the powers of the third branch (the Congress).

5. Roger H. Davidson, "The 104th Congress and Beyond," in *The 104th Congress: A Congressional Quarterly Reader*, eds. Roger H. Davidson and Walter J. Oleszek (Washington, D.C.: Congressional Quarterly Press, 1995), 3.

6. Davidson, "The 104th Congress," 3.

7. Ed Gillespie and Bob Schellhas, eds., *Contract with America: The Bold Plan by Rep. Newt Gingrich, Rep. Dick Armey and the House Republicans to Change the Nation*, (New York: Times Books, 1994).

8. Donna Cassata, "Republicans Bask in Success of Rousing Performance," *Congressional Quarterly Weekly Reports*, 8 April 1995, 988.

9. Linda Killian, *The Freshman: What Happened to the Republican Revolution?* (Boulder, Colo.: Westview Press, 1998), 5.

10. Gruenwald, "Shallow Tactics or Deep Issues."

11. Richard Morin, "Voters Repeat Their Simple Message About Government: Less is Better," *Washington Post*, 13 November 1994, sec. A, p. 1.

12. Gruenwald, "Shallow Tactics or Deep Issues."

13. Note that members of the House of Representatives are elected for two-year terms. Elections are held in even years; members of Congress are sworn in the following January. A "Congress" consists of two one-year "sessions," which have been numbered in consecutive order starting with the first Congress in 1790. So 1995 was the first session of the 104th Congress and 1996, the second session; and the election of 1996 led to the swearing in, in 1997, of the 105th Congress.

14. David S. Broder, "Vote May Signal GOP Return as Dominant Party," *Washington Post*, 10 November 1994, sec. A, p. 1.

15. Janet Hook, "Republicans Step Up to Power in Historic 40-Year Shift," *Congressional Quarterly Weekly Reports*, 7 January 1995, 92.

16. David S. Cloud, "GOP, to Its Own Great Delight, Enacts House Rules Changes," *Congressional Quarterly Weekly Reports*, 7 January 1995, 14.

17. Cloud, "GOP, to Its Own Great Delight," 13.

18. "GOP Plan for a Marathon January," *Congressional Quarterly Weekly Reports*, 31 December 1994, 3592. Note that congressional "recesses" are not exactly vacations. Members of Congress go home to meet with constituents and do other work in their districts, while Washington staff take the time to catch up on constituent mail and work out details of legislation.

19. Janet Hook, "Republicans Vote in Lock Step, But Unity May Not Last Long," *Congressional Quarterly Weekly Reports*, 18 February 1995, 495.

20. Hook, "Republicans Vote in Lock Step," 496.

21. Ornstein and Schenkenberg, "The 1995 Congress," 202.

22. Hook, "Republicans Vote in Lock Step," 497.

23. David S. Cloud, "House GOP Shows a United Front in Crossing 'Contract' Divide," *Congressional Quarterly Weekly Reports*, 22 February 1995, 527.

24. "GOP Agenda Hits Snag in Senate," *Congressional Quarterly Weekly Reports*, 4 February 1995, 333.

25. "House Speeds Pace on 'Contract'," *Congressional Quarterly Weekly Reports*, 11 February 1995, 437.

26. Guy Gugliotta, "Breakneck Pace Frazzles House," *Washington Post*, 7 March 1995, sec. A, p. 1.

27. Ornstein and Schenkenberg, "The 1995 Congress," 183.

28. Cassata, "Republicans Bask in Success," 986.

29. Legislation requiring Congress to comply with workplace laws was also signed by the president, but this was actually part of the preface and not one of the ten planks.

30. When a bill passes the House and Senate in different forms, the two versions are sent to a "conference" committee made up of members of both houses to work out the differences. The conference committee revision is then sent back to each chamber, where it must be voted on before being sent to the president.

31. Kenneth J. Cooper and Helen Dewar, "'100 Days Down, But Senate to Go for Most 'Contract' Items," *Washington Post*, 9 April 1995, sec. A, p. 6.

32. Robin Toner, "GOP Blitz of First 100 Days Now Brings Pivotal Second 100," *New York Times*, 9 April 1995, p. 18.

33. Steve Langdon, "'Contract' Dwarfs Senate GOP Pledge," *Congressional Quarterly Weekly Reports*, 25 February 1995, 578.

34. Jonathan D. Salant, "Senate Altering Its Course in Favor of Contract," *Congressional Quarterly Weekly Reports*, 29 April 1995, 1152.

35. Donald S. Cloud, "House Speeds Pace on Contract," *Congressional Quarterly Weekly Reports*, 11 February 1995, 437.

36. Salant, "Senate Altering Its Course," 1152.

37. Jeffrey L. Katz, "GOP Faces Unknown Terrain Without 'Contract' Map," *Congressional Quarterly Weekly Reports*, 8 April 1995, 981.

38. Jonathan D. Salant, "Gingrich Sounds Familiar Themes," *Congressional Quarterly Weekly Reports*, 8 April 1995, 981.

39. Ornstein and Schenkenberg, "The 1995 Congress," 206.

40. Gillian Peele, *Governing the UK*, 3d ed. (Oxford, U.K.: Blackwell, 1995), 21–22.

41. Ornstein and Schenkenberg, "The 1995 Congress," 206

42. Cassata, "Republicans Bask in Success," 990.

43. Cassata, "Republicans Bask in Success," 990.

44. Cassata, "Republicans Bask in Success," 990.

45. Peele, *Governing the UK*, 23.

4

....

What If American Democracy Functioned Without Checks and Balances?

If the United States were to adopt a British-type parliamentary system, the government would be accorded more power and be better able to respond to the demands of the electorate. At the same time the legislative majority in Washington, free from the various institutional limitations on its power, could imperil the rights of the minority out of power. At the Constitutional Convention in Philadelphia, the Framers decided that it was better to enable the minority with legislative means to block the initiatives of the majority rather than to risk the tyranny of the majority in power.

—Seymour Martin Lipset

How a British-Style Parliamentary System
Could Change American Politics

WE LEARNED IN CHAPTER 3 how the history of the Contract with America epitomizes this book's central dilemma: namely, that majority rule is often impeded by constitutional provisions for checks and balances among the three branches of government. The Constitution also protects the rights of the minority out of power. This chapter will take a different approach, and ask how politics and policy-outcomes could be different if American government functioned under a British-style parliamentary system, in which there are no checks and balances. Would a British parliamentary regime make American democracy more responsive? Would it solve legislative gridlock once and for all? What problems might such a system raise?

Expanding upon the model set forth in an essay by Joy Esberey,[1] this chapter seeks to examine how a British-style parliamentary system might have changed the course of American politics. Following a review of some of the main characteristics of this imagined American parliamentary regime, this hypothetical inquiry seeks to illustrate how a parliamentary arrangement could have changed American political development.

An Alternative Constitutional Convention

To begin, let us assume that a parliamentary system was introduced into the United States after the American Revolution.[2] In such a case, a different set of agreements would have been reached at the Constitutional Convention in Philadelphia. We have decided to dub our imaginary constitutional compromise leading to the establishment of an American parliamentary system the Westminster compromise, after the British parliamentary system. By the terms of this Westminster compromise, the Framers would have opted for two points that were actually under discussion at the Constitutional Convention in Philadelphia: from the Virginia plan, the executive would be chosen from the legislature, and legislative representation would be based upon population, not geography; from the New Jersey plan, there would be a representative assembly, a unicameral legislature rather than the American bicameral one. The net result of this arrangement would have been the implementation of a parliamentary form of government in 1789. As discussed in Chapter 2, Robert Dahl has observed that the actual debate over the Virginia plan brought the Framers to the brink of inventing a form of a parliamentary system because it advanced the idea that the executive be chosen by the national legislature.[3]

For the sake of simplicity, we envision four key alterations to the American system of government under this Westminster compromise. First, there would be no separation of powers. Rather, executive and legislative powers would be fused and sovereign. Second, there would only be one legislative chamber, not two, and it would be called the National Assembly. Third, the internal operating rules of this unicameral legislature would follow the Westminster system: the unicameral National Assembly both selects the prime minister and delegates to that executive official the national administration and the authority to direct the legislative branch. Fourth, the prime minister would choose a cabinet from among the ranks of the majority party in the legislature and would be able to dominate the parliament; and there would be no legal limitation on the actions of the legislature. As is the actual case of the United Kingdom, as long as the government has a legislative majority, it can expect to have all of its legislation passed without any revisions from the opposition. These four broad changes would significantly alter American political development.

How the United States Could Have
Ended Up with a Proportional System

Our Westminster compromise is based both on actual alternatives discussed at the American constitutional convention and on a British-style parliament. For purposes of argument, we would like to include one additional change: the use of a proportional system of elections rather than the single-member districts currently used by all fifty states. This change was not discussed at the Constitutional Convention, nor is it part of the British system, which, like the American system, relies on winner-take-all elections. Yet, a proportional system could have significantly altered election outcomes, as we will discuss later in the chapter. Since we are creating our own imaginary form of government, we would like to include proportional representation. And it is possible that our system could have evolved in that direction.

The American Constitution does not require the use of single-member districts to elect representatives to the House. The Constitution specified only that representation would be determined by population, not that each state would have the same number of congressional districts that it has seats in the House. In other words, the Framers of the Constitution did not specifically rule out proportional representation. The Framers never expected the United States to adopt proportional representation, but in like fashion, they also never expected American politics to be dominated by political parties. (In fact, the Framers were actually opposed to political parties.) The United States more or less invented political parties in the 1790s with the creation of the Federalist Party and the Democratic (or Jeffersonian) Republicans. And it could have developed its own proportional system (the idea existed prior to the founding of the United States) as it adapted to the increasing importance of political parties.

The history of political parties in the United States involves both struggles for domination by the parties and factionalization within parties. It is conceivable that at some point a proportional system could have been institutionalized as a way for some of the nondominant parties and factions to gain political control. For example, in the late 1800s, political parties represented urban interests, which dominated national politics. Hence, several rural parties were formed, including the Greenback Party and the People's Party (also know as the Populists) to counter the power of the urban parties. They were ultimately unsuccessful, although William Jennings Bryan, representing the Populist Party, came close to getting elected in 1896. A proportional system of elections would have given the newly formed agrarian parties more power in Congress. A parliamentary system could have forced the dominant parties to form a coalition with the agricultural parties.

By the turn of the century, the Progressive movement emerged and tried to eliminate political corruption and reform the party system. The Progressives questioned the usefulness of political parties, and even favored nonpartisan elections. It is possible to imagine slightly different tactics for the Progressive movement under a parliamentary system. Knowing that the majority party selects the prime minister in a parliamentary form of government, the Progressives might have attempted to take control of the legislature by entering into a coalition with other interests, such as the rural parties. As it was, Progressives favored changes to the political system, including the end of patronage and the institution of primary elections. Both of these reforms attempted to limit the power of political parties. In fact, the Progressives would have liked the elimination of political parties, but found that goal impossible to achieve. It is possible that under the Westminster compromise, Progressives might have proposed another reform: the use of proportional representation as a method of election. Instead of eliminating political parties, the Progressives might have attempted to dilute the power of parties through proportional elections. The Progressives could have lobbied for this change (as they did for others) at the state level, and may have changed the American electoral system in even more profound ways.

How American Political Development Could Have Been Different

Obviously, political institutional arrangements do not control or determine all aspects of a national political life. However, under the terms of this Westminster compromise, one can assume that there would have been some modifications to the pattern of political development in the United States. Arguably, there may have been some changes to the party system and to the political behavior of interest groups; the relationships among key government policymakers would have changed and the power of the majority party in the legislature would have increased.[4] Let us focus our inquiry on three main areas of change:

- alterations to American political culture,
- whether a proportional representation system could provide for better representation in the legislature, and
- the issue of effective responses to political scandals.

Alterations to American Political Culture

Political culture is characterized by the combination of beliefs, attitudes, expectations, feelings, and values held by a society concerning politics and government. In particular—and for a wide variety of political, social, economic, and cultural reasons—Americans have historically been preoccupied with their rights and with freedom from government restraints. One important contributing variable to this widespread distrust of government at the beginning of the American Republic was the dominant Protestant religious belief about how government should function. Specifically, the Protestant work ethic—which holds that a person should advance in society solely based on his or her individual abilities and hard work, and not due to family connections or class position—is hostile to governmental intrusions that seek to aid segments of the population.[5] Thus, among the world's peoples, Americans are particularly concerned about limiting governmental intrusions, except in certain critical areas. This generalized suspicion of government resonates with the constitutional guarantees of the inalienable rights to life, liberty, and the pursuit of happiness for every person, as well as with the protections of individual freedoms in the Bill of Rights. Accordingly, the ideas of liberty and individualism are pronounced features of American political culture and have generated a certain hostility toward government among people of varying political convictions. For example, saying that government should limit itself to social problems such as poverty and injustice, many liberals are concerned about the government's involvement in defense and military activities. More conservative critics would charge that programs devoted to such social problems themselves create unnecessary governmental intrusion into people's lives. Still others are concerned about limiting the government's role in individual decisions about such issues as religion, sexual activity, and reproduction. All sides have a political cultural bias that is deeply suspicious of government intrusion.

Under the terms of the Westminster compromise, this pronounced suspicion of government might have been somewhat mitigated. Had the Framers opted for the Westminster compromise, they would have decided to place the responsibility of governing squarely in the hands of the majority: There would have been no constitutional provisions hindering the rule of the majority, who would have been given the power and the authority to effectuate changes. Hence, the majority in our fictional National Assembly could make a real difference. As Seymour Martin Lipset points out in the quotation at the start of this chapter, American national government would be accorded more power and be better able to respond to the demands of the electorate under a parliamentary system. At the same time, this legislative majority could imperil the rights of the minority out of power. Under the terms of our Westminster compromise, the Framers would have decided that it is better to enable majority to rule than to hinder majority rule for the sake of minority rights. And they would have designed the legislative chamber to reflect and be responsive to the people.

Perhaps our Westminster compromise system might enable the government to be more positively viewed as an instrument for change rather than a perpetual threat to individual liberty. As Joy Esberey has noted:

> Under a parliamentary system of government, it is unlikely that Americans would be as suspicious of government as they are, even considering that many who came to this country did so to escape repressive regimes. They could not have equated democratic government with the autocratic governments they left behind; it is far more likely that they would have seen in democracy an opportunity to improve their conditions.[6]

Finally, under the Westminster compromise, when groups in society were not treated equally, the government would have had the power to quickly intervene to

A prime minister in Washington. British Prime Minister Margaret Thatcher addresses a joint session of Congress on 20 February 1985. Seated behind her are Vice President George Bush (L) and House Speaker Thomas "Tip" O'Neill. Photo courtesy of UPI/Corbis-Bettmann.

ensure equal opportunity. Such rapid response to societal ills could have won staunch supporters for governmental actions and diminished some of the current distrust of government. On the other hand, it may have also provoked a serious reaction against the national government, whose swift and decisive actions might have been viewed suspiciously. Indeed, such strong national government may have led to calls for secession early on in American political development. Regardless of its system of government, American society would probably still be more distrustful of government than are other societies. Indeed, it is also possible that Americans might be far more suspicious of government if the Framers had adopted the Westminster compromise, which grants the government more power than it has now.

A More Representative Polity?

When President Bill Clinton nominated lawyer Lani Guinier to be assistant attorney general in charge of the Civil Rights Division in 1993, the issue of the representation of all segments of the population was raised in a particularly contentious and adverse way. Due to the vociferousness of her opponents, President Clinton withdrew Guinier's nomination before the Senate started its consideration. Consequently, Guinier never was afforded the opportunity to spell out in public her view of how a single-member district plurality system, which allocates 100 percent of the power to 51 percent of the people is fundamentally unfair to those minority groups in the population.[7]

The question of representation is at the heart of the institutional question. As we discussed in Chapter 2, the U.S. single-member district system inhibits the ability of new political parties to win elections. American elections are won one district at a time, usually in contests between only two political parties. A proportional system, on the other hand, would create multimember districts and room for third parties. In the United States, a party that can garner just 20 percent of the vote has virtually no chance of representation in the legislature; in a proportional system, that party would make up 20 percent of the legislature. Further, under the Westminster compromise, one can imagine the formation of minority parties made up of labor, blacks, or other groups.

It is not unreasonable to assume that a system that accords seats on the basis of the proportion of votes received would have led to the development of a third party and/or several regional or ethnic parties at some point over the past two hundred years. Under those electoral rules, it is easy to imagine a third party starting in the early part of the twentieth century. As millions of people emigrated to the cities from abroad as well as from rural areas, they could quickly have formed a mass-based party, like the Labour Party in Great Britain. Other parties might have formed as well, including agrarian-based parties, progressive or reform-minded parties, and socialist, libertarian, anarchist, ethnic Catholic, Christian conservative, black, Hispanic, and militia parties. In such a system, the Democratic and Republican Parties would have faced a great deal of competition from significant minorities.

The Westminster compromise could have resulted in a very different legislative history for minorities in American history. Whereas the present single-member district plurality system favors the majority ethnic groups, it is reasonable to assume that there would be greater numbers of minorities in the National Assembly under a proportional representation system. For instance, under this scenario, black leaders could have formed a separate political party and charged into Washington with much influence.[8] The Democrats would not have been the majority party throughout much of the early twentieth century, and a third political party representing the interests of African-Americans, in exchange for their legislative support, could have had much more sway in negotiating with Democratic and/or Republican leaders for specific programs. This could have been a much better situation for blacks, who historically have voted in large numbers for the Democratic Party but who themselves do not make up the majority of the party. Democrats can count on the "black vote" but do not necessarily have to do much to court it. Blacks in the Democratic Party often feel that the party neglects them and lament that they have nowhere else to go. The Republican Party does even less to court blacks as a group; and if the group were to form its own political party, it would not have sufficient numbers to win elections. The case could be different in a parliamentary system with proportional representation, as Esberey notes:

> . . . at various times this century in which American blacks were denied their constitutional rights, president, Congress and the Court tried to do something to change the situation. On each situation they were frustrated by the checking power of the other branches. This situation would not arise in our parliamentary America. If we consider how much was achieved with everything in the political system working against the change, there can be no doubt that, with a system which facilitated change, the position of minorities would have been improved.[9]

Critics have noted, however, that if black political influence wholly depended on a separate black political party, it would never have gained the attention of the majority parties, nor made significant progress in civil rights legislation. This claim is perhaps true, but on the other hand, the existence of a separate black party could have been advantageous in one key area: It could have enabled the African-American legislative leadership to strike alliances with the leading majority parties in return for specific legislative goals. And even if there were not more

African-American representatives under this fictional system than there actually are under the present system, one could still argue that the Westminster compromise could have enabled African-Americans to be elected to the National Assembly and to coerce the majority party in our fictional National Assembly to confront the problems of racial injustice much earlier than was actually the case.

More Effective Response to Political Crises and Scandals?

It is also possible that the mechanisms available under a British-style parliamentary system would have enabled the American National Assembly to deal more easily with scandals. Let us look at how the Westminster compromise would have handled some recent political scandals.

Watergate occurred during the Nixon administration and resulted in a constitutional crisis for the office of the presidency. In 1972, a group of operatives working for the Republican Party and known as "the plumbers" was caught breaking into the Democratic national headquarters in the Watergate office building. They were apparently trying to get information on the Democratic strategy to win the presidential elections later that year. The investigation of this crime produced evidence that indicated President Nixon may have ordered the break-in or at the very least obstructed justice by covering up the crime. Democrats in Congress led the charge against President Nixon, and impeachment proceedings were initiated in 1974.

The nation was glued to televised coverage of the congressional impeachment proceedings, which were slow, painful, and difficult. One area of the congressional investigation focused on the White House tapes. These were tape recordings that the president had made for historical purposes of all discussions in the Oval Office. The investigators wanted to hear these taped conversations because they believed the conversations held clues as to the guilt or innocence of the president. President Nixon, however, refused to release private tape recordings of White House meetings, citing the principle of executive privilege. The president argued that by virtue of his office he was not required to release the tapes. Releasing the tapes, according to Nixon, would have set a bad precedent and threatened national security. This legislative-executive deadlock was settled by the unanimous decision of the Supreme Court that the president was obliged to release the tapes. Once the tapes were released, the information they contained implicated the president in the cover-up. Before the impeachment proceedings were over, Nixon resigned the presidency, and Vice President Ford was sworn in as president.

Under a British-style parliamentary system, Congress could have rid the nation of Nixon in 1974 with a simple vote of no confidence. The Watergate crisis, dubbed "our long national nightmare" by President Gerald Ford, could have been dealt with swiftly and decisively, and a new government could have been instituted immediately. Rather than having President Ford serve out an essentially lame duck presidency without the legitimacy of having been elected, the country could have seen a new leader emerge with the consent of the National Assembly. The adversarial relationship between the president and Congress—exacerbated by the Watergate scandal—would not exist in our Westminster compromise. However, it is also important to note that a parliament controlled by a Prime Minister Nixon could have had a negative side. The prime minister may have been able to prevent the National Assembly from acquiring the information necessary to institute impeachment procedures. As leader of both the party and the government, a Prime Minister Nixon could have exerted even more control than did President Nixon and would not have faced institutional checks on his power.

The Iran-Contra affair, which occurred during the Reagan administration, is another case in point. The adversarial relationship between the conservative Republican Reagan administration and the liberal Democratic Congress eventually led to this problem. In 1979 an armed left-wing rebel movement in Nicaragua, known as the Sandinistas, defeated the American-supported right-wing dictatorship of Somoza. At first, President Carter welcomed the victory of the Sandinistas, in the hope that they would bring about more respect for human rights than had been the case under Somoza. When Reagan came to office in January 1981 however, relations quickly cooled between Nicaragua and Washington. Reagan accused the Sandinistas of attempting to force Marxism on the Nicaraguan people and of fomenting revolution in the neighboring country of El Salvador. In the early 1980s, a group of anti-Sandinista Nicaraguans, agreeing with Reagan, decided that the only way to defeat the Sandinista leadership was by armed struggle, and so a civil conflict broke out. These rebels were against (or "contra" in Spanish) the Sandinistas, and thus became known as the Contras. The Reagan administration was very supportive of the Contras and sought to arm them. Nicaragua still had some support in the Democratic-controlled Congress, which sought to block Reagan's political and military initiatives against the country. Congress passed a law forbidding the administration from selling arms to the Nicaraguan Contras. Since Congress controls the purse strings, the Reagan administration was legally unable to help the Contras. With or without the president's knowledge, people in his administration, including Oliver North, resorted to illegal means to raise funds, purchase arms, and send them to the Contras. In a rather complicated plan involving Iran, administration officials privately raised funds to arm the Contras. Once the news of this illegal activity broke, there was talk of impeaching the president. Investigative hearings, much like those during the Watergate crisis, were held in Congress.

At first glance it seems that, had our Westminster compromise been in place, the government could have easily been righted by a vote of no confidence in Prime

Minister Reagan. But the larger point here is that the adversarial relationship between the executive and legislative branches would not have existed under the Westminster compromise and the scandal would probably never have occurred. Prime Minister Reagan, as leader of the majority party in the National Assembly, would have been able to arm the Contras through legal means and with parliamentary support. There would be no need to resort to illegal and covert means to accomplish the goal of arming the Contras. Of course, many Americans were glad that Democrats in Congress provided opposition to Reagan's plan to arm the Contras. Under a parliamentary system, such opposition could have been muted and there would have been no effective check on Prime Minister Reagan's power.

The Clinton presidency is plagued by scandal. While Watergate and Iran-Contra involved serious constitutional questions, President Clinton is faced with a series of charges and investigations into his personal life and financial dealings that so far have not proven to involve constitutional issues. The main scandal is known as Whitewater, a questionable financial deal in which President and Mrs. Clinton were involved in Arkansas. Using a law created in response to the Watergate scandal, Attorney General Janet Reno appointed an independent counsel to investigate Whitewater and related charges. The independent counsel, Kenneth Starr, is conducting an investigation of the president, acting as an additional check on the executive branch. The independent counsel must be appointed by the attorney general and approved by Congress. In this way, Congress is able to exert some control over an executive who may be abusing power.

How would the situation differ in a parliamentary system? An independent counsel would not be necessary, for at least two reasons. First, the Parliament automatically has control over the chief executive, since the prime minister is selected from its majority party. An American National Assembly would not need the additional check of an independent counsel to maintain control over the chief executive. Second, a vote of no confidence could send a prime minister from office. The United States has a long and cumbersome impeachment process that allows for removal from office only in the case of criminal activity. The president cannot be removed before his term of office ends on the grounds that he is politically unpopular or has the taint of scandal. Thus an independent counsel is needed to discover if there are any criminal charges to be made and, thus, if there is a basis for impeachment. Of course, the problem is the perception that the independent counsel is bent on finding anything that he or she can hang charges on. This perception dogged independent counsel in the Nixon and Reagan administrations and is currently hounding Kenneth Starr, whose initial probe into Whitewater led him to investigate a sex scandal involving the president and Monica Lewinsky, a college intern in the White House.

In a parliamentary system, such investigations would not have happened. Instead of a four-year inquiry by independent counsel Kenneth Starr into President Clinton's financial and sexual dealings, these situations could have been dealt with quickly and swiftly. If the National Assembly felt that Prime Minister Clinton had lost legitimacy in the eyes of the American people and could no longer govern effectively, it could remove him by a simple vote of no confidence. If, on the other hand, the National Assembly felt that too much was being made of these situations, and that it did not negatively influence Clinton's ability to govern, it could simply ignore the matter. Either way, this problem would not have resulted in long, drawn out deliberations with inconclusive results.

An independent counsel does make life difficult for the president, who may face embarrassing inquiries into his political and personal life, both past and present. Reagan Republicans and Clinton Democrats can agree that sometimes it seems as if an independent counsel is acting out some kind of a vendetta, trying to discover dirt on his political enemies. The post of independent counsel does reveal something about American politics: the citizens' basic distrust of government. The United States would rather err on the side of too much investigation of the president than risk the possibility of his taking on excessive powers. While a parliamentary system could easily remove a president from office, there is no guarantee that it would: What if the scandal or political crisis involved not only the prime minister but also his or her party in parliament? There would be no incentive to remove the prime minister from office or to bring forth information that might be damaging to the party. Americans would rather have an adversarial system with built-in checks than allow for excessive political power.

A parliamentary system would certainly have handled political scandals differently; and it would have had different electoral results as well. In the next section, we examine how a proportional voting system might have led to radically different election results, in terms of both the majority party in Congress and the actual person who became chief executive.

How Selected Election Outcomes May Have Been Different

How could a pure proportional voting system have changed American politics? Let us investigate some of the electoral outcomes in the twentieth century.

Such a reinterpretation of electoral results is a challenge: Obviously, if a different system were in place, a different trajectory would have followed each election. Hence, as we revisit each electoral outcome, we must also assume that in each case there were not past influences or trajectories. In other words, when we consider

Ronald Reagan's legislative program of the 1980s, we will not assume that any earlier period of Republican rule had already implemented Reagan's conservative agenda. Nor will we assume that a welfare state had been created by Teddy Roosevelt and was already in existence by the time his distant cousin became president.

As we begin this inquiry, one big caveat is in order: It is impossible to know whether, and to what extent, U.S. elections are national in character; that is, it actually may be impossible to meaningfully reinterpret electoral results garnered under a presidential system for the purposes of thinking about how things might have been different if a parliamentary system had been in place. One could try to examine the national aggregate totals of the congressional elections for this same purpose; but in most cases, congressional elections in the United States are dominated by local, pork-barrel concerns. In fact, the general consensus is that congressional elections are local elections won or lost on local issues. On the other hand, presidential elections do tend to focus on national issues; but in actuality, presidential electoral results are the product of both local and national concerns. These factors are so tightly interwoven in the United States that it is almost impossible to tease out which presidential outcome was decided on national issues. The presidential results are the only national elections held in the United States, and so they will have to do. Of course, a "what if" exercise can be fun, but we caution the reader that the following is an exercise of pure fancy designed to illustrate that an institutional arrangement can change policy outcomes.

For the sake of simplicity, we will assume that representation in the unicameral National Assembly is based on a pure proportional representation system drawn from the actual national vote totals of the presidential elections; this is the one true national vote we presently have for the head of government. Thus presidential election results serve as a "proxy" for a national vote in a parliamentary system.[10] Further, we will assume that the vote totals for the presidential elections were for a party list of candidates for the unicameral National Assembly, and we will ignore the actual results of the local elections. Let us now turn to the elections.

Case One: The Presidential Election of 1912

We start our "what ifs" with the election of 1912. The election is an appropriate starting point for at least two reasons. First, it involved the Progressive Party, which we have already imagined could have been the impetus for the institution of a proportional electoral system in our imaginary Westminster compromise. Second, the 1912 election was notable in that it involved one of the few serious

FIGURE 4.1   Case One: 1912

1912 National Vote Percentages
    Democratic: Woodrow Wilson, 41.9 percent
    Progressive (Bull Moose): Theodore Roosevelt, 27.4 percent
    Republican: William Harding Taft, 23.2 percent
    Socialist: Eugene Debs, 6 percent
Makeup of 63rd Congress
    House: Democrats 291; Republicans 127; Others 17
    Senate: Democrats 51; Republicans 44; Others 1

---

third party challenges in American history, this one waged by former President Theodore Roosevelt. It is important to remember that although the 1912 election was an atypical occurrence in the United States, the presence of a third-party candidate for the presidency does make it an interesting case for this exercise. (The 1912 election may also demonstrate how presidential elections would have occurred if, in fact, the Westminster compromise had been adopted along with a proportional representation system!)

Theodore Roosevelt, a Republican, was president from 1901 to 1908. He had been William McKinley's vice president, and when McKinley died early in his term, Roosevelt inherited the office. He then ran on his own in 1904 and, following precedent, did not run for a third consecutive term. William Henry Taft ran and won as the Republican candidate in 1908 and decided to run for reelection in 1912. Taft and Roosevelt disagreed politically and became personal and political enemies. Roosevelt, who was immensely popular with the public, decided to challenge Taft for the Republican nomination. When it became clear that the old-guard Republicans would support Taft and not him, Roosevelt left the party, taking his supporters with him. They found a home in the Progressive movement and created a national party known as the Progressives. Roosevelt, as the leader of the party, called himself "strong as a bull moose"; thus the nickname "bull moose" was given to both him and his party.

In his campaign, Roosevelt promised significant political and economic reforms, including plans to privilege human rights over property rights, to tax the wealthy in order to provide programs for the poor and unfortunate, to increase the power of the national government, and to create a welfare state. The former president delivered a fascinating speech—dubbed his political "confession of faith"—before the National Progressive Party presidential nominating convention on 6 August 1912. His comments give a clear idea about what he would have done in office. He stated clearly that "the time is ripe, and overripe, for a genuine Progressive movement, nation-wide and justice-loving."[11] And he then observed:

Now, friends, this is my confession of faith. . . . I believe in the larger use of the governmental power to help remedy industrial wrongs, because it has been borne in on me by actual experience that without the exercise of such power many of the wrongs will go unremedied. I believe in a larger opportunity for the people themselves directly to participate in government and to control their governmental agents, because long experience has taught me that without such control many of their agents will represent them badly.[12]

The conservative Republican establishment feared that these plans by their former president would lead to mob rule and to a generalized attack on property rights and social status. In response, the Republican candidate, President Taft, resisted most of Roosevelt's initiatives. The thrust of the Republican message was that change had to be controlled and limited. The divided Republican Party gave Woodrow Wilson, the Democratic Party's candidate, an opening. Wilson campaigned for some reforms as well. He supported the introduction of an income tax, the direct election of senators, and the protection of labor. Eugene Debs, representing the Socialist Party, presented a far-left political program, providing for the nationalization of most industries.[13]

Debs did not have enough votes to present much of a threat. The battle was fought between three candidates: Wilson, representing the Democratic Party; William Howard Taft, the official Republican candidate; and Roosevelt, the progressive Republican representing the Progressive (Bull Moose) Party. Roosevelt split the Republican vote, allowing Wilson to be elected. The Democrats controlled both the White House and the Congress. The Wilson administration, although Democratic, ended up enacting much of the Progressive Party's platform, leaving the Progressive Party without much reason for opposition. The Republicans were the minority party in Congress, and the Bull Moose Progressives eventually broke up. Theodore Roosevelt left the public scene, and the worst fears of the conservative Republicans never materialized. Further, as noted by George Mowry, "even though Debs had raised the total Socialist strength by over a third from that of the previous elections, his votes did not materially affect the results."[14] Congress remained dominated by two political parties, despite the strong showing of the Socialist Party. The political results in the Congress were in favor of stability and against change; the actual electoral results, however, indicate that the American population was in the mood for greater change. The Taft-led Republican Party, which stood for stability and the status quo, was clearly rejected by the electorate.

How might these electoral results have played out under the terms of the Westminster compromise? One can envision a much different political situation. A proportional representative system would have allocated seats in the National Assembly in proportion to the votes received. As the head of the party receiving a plurality of votes, Wilson would have presided over a minority government with 41.9 percent of the seats. On the other hand, it might have made more political sense for Wilson to form a coalition government with Theodore Roosevelt's Progressive Party, which received 27.4 percent of the seats. Perhaps he could have also included Eugene Debs's Socialist Party, which had won 6 percent of the seats. Arguably, the parties involved in the formation of this coalition government would have made some deals. Perhaps Wilson would have had to accept portions of the other party's platform in exchange for their support. In addition, Theodore Roosevelt and Eugene Debs could have been appointed to prominent cabinet posts.

However the accommodation was reached, this coalition government would certainly have been very powerful and would have diluted the power of the Republicans in Congress. Holding on to a combined 75 percent of the seats in the National Assembly, Woodrow Wilson could have presided over an effective government: It is not difficult to imagine that Wilson would have shepherded some reform legislation through the American National Assembly in the 1912–1916 legislative term, including a tax system predicated upon the idea that the wealthy should provide the money for poverty programs and the creation of a welfare state. Based on both the actual actions of Theodore Roosevelt when he was president (1901–1908) and the public statements of the socialist leader Eugene Debs, one can imagine that a cabinet including them would have sought antitrust laws, limiting the power of large monopoly groups. Also, this cabinet would most likely have been a strong supporter of workers' rights, including increased compensation, benefits, and the right to strike. This cabinet would probably have sought a pro-conservation agenda as well. Other reforms could have involved the abolition of child labor, the improvement of working conditions, and the institution of women's suffrage. Indeed, even if this coalition government were restricted to Wilson and Roosevelt, it is safe to assume that the net result of a shift in the American institutional structure from a presidential to a British-style parliamentary system would certainly have created a different—and more progressive—political trajectory in the United States following the 1912 elections.

The American system limited the power of a third-party candidate like Roosevelt. The entrenchment of two parties meant that there was little room for a third party to take hold. Teddy Roosevelt's Progressive Party candidacy did, however, have an impact on the American political system. Both major parties, fearful of the popular appeal of Roosevelt's ideas, adopted some progressive platforms for their candidates. And President Wilson instituted some, but not all, of Roosevelt's reforms. American government, with its checks and balances, did not experience dramatic change as a result of the election of 1912. The system did allow a somewhat modified version of Roosevelt's ideals to be absorbed into the existing parties. Perhaps the Framers would have feared the populist nature of Roosevelt's Bull Moose Party and the coalition that might have resulted from a proportional system of election in 1912. A coalition with 75 percent of the popular vote may have represented the tyranny of the majority that the Framers were trying to avoid.

Case Two: The Presidential Elections of 1932 and 1936

Let us now consider the results of both the historic 1932 and 1936 presidential elections. Franklin Roosevelt's victory of 1932 was solidified by his landslide re-election in 1936. In 1932, the public clearly showed its lack of confidence in Herbert Hoover, who appeared to believe that the Depression would work itself out without government intervention. Although it was not clear what exactly Roosevelt would do once in office, the public obviously believed he would do something, and that was more than they expected of Hoover.[15] Once elected, President Roosevelt sought immediate relief from the Depression by pushing Congress to pass new "big government" programs. By the time the 1936 election took place, the vote was considered a referendum on the New Deal, which was ratified overwhelmingly.[16] The difference between the two major political parties, which had been relatively indistinct in 1932, was now clearly delineated: Republicans wanted weak national government, and Democrats wanted strong national government. Big government won.[17]

According to the Democratic platform adopted in 1936, the Roosevelt administration planned an active governmental agenda. Among other things, they promised to create a structure of economic security for all (beyond the existing Social Security program), to secure for the consumer a fair value for and a fair spread between the price charged for a product and its cost, to provide decent adequate and affordable housing for all Americans, to enforce antitrust regulations, to guarantee government-supplied work when businesses failed to provide adequate jobs, and to protect the equal rights of all.[18] Many observers noted that the stakes were high for the 1936 elections: Would the Democrats become America's majority political party, would Americans accept big government, and how extensive would the welfare state become? The Democrats did become the majority party; Americans did at least partially accept big government; but the welfare state did not become as extensive as those that evolved in Europe. In spite of the Democrats best efforts to expand big government, the Republicans managed to slow down some of their initiatives. The structure of Congress, which encourages minority rights, compromise, and inaction, hindered Roosevelt in creating a true welfare state.

FIGURE 4.2   Case Two: 1932 and 1936

1932 Actual Vote Percentages
  Democrat: Franklin Roosevelt, 57.4 percent
  Republican: Herbert Hoover, 39.6 percent
  Socialist: Norman Thomas, 2.2 percent
Makeup of 73rd Congress
  House: Democrats 310; Republicans 117; other 5
  Senate: Democrats 60; Republicans 35; other 1
1936 National Vote Percentages
  Democrat: Franklin Roosevelt, 60.8 percent
  Republican: Alf London, 36.5 percent
  Union: William Lemke, 1.9 percent
  Socialist: Norman Thomas, 0.4 percent
Makeup of 74th Congress
  House: Democrats 319; Republicans 103; other 10
  Senate Democrats 69; Republicans 25; other 2

Nonetheless, President Franklin Roosevelt managed to create a new and expansive role for the federal government. He increased its regulation of business, he used public funds to provide immediate relief to persons out of work, he implemented a progressive income tax (whereby the rich pay a greater percentage than the poor), and he signed the Wagner Act into law, which gave workers many advantages over management in labor negotiations. In addition, Roosevelt proposed and implemented the Social Security system. As the above accomplishments clearly indicate, he presided over a very active and progressive presidency.

Under parliamentary rules, Roosevelt could have done even more. He would not have encountered any meaningful opposition from the Republicans. With such a wide margin in the National Assembly (57 percent in 1932 and 62 percent in 1936), Roosevelt would have had little problem getting broad new social programs passed. In addition, it is possible that the Democrats would have formed a coalition government with a socialist or workers party. Under a presidential system, the 2 percent of the national vote that those parties received reduced them to the status of a footnote on election results. Under a parliamentary system, 2 percent of the national vote would give such a party a toehold in the legislature, perhaps creating a launching pad for future gains. At the very least, a National Assembly in which 2 percent of its membership was socialist would have given some voice to an American leftist movement. Further, it is also possible that Roosevelt in coalition with the leading Democrats, would have appointed one or two socialists to his cabinet.

President Franklin D. Roosevelt, shown here acknowledging the cheers of a crowd. Despite his immense popularity, Roosevelt's legislative agenda was limited by the constitutional system of checks and balances. Photo courtesy of the Library of Congress.

While the New Deal actually resulted in something far less expansive than the European welfare state, a parliamentary system controlled by Rooseveltian Democrats could have resulted in more extensive social programs and increased federal involvement in the economy and in the lives of its citizens to a much greater extent than was actually the case in the New Deal. The Republican Party, which favored less government control, would not have had much power to stop the Democrats. A parliamentary system would not have had checks in place to stop the popular and powerful Franklin Roosevelt.

Case Three: The Presidential Elections of 1980 and 1984

Turning now to an examination of the 1980 and 1984 elections, we find that although President Reagan had different legislative priorities than President Franklin Roosevelt, he faced similar institutional obstacles.

In 1980 Ronald Reagan defeated the incumbent Jimmy Carter on a campaign that promised to return America to greatness by building up its defenses, cutting taxes and the bureaucracy, and balancing the budget. The Republican Party also

FIGURE 4.3   Case Three: 1980 and 1984

National Vote Percentages
    Republican: Ronald Reagan, 50.7 percent
    Democrat: Jimmy Carter, 41.0 percent
    Independent: John Anderson, 6.6 percent
Makeup of 97th Congress
    House: Democrats 243; Republicans 192
    Senate: Republicans 53; Democrats 46; other 1
National Vote Percentages
    Republican: Ronald Reagan, 58.7 percent
    Democrat: Walter Mondale, 40.5 percent
Makeup of 98th Congress
    House: Democrats 268; Republicans 166
    Senate: Republicans 55; Democrats 45

won control of the Senate. For their part, the Democrats retained control of the House of Representatives and were strongly opposed to the president's program. In 1984, Reagan was reelected president by a large margin, and the Republicans maintained the Senate.

Once elected, President Reagan sought immediate tax relief from "big government" by pushing Congress to cut New Deal programs. By the time the 1984 election took place, the vote was considered a referendum on Reagan's first four years, which were ratified overwhelmingly. The difference between the two major political parties that had been clearly delineated in 1932 stayed the same: Republicans wanted weak national government, and Democrats wanted strong national government. This time, however, the proponents of small government had the upper hand in the executive branch but were somewhat checked by a Democratic majority in the House of Representatives.

Reagan faced a Democratic-controlled House of Representatives. Tip O'Neill, the liberal Democratic Speaker of the House, along with a majority of the representatives, did not support the president's legislative package. O'Neill made it clear that they would block any measure they disagreed with. Reagan tried to outmaneuver O'Neill and the rest of his Democratic opposition by frequently claiming that the American people had granted him a national electoral "mandate" to implement his conservative legislative program.

Eventually, Reagan convinced Tip O'Neill not to block everything he was attempting to do, including tax cuts and increases in defense spending. O'Neill justified his cooperative position by stating that since the American people had voted for Reagan, he ought to let some of the right-wing agenda have a chance to work (or fail). O'Neill also gained some significant concessions from the president, who agreed not to slash spending on Social Security and on other human service programs. In sum, as we discussed in Chapter 1, Reagan and O'Neill decided to implement a legislative package that cut taxes, ended some governmental programs, maintained spending on Social Security, and increased defense spending—a combination that significantly augmented the national debt.

Both Republicans and Democrats have acknowledged that the national debt rapidly increased during the Reagan presidency, and they blame each other for it. What would have happened under the Westminster compromise?

Under a parliamentary system, the Republicans would have gained control of the National Assembly, and Reagan would have become the prime minister. There would have been no endless debates between Democrats and Republicans about the national debt: The chief of state under the Westminster compromise is responsible for the government and accountable for its policies. Since the burden of governing would be in the hands of the majority party under our parliamentary system, success or failure of Reagan's policies would be his. Governmental responsibility and accountability would have been squarely in Reagan's hands.

Consequently, it is possible that the national debt would not have increased under Prime Minister Reagan at all. As prime minister, he would not have had to make costly compromises with his opposition in the legislature; and so, he could have pursued his legislative goals in a more cost-efficient manner. Of course, we must also take into account that Reagan's electoral "mandate" was really not that commanding for the first four years. The Democrats, allied with the independents, would have totaled close to 49 percent of the representative body in 1980. In such a scenario, Reagan would have presided over a razor-slim majority and might have been more hesitant in his legislative initiatives. However, after the landslide election of 1984, Reagan would have had a commanding majority that could have been interpreted as a mandate.

Indeed, the very checks and balances that kept Franklin Roosevelt from implementing a large-scale welfare state on the European model also prevented Reagan from paring down government to the extent that he would have liked. Both Reagan and Roosevelt faced opposition from Congress. A Republican minority was able to slow down Roosevelt significantly in the 1930s; a Democratic majority was able to slow down Reagan in the 1980s.

Case Four: The Elections of 1992, 1994, and 1996

We will now examine the past three elections (two presidential, and one midterm) together. As in all the other cases, the presidential vote can be considered a proxy for a national vote in a parliamentary system. In this case, however, the midterm

FIGURE 4.4   Case Four: 1992, 1994, and 1996

1992 National Vote Percentages
   Democrat: Bill Clinton, 43 percent
   Republican: George Bush, 37.4 percent
   Independent: Ross Perot, 18.9 percent
Makeup of 103rd Congress
   House: Democrats 257; Republicans 176
   Senate: Democrats 56; Republicans 44
1994 Midterm Elections: Makeup of 104th Congress
   House: Republicans 235; Democrats 197; Independent 1
   Senate: Republicans 53; Democrats 47
1996 National Vote Percentages
   Democrat: Bill Clinton, 49 percent
   Republican: Bob Dole, 41 percent
   Reform Party: Ross Perot, 8 percent
   Green Party: Ralph Nader, 1 percent
   Libertarian Party: Harry Browne, 1 percent
Makeup of 105th Congress
   House: Republicans 225; Democrats 205; Independent 1; unresolved 4
   Senate: Republicans 55; Democrats 45

---

congressional election, in an unusual turn of events, can also be considered a proxy for a national vote.

In the United States, most congressional elections turn on the maxim, coined by former House Speaker Tip O'Neill, that "all politics is local." In 1994, Newt Gingrich succeeded in gaining a Republican majority in the House by nationalizing the elections. Although the elections clearly had a regional focus (Republican dominance of Congress came mostly from elections in the South), the 1994 congressional elections are the closest thing this country has seen to a national, parliamentary-style election. The Contract with America was the platform on which the party ran, and Representative Newt Gingrich, as the party's national leader, would have been its prime minister.

In 1992, Clinton clearly received no mandate (gaining substantially less than 50 percent of the vote), and yet he faced a Congress with his party in the majority. Had the 1992 presidential election been a national election, the hypothetical National Assembly would have had nearly as many Republicans as Democrats, and almost 20 percent of its membership would have been independent. The independents, led by Ross Perot (whose following actually became the Reform Party in 1996) would have been a powerful force in creating a coalition government, exacting compromises and holding out the power of their numbers as a prize to the party they eventually aligned themselves with. Throwing their weight with the Republicans, they would have created a coalition with 57 percent of the membership, a powerful majority, rivaling the 60 percent majority the Democrats actually had in the House and exceeding the 56 percent Democratic majority in the Senate.

It is not clear which party the independents would have aligned themselves with in 1992, nor who would have ended up prime minister. It is likely that they would have aligned with the Republicans and focused on fiscal conservatism and a balanced budget. On the other hand, had the independents aligned with the Democrats, and had Clinton been elected prime minister, national health care might well be the law of the land, and the more liberal welfare reform expected of Clinton in the early part of his first term would probably be in place.

In actuality, Clinton pursued a more liberal agenda from 1993 to 1994, with mixed results, than he did after 1994. In order to reduce the federal budget deficit in 1993, Congress passed his proposal to increase taxes and cut spending. Later that year, he won passage of the North American Free Trade Agreement and lost on a proposal to implement a sweeping national heath care system, which had envisioned a strong role for the federal government. After the Republicans won control of Congress in 1994, Clinton adopted a more centrist position. He supported an anticrime bill in 1995, and ended federal guarantees of support to the poor in his 1996 welfare reform program.[19]

So, who is the real Clinton? The one who proposed a large federal government involvement in his 1993 health care proposal, or the one who in 1996 ended a significant federal role in welfare? It is difficult to know. And what would he have done were he prime minister? The Republican Party and the independents were clearly unhappy with President Clinton by 1994 (both groups were upset with his liberalism, his "waffling," and his inability to work with Congress, particularly when it came to a budget package). Prime Minister Clinton would likely have faced a vote of confidence in 1994, and just as likely he would have lost it. The 1994 congressional election thus serves as an example of both a vote overthrowing the existing government and the subsequent vote to elect a new government.

Had the 1994 election actually been a national election under a parliamentary system, the result would not have been the gridlock that caused so much voter disgust from 1992 to 1994; instead, the Republican Contract with America would now be the law of the land. If we assume that Prime Minister Clinton would have emerged as the coalition leader after the 1992 elections, then we could possibly have seen the national health care program pass in 1993, only to be overturned in 1995. Similarly, a liberal welfare program might have been passed in 1993 only to be replaced by a block grant in 1995. Such a scenario illustrates the instability of a parliamentary system, which can easily result in rapid systemic change.

The 1996 election presents an interesting hypothetical for our imaginary system. The president received barely half of the national vote. The combination of the votes given to the Reform Party, the Green Party, and the Libertarian Party adds up to 10 percent, which, together with the 41 percent that the Republicans received in the national election, could have created a slim majority. However, if the third parties aligned themselves with the Democrats, they could have achieved a strong, 58 percent majority in the National Assembly. As in 1992, it is unclear who would have ended up prime minister in a parliamentary system after the 1996 election. Given that the voters sent back a Republican Congress (although voter decisions in congressional elections are more local than in presidential elections), the public clearly was ambivalent about the two political parties.

The question of the 1996 elections is whether they reflect a lack of confidence in House Speaker Newt Gingrich. Although he himself was reelected, and the Republicans maintained a majority in Congress, the presidential vote has been viewed as representing, if not a repudiation of the Republican Congress, then at least a message that the excesses of the Republicans should be balanced by the Democrats (and vice versa). It is possible under a parliamentary system that Prime Minister Clinton could be voted out of office and replaced by Prime Minister Gingrich, only to have his party returned to power two years later. In that case, policies easily passed by the Republican majority could just as easily be swept away by a Democratic majority, resulting in rapid and significant policy swings.

Conclusion

Arguably, this exploration of how American politics could function without checks and balances reveals in each case that the government in power could have been much more responsive to the demands of its constituency. Our proposed Westminster compromise may have strengthened third parties, given better representation to minorities, and left the Republican and Democratic Parties weakened, if indeed they managed to continue in their current forms. In addition, the blame-game, in which Democrats and Republicans each blame the other side for the deficit, would not be possible. In fact, the federal debt might not be as large, since spending and taxing compromises would not have been necessary with one party controlling both the presidency and the legislature. Either way, the Westminster compromise could lead to greater governmental accountability than is presently the case.

Further, under the fictional Westminster compromise it is quite possible that a European-style welfare state could have been created in the early 1900s, by Prime Minister Teddy Roosevelt, or during the Depression, under Prime Minister Franklin Roosevelt. If a national health care system had not been created then, it is possible that Prime Minister Bill Clinton could have been able to pass such legislation with a Democratic majority in the National Assembly in 1993. Alternatively, a Reform Party led by Ross Perot may have been able to pass term limits and curtail government spending at the height of his popularity in 1993. It is also quite possible that, following the 1994 legislative electoral results, the Contract with America would now be firmly established as the law of the land.

What cost would these changes have had? It is difficult to say. Perhaps the current American presidential form of government would be less stable. As American sentiment shifted from a preference toward big government in times of crisis to much more limited government in times of prosperity, the legislature and the laws passed therein could have lurched back and forth from one extreme to another. In addition, the minority out of power would not be in a position to act as a check for the legislative agenda of the majority in power, a circumstance certainly in opposition to what the Framers of the Constitution intended.

In conclusion, while we acknowledge that it is extremely risky business to make predictions about what might have been, we hope to have provided some food for thought regarding the question of whether institutional arrangements can have significant policy consequences.

Notes

1. Joy Esberey, "What If There Were a Parliamentary System?" in *What If the American Political System Were Different?* (Armonk, N.Y.: M. E. Sharpe, Inc., 1992).

2. Esberey, "What If," 103.

3. Robert A. Dahl, *Parliamentary Versus Presidential Government*, ed. Arend Lijphart (Oxford: Oxford University Press, 1992), 57–65.

4. Dahl, *Parliamentary Versus Presidential Government*, 95–147.

5. See Ralph Segalman, "The Protestant Ethic and Social Welfare," *Journal of Social Issues* 24 (1968), 123–130.

6. Esberey, "What If," 109.

7. See Lani Guinier, *The Tyranny of the Majority* (New York: Free Press, 1994).

8. Esberey, "What If," 130–131.

9. Esberey, "What If," 132.

10. Such a proxy is, naturally, incomplete; presumably voters' decisions would be impacted by whether they were voting for an individual to serve as president or a party to

serve as government. Note also that one could try this hypothetical exercise with reference to the aggregate congressional vote.

11. Theodore Roosevelt, "Address to National Progressive Party, Chicago, 6 August 1912," in *History of American Presidential Elections, 1789-1968*, eds. Arthur M. Schlesinger and Fred L. Israel, vol. 3 (New York: Chelsea House Publishers, 1971), 3:2222.

12. Roosevelt, "Address," 3:2222.

13. George E. Mowry, "The Election of 1912," in *History of American Presidential Elections, 1789-1968*, eds. Arthur M. Schlesinger and Fred L. Israel, vol. 3 (New York: Chelsea House Publishers, 1971).

14. Mowry, "The Election," 3:2163.

15. See William Leuchtenberg, *Franklin Roosevelt and the New Deal: 1932–1940* (New York: Harper and Row, 1963).

16. The 1936 election is known as a *realigning* election, because millions of voters changed their party loyalty from Republican to Democrat and remained Democrats for the rest of their lives.

17. Frank Freidel, "The Election of 1932," in *History of American Presidential Elections, 1789-1968*, eds. Arthur M. Schlesinger and Fred L. Israel, vol. 3 (New York: Chelsea House Publishers, 1971).

18. William E. Leuchtenburg, "Election of 1936," in *History of American Presidential Elections, 1789–1968*, eds. Arthur M. Schlesinger and Fred L. Israel, vol. 3 (New York: Chelsea House, 1971), 2851–2857.

19. See Anne Marie Cammisa, *From Rhetoric to Reform? Welfare Policy in American Politics* (Boulder, Colo.: Westview Press, 1998).

5

....

Some Ideas for the Reform of American Democracy

It is not enough that we have functioned longer under the ideals of 1776 and the Constitution of 1787 than any other nation. Is the system of divided, separate powers and functions workable in the complex social, economic and political environment of today and for the future?

—Warren E. Burger

The Problem Restated

YOU MAY REMEMBER when significant portions of the federal government were forced to shut down in 1996 because the president and Congress were unable to make a deal on the federal budget. That most recent version of gridlock infuriated the public, which itself was divided over whom to blame: A 1996 poll indicated that 48 percent of the population supported the president and 42 percent supported the Congress.[1] Certainly, the closing of the federal government was the direct result of the Democratic president having different budgetary priorities than the Republican Congress, but its origins may be traced to the American constitutional system of checks and balances.

Tired of divided government and gridlock, many observers have argued that the political system must be reformed to enable effective democratic governance. Critics have argued that the net result of gridlock has been a growing belief among the citizenry that it is not possible to change government and a consequent development of apathy, or even of antigovernmental activities in some extreme cases. The previous chapters have identified three central problems with the current institutional design of the American republic. These are

- divided government,
- gridlock, and
- a lack of any mechanism for quickly replacing a failed or deadlocked government.

This concluding chapter will restate and review these three main problems associated with the constitutional system and then present some ideas for its reform.

Problem One: Divided Government

Many Americans are frustrated that Congress and the president have been slow to pass and implement legislation supported by a majority of people, such as the Contract with America. Their reproach has focused on divided government, which occurs when there is an executive of a different party than the dominant party in the legislative branch. Although this situation nicely corresponds to the Framer's concern that power be divided and separated, this very structure has been held accountable by critics for a host of governmental problems, including the 104th Congress's inability to implement the ten provisions of the Contract with America. In his 1867 work entitled *The English Constitution,* the Englishman Walter Bagehot argued for the need of unified government (i.e., fused executive and legislative powers) in order to avoid the problems intrinsic to a divided power arrangement. He admonishes the American system for its fixed and inelastic nature, which, given its long and protracted procedures to respond during an unforeseen crisis, imperils its citizens. Further, Bagehot contends that the division of legislative and executive powers gives rise to the corollary problems of gridlock and lack of governmental accountability. Many contemporary observers echo Bagehot's critiques and have demanded that this situation be reformed.

The American system of divided powers naturally generates a related problem: the lack of governmental accountability. Since there is no central nucleus of power in Washington, it is quite possible for presidents and representatives to "pass the buck," informing concerned citizens that they had very little to do with almost any measure. Or, on the other hand, there is also nothing to keep a political leader from claiming full responsibility for a popular measure, when, in fact, the successful lawmaking process involves many people. For example, even though both the executive and legislative branches had a hand in the increase in the national debt in the 1980s, neither side accepted responsibility, and both have plausibly denied their role. This problem has led to poor policymaking and an erosion of people's confidence in the democratic process. Former President Harry S. Truman did his best to deal with the lack of governmental responsibility by proudly displaying a sign on his desk in the Oval Office that proclaimed that "the buck stops here." The problem of accountability is institutional, and absent a spunky president, only institutional changes will overcome it.

Problem Two: Gridlock

The problem of divided government is profoundly linked to the problem of gridlock, which may be defined as an impasse within or between the branches of government over legislative priorities. Gridlock transpires at numerous points: between the president and Congress, the president and one of the legislative houses, the Senate and the House, or within each legislative branch among the majority and minority parties. Gridlock prevents Congress from moving on legislative programs. There is a school of thought that does not think gridlock is a problem. As discussed in Chapter 1, in terms of getting important legislation passed, neither divided government nor gridlock are necessarily incompatible with effective governance.

Yet there are at least two dangers in the current constitutional arrangement. The first is that the Congress and the president will simply be unable to bring the national debt under control, leading the country to an economic disaster at some point in the not-too-distant future. Second, the divided power arrangement can prevent the president from effective action during a time of crisis somewhere in the world.[2]

Further, it is important to note that gridlock can occur under certain parliamentary arrangements as well. For example, in parliamentary systems with bicameral parliaments, one house may fall into one party's hands and the other house into the hands of another party, creating gridlock. Another problem might arise if no one party has either a majority in parliament or the ability to form a majority coalition. If the United States were to adopt a parliamentary system, perhaps it too would face the peril of minority governments and gridlock. There are simply no easy solutions.

Problem Three:
No Means to Quickly Replacing a Failed or
Deadlocked Administration

The American presidential system has been constitutionally unable to quickly remove a failed or deadlocked administration. As we saw in Chapter 4, given the separation of powers doctrine, Congress was unable to deal with the "long national nightmare" of Watergate swiftly and decisively and immediately institute a new government. Similarly, the congressional investigation into the Iran-Contra scandal in the 1980s lasted for several years and cost the government millions of dollars. Our current institutional arrangement leaves us no choice: Whenever there are serious questions raised about an administration, congressional investigation into the executive branch may last for years. Even though a special council has been occasionally appointed to lend impartiality to the inquiry and to speed up the process, the results have been less than satisfactory. Critics hold that short of institutional reform, we can look forward to more situations like these three well into the future.

Some Possible Solutions?

For three days in the spring of 1976, from April 5 to April 8, the American Academy of Political and Social Science invited a group of distinguished scholars, lawyers, judges, political leaders, and representatives of various interest groups to gather in Philadelphia for two reasons. The first was to celebrate the bicentennial of the American Declaration of Independence. The second was to reexamine the Constitution, including how well the separation of power mechanisms were working.

Conference participants met in various historical settings throughout Philadelphia during their discussions. Papers were delivered to four separate committees and subsequent discussions led to a consensus that several reforms, and some constitutional amendments, should be adopted.[3] In particular, Charles E. Gilbert's paper entitled "Shaping of Public Policy" suggested a series of institutional reforms, including the addition of both a legislative vote of confidence against the executive and a procedure whereby the executive could dissolve the legislature. Yet, in the over twenty years since the conference, no significant progress has been made on these recommendations. In more recent times, James L. Sundquist, an original participant in the 1976 meeting in Philadelphia, has suggested several remedies to the institutional problems associated with presidential government. Drawing on the suggested reforms offered both by the members of the 1976 bicentennial committee on the Constitution and by Sundquist, we have developed some ideas that may serve as a starting point in the search for remedies to the problems listed earlier. These three possible remedies are

- merge executive and legislative powers
- restore governmental accountability
- abandon fixed terms

We will now examine each one of these in turn.

Idea One: Merge Executive and Legislative Powers

The problem of divided government could possibly be modified if the executive and legislative branches were brought closer together. This solution envisions that the president would regularly attend legislative sessions with members of his cabinet, similar to the case of the British prime minister. Regularized executive-legislative contact could improve both communication and collegiality between the two branches of government. As suggested by both Gilbert and Sundquist in their respective works, it would also be a good idea to repeal Article I, section 6, paragraph 2 of the Constitution, so that cabinet officials might also simultaneously be members of Congress.[4] The net result of this change might be, first, that the executive and legislative branches would better understand each other and, second, that the House Speaker could emerge as a sort of congressional prime minister, focusing power and simplifying the lawmaking procedure. As George Gilbert notes, "the American system fragments 'powers' and confuses 'functions'; parliamentary systems consolidate 'power' and provide a more sophisticated institutionalization of functions. . . in which policy-shaping power in legislation and administrative coordination is more effective governmentally and more responsible politically." [5] Gilbert remarks further, and this is of particular interest, that perhaps some experimentation with the separation of powers be tried at the state level before any such reform be brought to Washington, D.C., noting that "if Pennsylvania could function with parliamentary government then, I suppose, so could any state."[6]

At the very least, removing the constitutional ban on members of Congress serving in the executive branch may lead to "constructive experimentation"[7] and to a less confrontational relationship between the two branches.

Idea Two:
Restoring Governmental Accountability

The 1992 presidential and congressional elections restored unified party government in Washington. With Democrat Bill Clinton in the White House and Democratic majorities in both the Senate and the House, many observers cheered the return of governmental accountability. Everyone knew who was in charge (the Democrats) and whom to blame if things went bad (the Democrats). The key question was whether these elections would finally end the bickering between the executive and legislative branches, or if Washington would return to the gridlock of the previous administrations. By 1994, however, and for a variety of reasons, the Democrats had failed, and the Republicans took majorities in both the Senate and the House. Their legislative package, known as the Contract with America, had won the day, and divided government was back. Why? What happened to the high hopes for unified government?

Many reasons were offered for the failure of Democratic-controlled unified government. Some have claimed that the Democrats overestimated their electoral strength after their presidential and congressional victories in 1992 and were not prepared for the Republican attacks. Others have argued that the 1994 election was a well-managed, effective Republican Party attack on the Democrats. Perhaps the most prescient explanation, however, was offered by former Reagan White House chief of staff, Kenneth M. Duberstein. At a meeting convened by the Committee on the Constitutional System and the Brookings Institution on 24 February 1993, he gave an institutional-based explanation for why the 1992 elections, which produced a Democratic president and Democratic majorities in the House and Senate, might not end gridlock and improve governmental accountability. In his view, gridlock and divided government are inevitable in our separated power situation:

> The good news is that on 3 November [1992]the American people clearly demon-strated that they wanted an end to gridlock, they want change, they want more ac-countability in our government—no excuses. The bad news is that now is about as best as it gets. . . . I hope that the American people will not be disappointed, but I am concerned that the end of gridlock is unlikely. The system is biased toward gridlock, not toward action. It is far, far easier to block something on Capitol Hill than it is to pass something affirmatively.[8]

Duberstein turned out to be correct, and gridlock has remained a pronounced feature of government in recent years. Although the divided powers system may occur when the president and the Congress are led by the same party, James Sundquist has argued that there is a greater likelihood for gridlock when the branches of government are also divided between parties. To guard against politi-cal-party-based gridlock, he suggests that a so-called team-ticket reform be adopted. In Sundquist's view, the team-ticket would combine each party's candi-dates for president, vice president, Senate, and House into a slate that would be voted for as a unit. This method would "eliminate ticket splitting that produces divided government."[9] This method of voting was used in the United States be-fore the advent of secret balloting, and some form of the party ballot was used up to the 1970s in several states, including Maine and Connecticut.

Alternatively, the United States could adopt a version of the d'Hondt system of proportional representation for national elections. An American variation of this system could see political parties presenting a closed list of candidates to the vot-ers for all of the positions in government, including the executive and legislative branches. Voters would choose a party list and could not divide their votes be-tween particular candidates from opposing parties. Once the vote totals were an-nounced, the d'Hondt system would allocate seats in the legislative assembly on the basis of a formula to determine the highest average of votes cast per party. This method of allocating seats in a legislature tends to favor larger parties, and so, arguably, the United States would continue to have two major parties. The ad-vantage would be to oblige the voter to make a clear choice about national legisla-tive priorities by freeing national elections from more narrow, local (pork-barrel) concerns.

A corollary to this proposal—which may have helped the Democrats overcome institutional gridlock after the 1992 election—would be to lengthen the terms of office for representatives and senators. In this regard, Sundquist has aptly observed:

> Even a united government is constantly distracted by the imminence of the next election, which is never more than two years away. The two-year life of the Congress—shortest of any national legislature in the world—normally limits an incoming president to barely a year as his "window of opportunity" to lead his party in enacting the program for which it sought its victory. To eliminate the midterm election and thereby lengthen the period of relative freedom from election pressure would require four-year House terms and either four-year or eight-year Senate terms, with the latter more in accord with the staggered-term tradition of the Senate. Presidents and Congresses alike would be better able to undertake short-term measures that might be unpopular, in order to achieve a greater long-run good, and the legislative process would benefit from a more deliberate tempo.[10]

A unified government with a clear electoral mandate and undistracted by the next election would certainly be better equipped to avoid the dangers of gridlock and provide effective governance than the current situation allows. Other useful proposals envision the implementation of a line-item presidential veto, a change in the Senate's filibuster and hold rules, the restoration of legislative veto, and a redefinition of governmental "powers." Each reform seeks to place clear responsibility in the hands of those making the decisions.

Idea Three: Abandon Fixed Terms

Perhaps one of the most frustrating political situations facing the American public is the development of a lame duck president or of an ineffective Congress. According to the current constitutional structure, all members of Congress and the president have the right to complete their term of office regardless of their performance in those roles, save for dire circumstances. The president can be removed from office by the Congress through the rare and difficult process of impeachment and only if he or she is found to have violated the Constitution during his or her term of office. The president may also be removed from office if he or she is found to be incapacitated and unable to perform the job per the terms of the Twenty-Fifth Amendment to the Constitution. Otherwise, for good or ill, the public is stuck with their president.

As we examined in Chapter 2, the American presidential system is a form of democratic government in which the executive branch is distinct and separated from the legislative branch. The chief executive, or president, is directly elected by the people (through the mechanism of the electoral college) and is granted independent power and authority by the Constitution. In general, the president may not be appointed nor dismissed by a legislative vote because executive power derives from the people and not from the legislature.[11] Further, the fixed nature of executive and legislative terms leads to a certain inflexibility of the American system, because no matter how ineffective or incompetent a president, representative, or senator may be, they have the right to stay in office until the end of their electoral term [12]

Perhaps it would be useful to reform this aspect of our presidential system with the introduction of a method for special elections to reconstitute a failed government. Certainly, if the United States were to adopt this so-called parliamentary safeguard (whereby governments can be dissolved at any time, and new elections can be scheduled quickly), weak or ineffective governments in office for long periods of time would become a thing of the past. This reform could promote effective governance.[13]

The organizing principle behind this sort of reform is that a constitutional amendment implementing a parliamentary mechanism for elections would free the current American presidential system from its confinement to the elections timetable. Then political leaders in Washington would be able to turn to new elections whenever they faced a legislative-executive impasse. Arguably, there are many ways to arrange a new electoral procedure. In general, this type of constitutional amendment would have two central provisions: It would allow the president to dissolve Congress and call for new elections if, in his view, Congress had lost the support of the people; and conversely, it would subject the president to a Congressional vote of confidence if, at any time, the legislature seriously doubted the continuing ability of a president to lead. These reforms would make the presidential system considerably less stable but would certainly result in a closer executive-legislative partnership, as both sides could face dissolution by the other.[14]

Conclusion: Revisiting the Constitutional Convention

To conclude, let us revisit the Constitutional Convention for a moment. As we discussed in Chapter 2, the origins of the dilemma of majority rule versus minority rights in American politics may be traced to the very founding of the nation in 1787. Having defeated the British King George III in the War of Independence, the Framers debated about the form and shape of their new democratic government at the Constitutional Convention in Philadelphia. Since there were no other viable functioning democratic models in the world to emulate, their deliberations were paving an unknown territory. And their solution to the dilemma was to wager that it was better to have executive–legislative gridlock than to chance either

The signing of the American Constitution—the start of an experiment in presidential democracy. Photo courtesy of the Architect of the Capitol.

the tyranny of the one or of the many. In that way the Framers launched an experiment in government predicated on divided and separated powers. We continue to live with this experiment.

Arguably, the threat of tyranny that so concerned the Framers is as valid today as ever. So should we really try to significantly alter this system of government? Americans always have the option to alter or amend the Constitution; prior to any change, however, it is incumbent upon us to carefully consider the pros and cons of the current arrangement and of the proposed change. The Framers struggled with how to organize their new democracy at the end of the eighteenth century, and they made their determination. Now the question is up to us. What should we do?

Our main purpose in this book has been to illustrate the importance of institutional arrangements. In particular, the American presidential system has been designed to be antagonistic to majority rule; this design has generated, among other difficulties, the problems of divided government, gridlock, and a lack of any mechanism for quickly replacing a failed or deadlocked government. Former President Woodrow Wilson understood these limitations of our Constitutional structure and suggested at the end of the last century that it would be better if the

United States adopted a British-style parliamentary system to suit the changing times. The three possible solutions suggested in this chapter echo Wilson's very concerns. Taken in aggregate, these reforms could, perchance, permit governmental leaders to quickly adopt new laws and adapt the government to the changing times. We suggest them as the start of a dialogue.

Notes

1. Poll results were reported in Karen O'Connor and Larry Sabato, *American Government: Continuity and Change,* 1997 alt. ed. (Boston: Allen and Bacon, 1997), 266.

2. James L. Sundquist, *Constitutional Reform and Effective Government,* rev. ed. (Washington, D.C.: Brookings Institution, 1992), 323.

3. The four topics were: on values and society in revolutionary America, effectiveness of governmental operations, shaping of public policy, and the United States and the world.

4. See Sundquist, *Constitutional Reform* and Charles E. Gilbert, "Shaping of Public Policy," in *The Revolution, the Constitution, and America's Third Century: The Bicentennial Conference on the United States Constitution,* vol. 1, *Conference Papers* (Philadelphia: American Academy of Political and Social Science by the University of Pennsylvania Press, 1976), 163–215.

5. Gilbert, "Shaping," 198.

6. Gilbert, "Shaping," 200.

7. Sundquist, *Constitutional Reform,* 324.

8. Kenneth Duberstein, in *Beyond Gridlock? Prospects for Governance in the Clinton Years—And After,* ed. James Sundquist, (Washington, D.C.: Brookings Institution, 1993), 17–18.

9. Sundquist, *Constitutional Reform,* 323.

10. Sundquist, *Constitutional Reform,* 323.

11. See Giovanni Sartori, *Comparative Constitutional Engineering: An Inquiry into Structures, Incentives and Outcomes* (New York: New York University Press, 1994), 101.

12. Juan J. Linz and Arturo Valenzuela, *The Failure of Presidential Democracy: Comparative Perspectives* (Baltimore: The Johns Hopkins University Press, 1994), 5–22.

13. Sundquist, *Constitutional Reform,* 199.

14. Sundquist, *Constitutional Reform,* 196–197.

Discussion Questions

Chapter 1

1. Have you found American government to be unresponsive?
2. Do you agree with President Wilson's critique of the presidential system?
3. Would a dual-executive system, such as the system in France, work in the United States?
4. In your view, would a parliamentary system make Washington more responsive?

Chapter 2

1. What was the Magna Carta? What difference did it make to British political development?
2. How did the industrial revolution change the British parliament?
3. What role does the British speaker play?
4. How are the powers of the British prime minister different from those of the American president?
5. What was the Virginia plan? Explain its significance in the development of a presidential system (as opposed to a parliamentary system) in the United States.

Chapter 3

1. What was the source of the Republican Contract with America? What difference did it make to the 1994 election?
2. Describe some of the major tenets of the contract.
3. What was the status of the contract at the end of the first one hundred days? What would the Framers have said about this?
4. Using the 104th Congress as an example, explain how the American Congress is unlike the British Parliament.

Chapter 4

1. Could our imagined "Westminster compromise" actually have happened? How?
2. Would a parliamentary system have really changed American political development? Explain.
3. Under the Westminster compromise, what would have happened to the 1994 Republican Contract with America?
4. Under the Westminster compromise, what would have happened during Watergate?

Chapter 5

1. Name and discuss the main problems associated with a presidential regime.
2. Name and discuss the main ideas offered as solutions for these problems.
3. Do you think the United States would be better off with a parliamentary system?

Appendices

1. Compare the introduction to the Magna Carta and the preamble to the United States Constitution. Who is granting liberties in the Magna Carta? Who is establishing the Constitution? What differences do you notice, and what impact do you think these differences would have on government?

2. Compare Cap. I of the Magna Carta to the second paragraph of the Declaration of Independence (especially the first two sentences). In each case, what is the origin of the rights?

3. Compare the Tenth Amendment of the Constitution to Article 2 of the Articles of Confederation. How are they similar? How are they different? Now find the "national supremacy clause" in Article VI of the Constitution. Does it refute the Tenth Amendment of the Constitution? Why or why not?

4. Examine Article 7 of the Virginia Plan. Compare it to Article II, section 1, of the Constitution. How do they differ from each other in terms of the manner by which the president is selected? What is the significance of the difference?

5. Read Federalist No. 10. What does Madison mean by "faction"? How does he propose to mitigate the effects of a faction? Do you think that his precautions against factions are necessary today? Why or why not?

6. Find the section of Federalist No. 51 where Madison says the following: "If men were angels, no government would be necessary. If angels were to govern men, neither external nor internal controls would be necessary." What does Madison mean by this? What controls does he suggest to counteract the risks of a government controlled by humans rather than by angels?

Appendixes

Appendix A:
Magna Carta

The following text is taken from *Statutes at Large,* ed. O. Ruffhead, revised C. Runnington (1786–1800), i. 1–10.

Edward by the grace of God King of *England,* Lord of *Ireland,* and Duke of *Guyan,* to all *Archbishops, Bishops,* etc. We have seen the Great Charter of the Lord *Henry,* sometimes King of *England,* our father, of the Liberties of *England,* in these words: HENRY by the grace of God, King of *England,* Lord of *Ireland,* Duke of *Normandy* and *Guyan,* and Earl of *Anjou,* to all Archbishops, Bishops, Abbots, Priors, Earls, Barons, Sheriffs, Provosts, Officers, and to all Bailiffs and other our faithful Subjects, which shall see this present Charter, Greeting. Know ye that we, unto the Honour of Almighty God, and for the salvation of the souls of our progenitors and successors, *Kings of England,* to the advancement of holy Church, and amendment of our Realm, of our meer and free will, have given and granted to all Archbishops, Bishops, Abbots, Priors, Earls, Barons, and to all freemen of this our realm, these liberties following, to be kept in our kingdom of *England* for ever.

Cap. I

A Confirmation of Liberties

First, We have granted to God, and by this our present Charter have confirmed, for us and our Heirs for ever, That the Church of *England* shall be free, and shall have her whole rights and liberties inviolable. (2) We have granted also, and given to all the freemen of our realm, for us and our Heirs for ever, these liberties underwritten, to have and to hold to them and their Heirs, of us and our Heirs for ever.

Cap. II

The Relief of the King's Tenant of full Age

If any of our Earls or Barons, or any other, which holdeth of Us in chief by Knights service, die and at the time of his death his heir be of full age, and oweth us Relief, he shall have his inheritance by the old Relief; that is to say, the heir or heirs of an Earl, for a whole Earldom, by one hundred pound; the heir or heirs of a Baron, for an whole Barony, by one hundred

159

marks; the heir or heirs of a Knight, for one while Knights fee, one hundred shillings at the most; and he that hath less, shall give less, according to the old custom of the fees.

Cap. III

The Wardship of an Heir within Age. The Heir a Knight

But if the Heir of any such be within age, his Lord shall not have the ward of him, nor of his land, before that he hath taken of him homage. (2) And after that such an heir hath been in ward (when he is come of full age) that is to say, to the age of one and twenty years, he shall have his inheritance without Relief, and without Fine; so that if such an heir, being within age, be made Knight, yet nevertheless his land shall remain in the keeping of his Lord unto the term of aforesaid.

Cap. IV

No Waste shall be made by a Guardian in Wards Lands

The keeper of the land of such an heir, being within age, shall not take of the lands of the heir, but reasonable issues, reasonable customs, and reasonable services, and that without destruction and waste of his men and his goods. (2) And if we commit the custody of any such land to the Sheriff, or to any other, which is answerable unto us for the issues of the same land, and he make destruction or waste of those things that he hath in custody, we will take of him amends *and recompence therefore,* (3) and the land shall be committed to two lawful and discreet men of that fee, which shall answer unto us for the issues of the same land, or unto him whom we will assign. (4) And if we give or sell to any man the custody of any such land, and he therein do make destruction or waste, he shall lose the same custody; and it shall be assigned to two lawful and discreet men of that fee, which also in like manner shall be answerable to us, as afore is said.

Cap. V

Guardians shall maintain the Inheritance of their Wards; and of Bishoprics, etc.

The keeper, so long as he hath the custody of the land of such an heir, shall keep up the houses, parks, warrens, ponds, mills, and other things pertaining to the same land, with the issues of the said land; and he shall deliver to the Heir, when he cometh to his full age, all his land stored with ploughs, and all other things, at the least as he received it. All these things shall be observed in the custodies of Archbishopricks, Bishopricks, Abbeys, Priories, Churchs, and Dignities vacant, which appertain to us; except this, that such custody shall not be sold.

Cap. VI

Heirs shall be married without Disparagement

Heirs shall be married without Disparagement.

Cap. VII

A Widow shall have her Marriage, Inheritance, and Quarentine. The King's Widow, etc.

A Widow, after the death of her husband, incontinent, and without any Difficulty, shall have her marriage and her inheritance, (2) and shall give nothing for her dower, her marriage, or her inheritance, which her husband and she held the day of the death of her husband, (3) and she shall tarry in the chief house of her husband by forty days after the death of her husband, within which days her dower shall be assigned her (if it were not assigned her before) or that the house be a castle; (4) and if she depart from the castle, then a competent house shall be forthwith provided for her, in the which she may honestly dwell, until her dower be to her assigned, as it is aforesaid; and she shall have in the meantime her reasonable estovers of the common; (5) and for her dower shall be assigned unto her the third part of all the lands of her husband, which were his during coverture, except she were endowed of less at the Church-door. (6) No widow shall be distrained to marry herself: nevertheless she shall find surety, that she shall not marry without our licence and assent (if she hold of us) nor without the assent of the Lord, if she hold of another.

Cap. VIII

How Sureties shall be charged to the King

We or our Bailiffs shall not seize any land or rent for any debt, as long as the present Goods and Chattels of the debtor do suffice to pay the debt, and the debtor himself be ready to satisfy therefore. (2) Neither shall the pledges of the debtor be distrained, as long as the principal debtor is sufficient for the payment of the debt. (3) And if the principal debtor fail in the payment of the debt, having nothing wherewith to pay, or will not pay where he is able, the pledges shall answer for the debt. (4) And if they will, they shall have the lands and rents of the debtor, until they be satisfied of *that* which they before paid for him, except that the debtor can show himself to be acquitted against the said sureties.

Cap. IX

The Liberties of London, and other Cities and Towns confirmed

The city of *London* shall have all *the* old liberties and customs, *which it hath been used to have*. Moreover we will and grant, that all other Cities, Boroughs, Towns, and the Barons of the Five Ports, and all other Ports, shall have all their liberties and free customs.

Cap. X

None shall distrain for more Service than is due

No man shall be distrained to do more service for a Knights fee, nor any freehold, than therefore is due.

Cap. XI

Common Pleas shall not follow the King's Court

Common Pleas shall not follow our Court, but shall be holden in some place certain.

Cap. XII

Where and before whom Assises shall be taken. Adjournment for Difficulty

Assises of *novel disseisin,* and of *Mortdancestor,* shall not be taken but in the shires, and after this manner: If we be out of this Realm, our chief Justicer shall send our Justicers through every County once in the Year, which, with the Knights of the shires, shall take the said Assises in those counties; (2) and those things that at the coming of our foresaid Justicers, being sent to take those Assises in the counties, cannot be determined, shall be ended by them in some other place in their circuit; (3) and those things, which for difficulty of some articles cannot be determined by them, shall be referred to our Justicers of the Bench, and there shall be ended.

Cap. XIII

Assises of Darrein Presentment

Assises of *Darrein Presentment* shall be alway taken before our Justices of the Bench, and there shall be determined.

Cap. XIV

How Men of all Sorts shall be amerced, and by whom

A Freeman shall not be amerced for a small fault, but after the manner of the fault; and for a great fault after the greatness thereof, saving to him his contenement; (2) and a Merchant likewise, saving to him his Merchandise; (3) and any other's villain than ours shall be likewise amerced, saving his wainage, if he falls into our mercy. (4) And none of the said amerciaments shall be assessed, but by the oath of honest and lawful men of the vicinage. (5) Earls and Barons shall not be amerced but by their Peers, and after the manner of their offence. (6) No man of the Church shall be amerced after the quantity of his spiritual Benefice, but after his Lay-tenement, and after the quantity of his offence.

Cap. XV

Making of Bridges and Banks

No Town or Freeman shall be distrained to make Bridges nor Banks, but such as of old time and of right have been accustomed to make them in the time of King *Henry* our Grandfather.

Cap. XVI

Defending of Banks

No Banks shall be defended from henceforth, but such as were in defence in the time of King Henry our Grandfather, by the same places, and the same bounds, as they were wont to be in his time.

Cap. XVII

Holding Pleas of the Crown

No Sheriff, Constable, Escheator, Coroner, nor any other our Bailiffs, shall hold Pleas of our Crown.

Cap. XVIII

The King's Debtor dying, the King shall be first paid

If any that holdeth of us Lay-fee do die, and our Sheriff or Bailiff do show our Letters Patents of our summon for Debt, which the dead man did owe to us; it shall be lawful to our Sheriff or Bailiff to attach or inroll all the goods and chattels of the dead, being found in the said fee, to the Value of the same Debt, by the sight *and testimony* of lawful men, so that nothing thereof shall be taken away, until we be clearly paid off the debt; (2) and the residue shall remain to the Executors to perform the testament of the dead; (3) and if nothing be owing unto us, all the chattels shall go to the use of the dead (saving to his wife and children their reasonable parts).

Cap. XIX

Purveyance for a Castle

No Constable, nor his Bailiff, shall take corn or other chattels of any man, if the man be not of the Town where the Castle is, but he shall forthwith pay for the same, unless that the will of the seller was to respite the payment; (2) and if he be of the same Town, the price shall be paid unto him within forty days.

Cap. XX

Doing of Castle-ward

No Constable shall distrain any Knight to give money for keeping of his Castle, if he himself will do it in his proper person, or cause it to be done by another sufficient man, if he may not do it himself for a reasonable cause. (2) And if we lead or send him to an army, he shall be free from Castle-ward for the time that he shall be with us in fee in our host, for the which he hath done service in our wars.

Cap. XXI

Taking of Horses, Carts, and Wood

No Sheriff nor Bailiff of ours, or any other, shall take the Horses or Carts of any man to make carriage, except he pay the old price limited, that is to say, for carriage with two horse, x.d. a day; for three horse, xiv.d. a day. (2) No demesne Cart of any Spiritual person or Knight, or any Lord, shall be taken by our Bailiffs; (3) nor we, nor our Bailiffs, nor any other, shall take any man's wood for our Castles, or other our necessaries to be done, but by the licence of him whose wood it shall be.

Cap. XXII

How long Felons Lands shall be holden by the King

We will not hold the Lands of them that be convict of Felony but one year and one day, and then those Lands shall be delivered to the Lords of the fee.

Cap. XXIII

In what Places Wears shall be put down

All Wears from henceforth shall be utterly put down by *Thames* and *Medway*, and through all *England*, but only by the Sea-coasts.

Cap. XXIV

In what Case a Praecipe in Capite is not grantable

The Writ that is called *Praecipe in capite* shall be from henceforth granted to no person of any freehold, whereby any freeman may lose his Court.

Cap. XXV

There shall be but one Measure throughout the Realm

One measure of Wine shall be through our Realm, and one measure of Ale, and one measure of Corn, that is to say, the Quarter of *London;* and one breadth of dyed Cloth, Russets, and Haberjects, that is to say, two Yards within the lists. (2) And it shall be of Weights as it is of Measures.

Cap. XXVI

Inquisition of Life and Member

Nothing from henceforth shall be given for a Writ of Inquisition, nor taken of him that prayeth Inquisition of Life, or of Member, but it shall be granted freely, and not denied.

Cap. XXVII

Tenure of the King in Socage, and of another by Knights Service. Petit Serjeanty

If any do hold of us by Fee-ferm, or by Socage, or Burgage, and he holdeth Lands of another by Knights Service, we will not have the Custody of his Heir, nor of his Land, which is holden of the Fee of another, by reason of that Fee-ferm, Socage, or Burgage. (2) Neither will we have the custody of such Fee-ferm, or Socage, or Burgage, except Knights Service be due unto us out of the same Fee-ferm. (3) We will not have the custody of the Heir, or of any Land, by occasion of any Petit Serjeanty, that any man holdeth of us by Service to pay a Knife, an Arrow, or the like.

Cap. XXVIII

Wager of Law shall not be without Witness

No Bailiff from henceforth shall put any man to his open Law, nor to an Oath, upon his own bare saying, without faithful Witnesses brought in for the same.

Cap. XXIX

None shall be condemned without Trial.
Justice shall not be sold or deferred

No Freeman shall be taken, or imprisoned, or be disseised of his Freehold, or Liberties, or free Customs, or be outlawed, or exiled, or any otherwise destroyed; *nor will we pass upon him, nor condemn him,* but by lawful Judgment of his Peers, or by the Law of the Land. (2) We will sell to no man, we will not deny or defer to any man either Justice or Right.

Cap. XXX

Merchant Strangers coming into this Realm shall be well used

All Merchants (if they were not openly prohibited before) shall have their safe and sure Conduct to depart out of *England,* to come into *England,* to tarry in, and go through *England,* as well by Land as by Water, to buy and sell without any manner of evil Tolts, by the old and rightful Customs, except in Time of War. (2) And if they be of a land making War against us, and such be found in our Realm at the beginning of the Wars, they shall be attached without harm of body or goods, until it be known unto us, or our Chief Justice, how our Merchants be intreated there in the land making War against us; (3) and if our Merchants be well intreated there, theirs shall be likewise with us.

Cap. XXXI

Tenure of a Barony coming into the King's Hands by Eschete

If any man hold of any Eschete, as of the honour of *Wallingford, Nottingham, Boloin,* or of any other Eschetes which be in our hands, and are Baronies, and die, his Heir shall give none other Relief, nor do none other Service to us, than he should to the Baron, if it were in the Baron's hand. (2) And we in the same wise shall hold it as the Baron held it; neither shall we have, by occasion of any such Barony or Eschete, any Eschete or keeping of any of our men, unless he that held the Barony or Eschete hold of us in chief.

Cap. XXXII

Lands shall not be alienated to the Prejudice of the Lord's Service

No Freeman from henceforth shall give or sell any more of his Land, but so that of the residue of the Lands the Lord of the Fee may have the Service due to him, which belongeth to the Fee.

Cap. XXXIII

Patrons of Abbies shall have the Custody of them in the time of Vacation

All Patrons of Abbies, which have the King's Charters of *England* of Advowson, or have old Tenure or Possession in the same, shall have the Custody of them when they fall void, as it hath been accustomed, and as it is afore declared.

Cap. XXXIV

In what Case only a Woman shall have an Appeal of Death

No Man shall be taken or imprisoned upon the Appeal of a Woman for the Death of any other, than of her husband.

Cap. XXXV

At what Time shall be kept a County Court, Sheriff's Turn, and a Leet

No County Court from henceforth shall be holden, but from Month to Month; and where greater time hath been used, there shall be greater: Nor any Sheriff, or his Bailiff, shall keep his Turn in the Hundred but twice in the Year; and nowhere but in due place, and accustomed; that is to say, once after *Easter*, and again after the Feast of St. *Michael.* And the View of Frankpledge shall be likewise at the Feast of St. *Michael* without occasion; so that every man may have his Liberties which he had, or used to have, in the time of King HENRY our Grandfather, or which he hath purchased since: but the View of Frankpledge shall be so done, that our Peace may be kept; and that the Tything be wholly kept as it hath been accustomed; and that the Sheriff seek no Occasions, and that he be content with so much as the Sheriff was wont to have for his Viewmaking in the time of King HENRY our Grandfather.

Cap. XXXVI

No Land shall be given in Mortmain

It shall not be lawful from henceforth to any to give his Lands to any Religious House, and to take the same Land again to hold of the same House. Nor shall it be lawful to any House of Religion to take the Lands of any, and to lease the same to him of whom he received it. If any from henceforth give his Lands to any Religious House, and thereupon be convict, the Gift shall be utterly void, and the Land shall accrue to the Lord of the Fee.

Cap. XXXVII

A Subsidy in respect of this Charter, and the Charter of the Forest, granted to the King

Escuage from henceforth shall be taken like as it was wont to be in the time of King HENRY our Grandfather; reserving to all Archbishops, Bishops, Abbots, Priors, Templers, Hospitallers, Earls, Barons, and all persons, as well Spiritual as Temporal, all their free liberties and free Customs, and Liberties aforesaid, which we have granted to be holden within this our Realm, as much as appertaineth to us *and our Heirs, we shall observe;* and all Men of this our Realm, as well Spiritual as Temporal (as much as in them is) shall observe the same against all persons in like wise. And for this our Gift and Grant of these Liberties, and of other contained in our Charter of Liberties of our Forest, the Archbishops, Bishops, Abbots, Priors, Earls, Barons, Knights, Freeholders, and other our Subjects, have given unto us the Fifteenth Part of all their Moveables. And we have granted unto them for us and our Heirs, that neither we, nor our Heirs shall procure or do anything whereby the Liberties in this Charter contained shall be infringed or broken; and if anything be procured by any person contrary to the premises, it shall be had of no force nor effect. These being Witnesses; Lord B. Archbishop of *Canterbury,* E. Bishop of *London,* J. Bishop of *Bathe,* P. of *Winchester,* H. of *Lincoln,* R. of *Salisbury,* W. of *Rochester,* W. of *Worcester,* J. of *Ely,* H. of *Hereford,* R. of *Chichester,* W. of *Exeter,* Bishops; the Abbot of St. *Edmunds,* the Abbot of St. *Albans,* the Abbot of *Bello,* the Abbot of St. *Augustines* in *Cantebury,* the Abbot of *Evesham,* the Abbot of *Westminster,* the Abbot of *Bourgh* St. *Peter,* the Abbot of *Reading,* the Abbot of *Abindon,* the Abbot of *Malmsbury,* the Abbot of *Winchcomb,* the Abbot of *Hyde,* the Abbot of *Certefey,* the Abbot of *Sherburn,* the Abbot of *Cerne,* the Abbot of *Abbotebir,* the Abbot of *Middleton,* the Abbot of *Seleby,* the Abbot of *Cirencester;* H. *de Burgh* Justice, H. Earl of *Chester* and *Lincoln,* W. Earl of *Salisbury,* W. Earl of *Warren,* G. *de Clare* Earl of *Gloucester* and *Hereford,* W. *de Ferrars* Earl of *Derby,* W. *de Mandeville* Earl of *Essex,* H. *de Bygod* Earl of *Norfolk,* W. Earl of *Albermarle,* H. Earl of *Hereford,* J. Constable of *Chester, R. de Ros, R. Fitzwalter, R. de Vyponte, W. de Bruer, R. de Muntefichet, P. Fitzherbert, W. de Aubenie, F. Grefly, F. de Breus, J. de Monemue, J. Fitzallen, H. de Mortimer, W. de Beauchamp, W. de St. John, P. de Mauly, Brian de Lisle, Thomas de Multon, R. de Argenteyn, G. de Nevil, W. de Mauduit, J. de Balun,* and others.

II. We, ratifying and approving these Gifts and Grants aforesaid, confirm and make strong all the same for us and our Heirs perpetually, and, by the Tenour of these Presents, do renew the same; willing and granting for us and our Heirs, that this Charter, and all and singular his Articles, for ever shall be stedfastly, firmly, and inviolably observed; *although some Articles in the same Charter contained, yet hitherto peradventure have not been kept, we will, and by Authority* Royal command, from henceforth firmly they be observed. In witness whereof we have caused these our Letters Patents to be made. T. EDWARD our Son at *Westminster, the Twenty-eighth Day* of March, *in the Twenty-eighth Year of our Reign.*

Appendix B:
Declaration of Independence

Action of Second Continental Congress, July 4, 1776

The unanimous Declaration of the thirteen United States of America

WHEN in the Course of human Events, it becomes necessary for one People to dissolve the Political Bands which have connected them with another, and to assume among the Powers of the Earth, the separate and equal Station to which the Laws of Nature and of Nature's God entitle them, a decent Respect to the Opinions of Mankind requires that they should declare the causes which impel them to the Separation.

WE hold these Truths to be self-evident, that all Men are created equal, that they are endowed by their Creator with certain unalienable Rights, that among these are Life, Liberty and the Pursuit of Happiness—That to secure these Rights, Governments are instituted among Men, deriving their just Powers from the Consent of the Governed, that whenever any Form of Government becomes destructive of these Ends, it is the Right of the People to alter or to abolish it, and to institute new Government, laying its Foundation on such Principles, and organizing its Powers in such Form, as to them shall seem most likely to effect their Safety and Happiness. Prudence, indeed, will dictate that Governments long established should not be changed for light and transient Causes; and accordingly all Experience hath shewn, that Mankind are more disposed to suffer, while Evils are sufferable, than to right themselves by abolishing the Forms to which they are accustomed. But when a long Train of Abuses and Usurpations, pursuing invariably the same Object, evinces a Design to reduce them under absolute Despotism, it is their Right, it is their Duty, to throw off such Government, and to provide new Guards for their future Security. Such has been the patient Sufferance of these Colonies; and such is now the Necessity which constrains them to alter their former Systems of Government. The History of the present King of Great-Britain is a History of repeated Injuries and Usurpations, all having in direct Object the Establishment of an absolute Tyranny over these States. To prove this, let Facts be submitted to a candid World.

HE has refused his Assent to Laws, the most wholesome and necessary for the public Good.

HE has forbidden his Governors to pass Laws of immediate and pressing Importance, unless suspended in their Operation till his Assent should be obtained; and when so suspended, he has utterly neglected to attend to them.

HE has refused to pass other Laws for the Accommodation of large Districts of People, unless those People would relinquish the Right of Representation in the Legislature, a Right inestimable to them, and formidable to Tyrants only.

HE has called together Legislative Bodies at Places unusual, uncomfortable, and distant from the Depository of their public Records, for the sole Purpose of fatiguing them into Compliance with his Measures.

HE has dissolved Representative Houses repeatedly, for opposing with manly Firmness his Invasions on the Rights of the People.

HE has refused for a long Time, after such Dissolutions, to cause others to be elected; whereby the Legislative Powers, incapable of the Annihilation, have returned to the People at large for their exercise; the State remaining in the mean time exposed to all the Dangers of Invasion from without, and the Convulsions within.

HE has endeavoured to prevent the Population of these States; for that Purpose obstructing the Laws for Naturalization of Foreigners; refusing to pass others to encourage their Migrations hither, and raising the Conditions of new Appropriations of Lands.

HE has obstructed the Administration of Justice, by refusing his Assent to Laws for establishing Judiciary Powers.

HE has made Judges dependent on his Will alone, for the Tenure of their Offices, and the Amount and Payment of their Salaries.

HE has erected a Multitude of new Offices, and sent hither Swarms of Officers to harrass our People, and eat out their Substance.

HE has kept among us, in Times of Peace, Standing Armies, without the consent of our Legislatures.

HE has affected to render the Military independent of and superior to the Civil Power.

HE has combined with others to subject us to a Jurisdiction foreign to our Constitution, and unacknowledged by our Laws; giving his Assent to their Acts of pretended Legislation:

FOR quartering large Bodies of Armed Troops among us;

FOR protecting them, by a mock Trial, from Punishment for any Murders which they should commit on the Inhabitants of these States:

FOR cutting off our Trade with all Parts of the World:

FOR imposing Taxes on us without our Consent:

FOR depriving us, in many Cases, of the Benefits of Trial by Jury:

FOR transporting us beyond Seas to be tried for pretended Offences:

FOR abolishing the free System of English Laws in a neighbouring Province, establishing therein an arbitrary Government, and enlarging its Boundaries, so as to render it at once an Example and fit Instrument for introducing the same absolute Rules into these Colonies:

FOR taking away our Charters, abolishing our most valuable Laws, and altering fundamentally the Forms of our Governments:

FOR suspending our own Legislatures, and declaring themselves invested with Power to legislate for us in all Cases whatsoever.

HE has abdicated Government here, by declaring us out of his Protection and waging War against us.

HE has plundered our Seas, ravaged our Coasts, burnt our Towns, and destroyed the Lives of our People.

HE is, at this Time, transporting large Armies of foreign Mercenaries to compleat the Works of Death, Desolation, and Tyranny, already begun with circumstances of Cruelty and Perfidy, scarcely paralleled in the most barbarous Ages, and totally unworthy the Head of a civilized Nation.

HE has constrained our fellow Citizens taken Captive on the high Seas to bear Arms against their Country, to become the Executioners of their Friends and Brethren, or to fall themselves by their Hands.

HE has excited domestic Insurrections amongst us, and has endeavoured to bring on the Inhabitants of our Frontiers, the merciless Indian Savages, whose known Rule of Warfare, is an undistinguished Destruction, of all Ages, Sexes and Conditions.

IN every stage of these Oppressions we have Petitioned for Redress in the most humble Terms: Our repeated Petitions have been answered only by repeated Injury. A Prince, whose Character is thus marked by every act which may define a Tyrant, is unfit to be the Ruler of a free People.

NOR have we been wanting in Attentions to our British Brethren. We have warned them from Time to Time of Attempts by their Legislature to extend an unwarrantable Jurisdiction over us. We have reminded them of the Circumstances of our Emigration and Settlement here. We have appealed to their native Justice and Magnanimity, and we have conjured them by the Ties of our common Kindred to disavow these Usurpations, which, would inevitably interrupt our Connections and Correspondence. They too have been deaf to the Voice of Justice and of Consanguinity. We must, therefore, acquiesce in the Necessity, which denounces our Separation, and hold them, as we hold the rest of Mankind, Enemies in War, in Peace, Friends.

WE, therefore, the Representatives of the UNITED STATES OF AMERICA, in GENERAL CONGRESS, Assembled, appealing to the Supreme Judge of the World for the Rectitude of our Intentions, do, in the Name, and by Authority of the good People of these Colonies, solemnly Publish and Declare, That these United Colonies are, and of Right ought to be, FREE AND INDEPENDENT STATES; that they are absolved from all Allegiance to the British Crown, and that all political Connection between them and the State of Great-Britain, is and ought to be totally dissolved; and that as FREE AND INDEPENDENT STATES, they have full Power to levy War, conclude Peace, contract Alliances, establish Commerce, and to do all other Acts and Things which INDEPENDENT STATES may of right do. And for the support of this Declaration, with a firm Reliance on the Protection of divine Providence, we mutually pledge to each other our Lives, our Fortunes, and our sacred Honor.

John Hancock.
GEORGIA, Button Gwinnett, Lyman Hall, Geo. Walton.
NORTH-CAROLINA, Wm. Hooper, Joseph Hewes, John Penn.
SOUTH-CAROLINA, Edward Rutledge, Thos Heyward, junr.,
Thomas Lynch, junr., Arthur Middleton.
MARYLAND, Samuel Chase, Wm. Paca, Thos. Stone, Charles Carroll, of Carrollton.
VIRGINIA, George Wythe, Richard Henry Lee, Ths. Jefferson, Benja. Harrison,
Thos. Nelson, jr., Francis Lightfoot Lee, Carter Braxton.

PENNSYLVANIA, Robt. Morris, Benjamin Rush, Benja. Franklin, John Morton, Geo. Clymer,
Jas. Smith, Geo. Taylor, James Wilson, Geo. Ross.
DELAWARE, Caesar Rodney, Geo. Read.
NEW-YORK, Wm. Floyd, Phil. Livingston, Frank Lewis, Lewis Morris.
NEW-JERSEY, Richd. Stockton, Jno. Witherspoon, Fras. Hopkinson, John Hart, Abra. Clark.
NEW-HAMPSHIRE, Josiah Bartlett, Wm. Whipple, Matthew Thornton.
MASSACHUSETTS-BAY, Saml. Adams, John Adams, Robt. Treat Paine, Elbridge Gerry.
RHODE-ISLAND AND PROVIDENCE, C. Step. Hopkins, William Ellery.
CONNECTICUT, Roger Sherman, Saml. Huntington, Wm. Williams, Oliver Wolcott.

IN CONGRESS, JANUARY 18, 1777.

Appendix C:
Articles of Confederation

Articles of Confederation and Perpetual Union between the States of New Hampshire, Massachusetts Bay, Rhode Island and Providence Plantations, Connecticut, New York, New Jersey, Pennsylvania, Delaware, Maryland, Virginia, North Carolina, South Carolina, and Georgia.

Article One

The style of this Confederacy shall be "The United States of America."

Article Two

Each State retains its sovereignty, freedom, and independence, and every power, jurisdiction, and right, which is not by this Confederation expressly delegated to the United States in Congress assembled.

Article Three

The said States hereby severally enter into a firm league of friendship with each other, for their common defence, the security of their liberties, and their mutual and general welfare, binding themselves to assist each other against all force offered to, or attacks made upon them, or any of them, on account of religion, sovereignty, trade, or any other pretence whatever.

Article Four

The better to secure and perpetuate mutual friendship and intercourse among the people of the different States in this Union, the free inhabitants of each of these States, paupers, vagabonds, and fugitives from justice excepted, shall be entitled to all the privileges and immunities of free citizens in the several States, and the people of each State shall have free ingress and regress to and from any other State, and shall enjoy therein all the privileges of trade and commerce, subject to the same duties, impositions, and restrictions as the inhabitants thereof respectively, provided that such restrictions shall not extend so far as to prevent the removal of property imported into any State, to any other State of which the owner is an inhabitant; provided also, that no imposition, duties, or restriction shall be laid by any State, on the property of the United States, or either of them.

If any person guilty of or charged with treason, felony, or other high misdemeanor in any State, shall flee from justice, and be found in any of the United States, he shall, upon demand of the governor or executive power of the State from which he fled, be delivered up and removed to the State having jurisdiction of his offence.

Full faith and credit shall be given in each of these States to the records, acts, and judicial proceedings of the courts and magistrates of every other State.

Article Five

For the more convenient management of the general interests of the United States, delegates shall be annually appointed in such manner as the legislature of each State shall direct, to meet in Congress on the first Monday in November, in every year, with a power reserved to each State to recall its delegates, or any of them, at any time within the year, and to send others in their stead, for the remainder of the year.

No State shall be represented in Congress by less than two, nor by more than seven members; and no person shall be capable of being a delegate for more than three years in any term of six years, nor shall any person, being a delegate, be capable of holding any office under the United States for which he or another for his benefit receives any salary, fees, or emolument of any kind.

Each State shall maintain its own delegates in a meeting of the States, and while they act as members of the committee of the States.

In determining questions in the United States, in Congress assembled, each State shall have one vote.

Freedom of speech and debate in Congress shall not be impeached or questioned in any court or place out of Congress, and the members of Congress shall be protected in their persons from arrests and imprisonments, during the time of their going to or from, and attendance on, Congress, except for treason, felony, or breach of the peace.

Article Six

No State, without the consent of the United States in Congress assembled, shall send any embassy to, or receive any embassy from, or enter into any conference, agreement, alliance, or treaty with, any king, prince, or state; nor shall any person holding any office of profit or trust under the United States, or any of them, accept of any present, emolument, office, or title of any kind whatever from any king, prince, or foreign state; nor shall the United States in Congress assembled, or any of them, grant any title of nobility.

No two or more States shall enter into any treaty, confederation, or alliance whatever between them, without the consent of the United States in Congress assembled, specifying accurately the purposes for which the same is to be entered into, and how long it shall continue.

No State shall lay any imposts or duties, which may interfere with any stipulations in treaties entered into by the United States in Congress assembled, with any king, prince, or state, in pursuance of any treaties already proposed by Congress, to the courts of France and Spain.

No vessels of war shall be kept in time of peace by any State, except such number only as shall be deemed necessary by the United States in Congress assembled, for the defence of such State or its trade; nor shall any body of forces be kept up by any State, in time of peace, except such number only as in the judgment of the United States in Congress assembled shall be deemed requisite to garrison the forts necessary for the defence of such State; but every State shall always keep up a well regulated and disciplined militia, sufficiently armed and accounted, and shall provide and constantly have ready for use, in public stores, a due number of field-pieces and tents, and a proper quantity of arms, ammunition, and camp equipage.

No State shall engage in any war without the consent of the United States in Congress assembled, unless such State be actually invaded by enemies, or shall have received certain advice of a resolution being formed by some nation of Indians to invade such State, and the danger is so imminent as not to admit of a delay till the United States in Congress assembled can be consulted; nor shall any State grant commissions to any ships or vessels of war, nor letters of marque or reprisal, except it be after a declaration of war by the United States in Congress assembled, and then only against the kingdom or state, and the subjects thereof, against which war has been so declared, and under such regulations as shall be established by the United States in Congress assembled, unless such State be infested by pirates, in which case vessels of war may be fitted out for that occasion, and kept so long as the danger shall continue, or until the United States in Congress assembled shall determine otherwise.

Article Seven

When land forces are raised by any State for the common defence, all officers of or under the rank of colonel shall be appointed by the legislature of each State respectively, by whom such forces shall be raised, or in such manner as such State shall direct; and all vacancies shall be filled up by the State which first made the appointment.

Article Eight

All charges of war and all other expenses that shall be incurred for the common defence or general welfare, and allowed by the United States in Congress assembled, shall be defrayed out of a common treasury, which shall be supplied by the several States, in proportion to the value of all land within each State, granted to or surveyed for any person, and such land and the buildings and improvements thereon shall be estimated according to such mode as the United States in Congress assembled shall from time to time direct and appoint.

The taxes for paying that proportion shall be laid and levied by the authority and direction of the legislatures of the several States within the time agreed upon by the United States in Congress assembled.

Article Nine

The United States in Congress assembled shall have the sole and exclusive right and power of determining on peace and war, except in the cases mentioned in the sixth article—of sending and receiving ambassadors—entering into treaties and alliances, provided that no treaty of commerce shall be made whereby the legislative power of the respective States shall be restrained from imposing such imposts and duties on foreigners as their own people are subjected to, or from prohibiting the exportation or importation of any species of goods or commodities whatsoever—of establishing rules for deciding, in all cases, what captures on land or water shall be legal, and in what manner prizes taken by land or naval forces in the service of the United States shall be divided or appropriated—of granting letters of marque and reprisal in times of peace—appointing courts for the trial of piracies and felonies committed on the high seas, and establishing courts for receiving and determining finally appeals in all cases of captures, provided that no member of Congress shall be appointed a judge of any of the said courts.

The United States in Congress assembled shall also be the last resort on appeal in all disputes and differences now subsisting or that hereafter may arise between two or more States concerning boundary, jurisdiction, or any other cause whatever; which authority shall always be exercised in the manner following:—Whatever the legislative or executive authority or lawful agent of any State in controversy with another shall present a petition to Congress stating the matter in question and praying for a hearing, notice thereof shall be given by order of Congress to the legislative or executive authority of the other State in controversy, and a day assigned for the appearance of the parties by their lawful agents, who shall then be directed to appoint, by joint consent, commissioners or judges to constitute a court for hearing and determining the matter in question; but if they cannot agree, Congress shall name three persons out of each of the United states, and from the list of such persons each party shall alternately strike out one, the petitioners beginning, until the number shall be reduced to thirteen; and from that number not less than seven nor more than nine names, as Congress shall direct, shall, in the presence of Congress, be drawn out by lot, and the persons whose names shall be so drawn, or any five of them, shall be commissioners or judges, to hear and finally determine the controversy, so always as a major part of the judges who shall hear the cause shall agree in the determination; and if either party shall neglect to attend at the day appointed, without showing reasons, which Congress shall judge sufficient, or, being present, shall refuse to strike, the Congress shall proceed to nominate three persons out of each State, and the Secretary of Congress shall strike in behalf of such party absent or refusing; and the judgment and sentence of the court to be appointed, in the manner before prescribed, shall be final and conclusive; and if any of the parties shall refuse to submit to the authority of such court, or to appear or defend their claim or cause, the court shall nevertheless proceed to pronounce sentence or judgment, which shall in like manner be final and decisive, the judgment or sentence and other proceedings being in either case transmitted to Congress, and lodged among the acts of Congress for the security of the parties concerned: provided that every commissioner, before he sits in judgment, shall take an oath, to be administered by one of the judges of the Supreme or Superior Court of the State where the cause shall be tried, "*well and truly to hear and determine the matter in question according to the best of his judgment, without favor, affection, or hope of reward,*" provided also that no State shall be deprived territory for the benefit of the United States.

All controversies concerning the private right of soil, claimed under different grants of two or more States, whose jurisdictions as they may respect such lands and the States which passed such grants are adjusted, the said grants or either of them being at the same time claimed to have originated antecedent to such settlement of jurisdiction, shall, on the petition of either party to the Congress of the United States, be finally determined as near as may be in the same manner as is before prescribed for deciding disputes respecting territorial jurisdiction between different States.

The United States in Congress assembled shall also have the sole and exclusive right and power of regulating the alloy and value of coin struck by their own authority, or by that of the respective States—fixing the standard of weights and measures throughout the United States—regulating the trade and managing all affairs with the Indians, not members of any of the States, provided that the legislative right of any State within its own limits be not infringed or violated—establishing and regulating post-offices from one State to another, throughout all the United States, and exacting such postage on the papers passing through the same as may be requisite to defray the expenses of the said office—appointing all officers of the land forces in the service of the United States, excepting regimental officers—appointing all the officers of the naval forces, and commissioning all officers whatever in the service of the United States—making rules for the government and regulation of the said land and naval forces, and directing their operations.

The United States in Congress assembled shall have authority to appoint a committee, to sit in the recess of Congress, to be denominated "A Committee of the States," and to consist of one delegate from each State; to appoint such other committees and civil officers as may be necessary for managing the general affairs of the United States under their direction; and to appoint one of their number to preside, provided that no person be allowed to serve in the office of president more than one year in any term of three years—to ascertain the necessary sums of money to be raised for the service of the United States, and to appropriate and apply the same for defraying the public expenses—to borrow money, or emit bills on the credit of the United States, transmitting every half-year to the respective States an account of the sums of money so borrowed or emitted—to build and equip a navy—to agree upon the number of land forces, and to make requisitions from each State for its quota, in proportion to the number of white inhabitants in such State; which requisition shall be binding, and thereupon the legislature of each State shall appoint the regimental officers, raise the men, and clothe, arm, and equip them in a soldier-like manner, at the expense of the United States, and the officers and men so clothed, armed, and equipped shall march to the place appointed, and within the time agreed on by the United States in Congress assembled; but if the United States in Congress assembled shall, on consideration of circumstances, judge proper that any State should not raise men, or should raise a smaller number than its quota, and that any other State should raise a greater number of men than the quota thereof, such extra number shall be raised, officered, clothed, armed, and equipped in the same manner as the quota of such State, unless the legislature of such State shall judge that such extra number cannot be safely spared out of the same, in which case they shall raise, officer, clothe, arm, and equip as many of such extra number as they judge can be safely spared: and the officers and men, so clothed, armed, and equipped shall march to the place appointed, and within the time agreed on, by the United States in Congress assembled.

The United States in Congress assembled shall never engage in a war, nor grant letters of marque and reprisal in time of peace, nor enter into any treaties or alliances, nor coin money, nor regulate the value thereof, nor ascertain the sums and expenses necessary for the defence and welfare of the United States, or any of them, nor emit bills, nor borrow money on the credit of the United States, nor appropriate money, nor agree upon the number of vessels of war to be built or purchased, or the number of land or sea forces to be raised, nor appoint a commander-in-chief of the army or navy, unless nine States assent to the same; nor shall a question on any other point, except for adjourning from day to day, be determined, unless by the votes of a majority of the United States in Congress assembled.

The Congress of the United States shall have power to adjourn to any time within the year, and to any place within the United States, so that no period of adjournment be for a longer duration than the space of six months, and shall publish the journal of their proceedings monthly, except such parts thereof relating to treaties, alliances, or military operations, as in their judgment require secrecy, and the yeas and nays of the delegates of each State on any question shall be entered on the journal, when it is desired by any delegate; and the delegates of a State, or any of them, at his or their request, shall be furnished with a transcript of the said journal, except such parts as are above excepted to lay before the legislatures of the several States.

Article Ten

The Committee of the States, or any nine of them, shall be authorized to execute, in the recess of Congress, such of the powers of Congress as the United States in Congress assembled, by the consent of nine States, shall from time to time think expedient to vest them with: provided that no power be delegated to the said Committee, for the exercise of which, by the Articles of Confederation, the voice of nine States in the Congress of the United States assembled is requisite.

Article Eleven

Canada, acceding to this Confederation, and joining in the measures of the United States, shall be admitted into and entitled to all the advantages of this Union; but no other colony shall be admitted into the same, unless such admission be agreed to by nine States.

Article Twelve

All bills of credit emitted, moneys borrowed, and debts contracted by or under the authority of Congress, before the assembling of the United States in pursuance of the present Confederation, shall be deemed and considered as a charge against the United States, for payment and satisfaction whereof the said United States and the public faith are hereby solemnly pledged.

Article Thirteen

Every State shall abide by the determinations of the United States in Congress assembled, on all questions which by this Confederation are submitted to them. And the Articles of this Confederation shall be inviolably observed by every State, and the Union shall be perpetual; nor shall any alteration at any time hereafter be made in any of them, unless such alteration be agreed to in a Congress of the United States, and be afterwards confirmed by the legislatures of every State.

And whereas it hath pleased the Great Governor of the world to incline the hearts of the legislatures we respectfully represent in Congress to approve of and to authorize us to ratify the said Articles of Confederation and perpetual Union, Know Ye, That we, the undersigned delegates, by virtue of the power and authority to us given for that purpose, do by these presents, in the name and in behalf of our respective constituents, fully and entirely ratify and confirm each and every of the said Articles of Confederation and perpetual Union, and all and singular the matters and things therein contained: and we do further solemnly plight and engage the faith of our respective constituents that they shall abide by the determinations of the United States in Congress assembled, on all questions which by the said Confederation are submitted to them. And that the Articles thereof shall be inviolably observed by the States we respectively represent, and the Union shall be perpetual.

George Washington

Appendix D:
Federalist No. 10

The Same Subject Continued:
The Union as a Safeguard Against Domestic Faction and Insurrection
From the New York Packet.
Friday, November 23, 1787.

Author: James Madison

To the People of the State of New York:

AMONG the numerous advantages promised by a well-constructed Union, none deserves to be more accurately developed than its tendency to break and control the violence of faction. The friend of popular governments never finds himself so much alarmed for their character and fate, as when he contemplates their propensity to this dangerous vice. He will not fail, therefore, to set a due value on any plan which, without violating the principles to which he is attached, provides a proper cure for it. The instability, injustice, and confusion introduced into the public councils, have, in truth, been the mortal diseases under which popular governments have everywhere perished; as they continue to be the favorite and fruitful topics from which the adversaries to liberty derive their most specious declamations. The valuable improvements made by the American constitutions on the popular models, both ancient and modern, cannot certainly be too much admired; but it would be an unwarrantable partiality, to contend that they have as effectually obviated the danger on this side, as was wished and expected. Complaints are everywhere heard from our most considerate and virtuous citizens, equally the friends of public and private faith, and of public and personal liberty, that our governments are too unstable, that the public good is disregarded in the conflicts of rival parties, and that measures are too often decided, not according to the rules of justice and the rights of the minor party, but by the superior force of an interested and overbearing majority. However anxiously we may wish that these complaints had no foundation, the evidence, of known facts will not permit us to deny that they are in some degree true. It will be found, indeed, on a candid review of our situation, that some of the distresses under which we labor have been erroneously charged on the operation of our governments; but it will be found, at the same time, that other causes will not alone account for many of our heaviest misfortunes; and, particularly, for that prevailing and increasing distrust of public engagements, and alarm for private rights, which are echoed from one end of the continent to the other. These must be chiefly, if not wholly, effects of the unsteadiness and injustice with which a factious spirit has tainted our public administrations.

By a faction, I understand a number of citizens, whether amounting to a majority or a minority of the whole, who are united and actuated by some common impulse of passion, or of interest, adversed to the rights of other citizens, or to the permanent and aggregate interests of the community.

There are two methods of curing the mischiefs of faction: the one, by removing its causes; the other, by controlling its effects.

There are again two methods of removing the causes of faction: the one, by destroying the liberty which is essential to its existence; the other, by giving to every citizen the same opinions, the same passions, and the same interests.

It could never be more truly said than of the first remedy, that it was worse than the disease. Liberty is to faction what air is to fire, an aliment without which it instantly expires. But it could not be less folly to abolish liberty, which is essential to political life, because it nourishes faction, than it would be to wish the annihilation of air, which is essential to animal life, because it imparts to fire its destructive agency.

The second expedient is as impracticable as the first would be unwise. As long as the reason of man continues fallible, and he is at liberty to exercise it, different opinions will be formed. As long as the connection subsists between his reason and his self-love, his opinions and his passions will have a reciprocal influence on each other; and the former will be objects to which the latter will attach themselves. The diversity in the faculties of men, from which the rights of property originate, is not less an insuperable obstacle to a uniformity of interests. The protection of these faculties is the first object of government. From the protection of different and unequal faculties of acquiring property, the possession of different degrees and kinds of property immediately results; and from the influence of these on the sentiments and views of the respective proprietors, ensues a division of the society into different interests and parties.

The latent causes of faction are thus sown in the nature of man; and we see them everywhere brought into different degrees of activity, according to the different circumstances of civil society. A zeal for different opinions concerning religion, concerning government, and many other points, as well of speculation as of practice; an attachment to different leaders ambitiously contending for pre-eminence and power; or to persons of other descriptions whose fortunes have been interesting to the human passions, have, in turn, divided mankind into parties, inflamed them with mutual animosity, and rendered them much more disposed to vex and oppress each other than to cooperate for their common good. So strong is this propensity of mankind to fall into mutual animosities, that where no substantial occasion presents itself, the most frivolous and fanciful distinctions have been sufficient to kindle their unfriendly passions and excite their most violent conflicts. But the most common and durable source of factions has been the various and unequal distribution of property. Those who hold and those who are without property have ever formed distinct interests in society. Those who are creditors, and those who are debtors, fall under a like discrimination. A landed interest, a manufacturing interest, a mercantile interest, a moneyed interest, with many lesser interests, grow up of necessity in civilized nations, and divide them into different classes, actuated by different sentiments and views. The regulation of these various and interfering interests forms the principal task of modern legislation, and involves the spirit of party and faction in the necessary and ordinary operations of the government.

No man is allowed to be a judge in his own cause, because his interest would certainly bias his judgment, and, not improbably, corrupt his integrity. With equal, nay with greater reason, a body of men are unfit to be both judges and parties at the same time; yet what are many of the most important acts of legislation, but so many judicial determinations, not indeed concerning the rights of single persons, but concerning the rights of large bodies of citizens? And what are the different classes of legislators but advocates and parties to the causes which they determine? Is a law proposed concerning private debts? It is a question to which the creditors are parties on one side and the debtors on the other. Justice ought to hold the balance between them. Yet the parties are, and must be, themselves the judges; and the most numerous party, or, in other words, the most powerful faction must be expected to prevail. Shall domestic manufactures be encouraged, and in what degree, by restrictions on foreign manufactures? are questions which would be differently decided by the landed and the manufacturing classes, and probably by neither with a sole regard to justice and the public good. The apportionment of taxes on the various descriptions of property is an act which seems to require the most exact impartiality; yet there is, perhaps, no legislative act in which greater opportunity and temptation are given to a predominant party to trample on the rules of justice. Every shilling with which they overburden the inferior number, is a shilling saved to their own pockets.

It is in vain to say that enlightened statesmen will be able to adjust these clashing interests, and render them all subservient to the public good. Enlightened statesmen will not always be at the helm. Nor, in many cases, can such an adjustment be made at all without taking into view indirect and remote considerations, which will rarely prevail over the immediate interest which one party may find in disregarding the rights of another or the good of the whole.

The inference to which we are brought is, that the CAUSES of faction cannot be removed, and that relief is only to be sought in the means of controlling its EFFECTS.

If a faction consists of less than a majority, relief is supplied by the republican principle, which enables the majority to defeat its sinister views by regular vote. It may clog the administration, it may convulse the society; but it will be unable to execute and mask its violence under the forms of the Constitution. When a majority is included in a faction, the form of popular government, on the other hand, enables it to sacrifice to its ruling passion or interest both the public good and the rights of other citizens. To secure the public good and private rights against the danger of such a faction, and at the same time to preserve the spirit and the form of popular government, is then the great object to which our inquiries are directed. Let me add that it is the great desideratum by which this form of government can be rescued from the opprobrium under which it has so long labored, and be recommended to the esteem and adoption of mankind.

By what means is this object attainable? Evidently by one of two only. Either the existence of the same passion or interest in a majority at the same time must be prevented, or the majority, having such coexistent passion or interest, must be rendered, by their number and local situation, unable to concert and carry into effect schemes of oppression. If the impulse and the opportunity be suffered to coincide, we well know that neither moral nor religious motives can be relied on as an adequate control. They are not found to be such on the injustice and violence of individuals, and lose their efficacy in proportion to the number combined together, that is, in proportion as their efficacy becomes needful.

From this view of the subject it may be concluded that a pure democracy, by which I mean a society consisting of a small number of citizens, who assemble and administer the government in person, can admit of no cure for the mischiefs of faction. A common passion or interest will, in almost every case, be felt by a majority of the whole; a communication and concert result from the form of government itself; and there is nothing to check the inducements to sacrifice the weaker party or an obnoxious individual. Hence it is that such democracies have ever been spectacles of turbulence and contention; have ever been found incompatible with personal security or the rights of property; and have in general been as short in their lives as they have been violent in their deaths. Theoretic politicians, who have patronized this species of government, have erroneously supposed that by reducing mankind to a perfect equality in their political rights, they would, at the same time, be perfectly equalized and assimilated in their possessions, their opinions, and their passions.

A republic, by which I mean a government in which the scheme of representation takes place, opens a different prospect, and promises the cure for which we are seeking. Let us examine the points in which it varies from pure democracy, and we shall comprehend both the nature of the cure and the efficacy which it must derive from the Union.

The two great points of difference between a democracy and a republic are: first, the delegation of the government, in the latter, to a small number of citizens elected by the rest; secondly, the greater number of citizens, and greater sphere of country, over which the latter may be extended.

The effect of the first difference is, on the one hand, to refine and enlarge the public views, by passing them through the medium of a chosen body of citizens, whose wisdom may best discern the true interest of their country, and whose patriotism and love of justice will be least likely to sacrifice it to temporary or partial considerations. Under such a regulation, it may well happen that the public voice, pronounced by the representatives of the people, will be more consonant to the public good than if pronounced by the people themselves, convened for the purpose. On the other hand, the effect may be inverted. Men of factious tempers, of local prejudices, or of sinister designs, may, by intrigue, by corruption, or by other means, first obtain the suffrages, and then betray the interests, of the people. The question resulting is, whether small or extensive republics are more favorable to the election of proper guardians of the public weal; and it is clearly decided in favor of the latter by two obvious considerations:

In the first place, it is to be remarked that, however small the republic may be, the representatives must be raised to a certain number, in order to guard against the cabals of a few;

and that, however large it may be, they must be limited to a certain number, in order to guard against the confusion of a multitude. Hence, the number of representatives in the two cases not being in proportion to that of the two constituents, and being proportionally greater in the small republic, it follows that, if the proportion of fit characters be not less in the large than in the small republic, the former will present a greater option, and consequently a greater probability of a fit choice.

In the next place, as each representative will be chosen by a greater number of citizens in the large than in the small republic, it will be more difficult for unworthy candidates to practice with success the vicious arts by which elections are too often carried; and the suffrages of the people being more free, will be more likely to centre in men who possess the most attractive merit and the most diffusive and established characters.

It must be confessed that in this, as in most other cases, there is a mean, on both sides of which inconveniences will be found to lie. By enlarging too much the number of electors, you render the representatives too little acquainted with all their local circumstances and lesser interests; as by reducing it too much, you render him unduly attached to these, and too little fit to comprehend and pursue great and national objects. The federal Constitution forms a happy combination in this respect; the great and aggregate interests being referred to the national, the local and particular to the State legislatures.

The other point of difference is, the greater number of citizens and extent of territory which may be brought within the compass of republican than of democratic government; and it is this circumstance principally which renders factious combinations less to be dreaded in the former than in the latter. The smaller the society, the fewer probably will be the distinct parties and interests composing it; the fewer the distinct parties and interests, the more frequently will a majority be found of the same party; and the smaller the number of individuals composing a majority, and the smaller the compass within which they are placed, the more easily will they concert and execute their plans of oppression. Extend the sphere, and you take in a greater variety of parties and interests; you make it less probable that a majority of the whole will have a common motive to invade the rights of other citizens; or if such a common motive exists, it will be more difficult for all who feel it to discover their own strength, and to act in unison with each other. Besides other impediments, it may be remarked that, where there is a consciousness of unjust or dishonorable purposes, communication is always checked by distrust in proportion to the number whose concurrence is necessary.

Hence, it clearly appears, that the same advantage which a republic has over a democracy, in controlling the effects of faction, is enjoyed by a large over a small republic,—is enjoyed by the Union over the States composing it. Does the advantage consist in the substitution of representatives whose enlightened views and virtuous sentiments render them superior to local prejudices and schemes of injustice? It will not be denied that the representation of the Union will be most likely to possess these requisite endowments. Does it consist in the greater security afforded by a greater variety of parties, against the event of any one party being able to outnumber and oppress the rest? In an equal degree does the increased variety of parties comprised within the Union, increase this security. Does it, in fine, consist in the greater obstacles opposed to the concert and accomplishment of the secret wishes of an unjust and interested majority? Here, again, the extent of the Union gives it the most palpable advantage.

The influence of factious leaders may kindle a flame within their particular States, but will be unable to spread a general conflagration through the other States. A religious sect may degenerate into a political faction in a part of the Confederacy; but the variety of sects dispersed over the entire face of it must secure the national councils against any danger from that source. A rage for paper money, for an abolition of debts, for an equal division of property, or for any other improper or wicked project, will be less apt to pervade the whole body of the Union than a particular member of it; in the same proportion as such a malady is more likely to taint a particular county or district, than an entire State.

In the extent and proper structure of the Union, therefore, we behold a republican remedy for the diseases most incident to republican government. And according to the degree of pleasure and pride we feel in being republicans, ought to be our zeal in cherishing the spirit and supporting the character of Federalists.

PUBLIUS.

Appendix E:
Federalist No. 51

The Structure of the Government Must Furnish the Proper Checks
and Balances Between the Different Departments
From the New York Packet.
Friday, February 8, 1788.

Author: Alexander Hamilton or James Madison

To the People of the State of New York:

TO WHAT expedient, then, shall we finally resort, for maintaining in practice the necessary partition of power among the several departments, as laid down in the Constitution? The only answer that can be given is, that as all these exterior provisions are found to be inadequate, the defect must be supplied, by so contriving the interior structure of the government as that its several constituent parts may, by their mutual relations, be the means of keeping each other in their proper places. Without presuming to undertake a full development of this important idea, I will hazard a few general observations, which may perhaps place it in a clearer light, and enable us to form a more correct judgment of the principles and structure of the government planned by the convention. In order to lay a due foundation for that separate and distinct exercise of the different powers of government, which to a certain extent is admitted on all hands to be essential to the preservation of liberty, it is evident that each department should have a will of its own; and consequently should be so constituted that the members of each should have as little agency as possible in the appointment of the members of the others. Were this principle rigorously adhered to, it would require that all the appointments for the supreme executive, legislative, and judiciary magistracies should be drawn from the same fountain of authority, the people, through channels having no communication whatever with one another. Perhaps such a plan of constructing the several departments would be less difficult in practice than it may in contemplation appear. Some difficulties, however, and some additional expense would attend the execution of it. Some deviations, therefore, from the principle must be admitted. In the constitution of the judiciary department in particular, it might be inexpedient to insist rigorously on the principle: first, because peculiar qualifications being essential in the members, the primary consideration ought to be to select that mode of choice which best secures these qualifications; secondly, because the permanent tenure by which the appointments are held in that department, must soon destroy all sense of dependence on the authority conferring them. It is equally evident, that the members of each department should be as little dependent as possible on those of the others, for the emoluments annexed to their offices. Were the executive magistrate, or the judges, not independent of the legislature in this particular, their independence in every other would be merely nominal. But the great security against a gradual concentration of the several powers in the same department, consists in giving to those who administer each department the necessary constitutional means and personal motives to resist encroachments of the others. The provision for defense must in this, as in all other cases, be made commensurate to the danger of attack. Ambition must be made to counteract ambition. The interest of the man must be connected with the constitutional rights of the place. It may be a reflection on human nature, that such devices should be necessary to control the abuses of government. But what is government itself, but the greatest of all reflections on human nature? If men were angels, no government would be necessary. If angels were to govern men, neither external nor internal controls on government would be necessary. In framing a government which is to be administered by men over men, the great difficulty lies in this: you must first enable the government to control the governed; and in the next place oblige it to control itself. A dependence on the people is, no doubt, the primary control on the government; but experience has taught mankind the necessity of auxiliary precautions. This policy of supplying, by opposite and rival interests, the defect of better motives, might be traced through the whole system of human affairs, private as well as public. We see it particularly displayed in all the subordinate distributions of power, where the constant aim is to divide and arrange the several offices in such a manner as that each may be a check on the other that the private interest of every individual may be a sentinel over the public rights. These inventions of prudence cannot be less requisite in the distribution of the supreme powers of the State. But it is not possible to give to each department an equal power of self-defense. In republican government, the legislative authority necessarily predominates. The remedy for this inconveniency is to divide the legislature into different branches; and to render them, by different modes of election and different principles of action, as little connected with each other as the nature of their common functions and their common dependence on the society will admit. It may even be necessary to guard against dangerous encroachments by still further precautions. As the weight of the legislative authority requires that it should be thus divided, the weakness of the executive may require, on the other hand, that it should be fortified. An absolute negative on the legislature appears, at first view, to be the natural defense with which the executive magistrate should be armed. But perhaps it would be neither altogether safe nor alone sufficient. On ordinary occasions it might not be exerted with the requisite firmness, and on extraordinary occasions it might be perfidiously abused. May not this defect of an absolute negative be supplied by some qualified connection between this weaker department and the weaker branch of the stronger department, by which the latter may be led to support the constitutional rights of the former, without being too much detached from the rights of its own department? If the principles on which these observations are founded be just, as I persuade myself they are, and they be applied as a criterion to the several State constitutions, and to the federal Constitution it will be found that if the latter does not perfectly correspond with them, the former are infinitely less able to bear such a test. There are, moreover, two considerations particularly applicable to the federal system of America, which place that system in a very interesting point of view. First. In a single republic, all the power surrendered by the people is submitted to the administration of a single government; and the usurpations are guarded against by a division of the government into distinct and separate departments. In the compound republic of America, the power surrendered by the people is first divided between two distinct governments, and then the portion allotted to each subdivided among distinct and separate departments. Hence a double security arises to the rights of the people. The different governments will control each other, at the same time that each will be controlled by itself. Second. It is of great importance in a republic not only to guard the society against the oppression of its rulers, but to guard one part of the society against the injustice of the other part. Different interests necessarily exist in different classes of citizens. If a majority be united by a common interest, the rights of the minority will be insecure. There are but two methods of providing against this evil: the one by creating a will in the community independent of the majority that is, of the society itself; the other, by comprehending in the society so many separate descriptions of citizens as will render an unjust combination of a majority of the whole very improbable, if not impracticable. The first method prevails in all governments possessing an hereditary or self-appointed authority. This, at best, is but a precarious security; because a power independent of the society may as well espouse the unjust views of the major, as the rightful interests of the minor party, and may possibly be turned against both parties. The second method will be exemplified in the federal republic of the United States. Whilst all authority in it will be derived from and dependent on the society, the society itself will be broken into so many parts, interests, and classes of citizens, that the rights of individuals, or of the minority, will be in little danger from interested combinations of the majority. In a free government the security for civil rights must be the same as that for religious rights. It consists in the one case in the multiplicity of interests, and in the other in the multiplicity of sects. The degree of security in both cases will depend on the number of interests and sects; and this may be presumed to depend on the extent of country and number of people comprehended under the same government. This view of the subject must particularly recommend a proper federal system to all the sincere and considerate friends of republican government, since it shows that in exact proportion as the territory of the Union may be formed into more circumscribed Confederacies, or States oppressive combinations of a majority will be facilitated: the best security, under the republican forms, for the rights of every class of citizens, will be diminished: and consequently the stability and independence of some member of the government, the only other security, must be proportionately increased. Justice is the end of government. It is the end of civil society. It ever has been and ever will be pursued until it be obtained, or until liberty be lost in the pursuit. In a society under the forms of which the stronger faction can readily unite and oppress the weaker, anarchy may as truly be said to reign as in a state of nature, where the weaker individual is not secured against the violence of the stronger; and as, in the latter state, even the stronger individuals are prompted, by the uncertainty of their condition, to submit to a government which may protect the weak as well as themselves; so, in the former state, will the more powerful factions or parties be gradually induced, by a like motive, to wish for a government which will protect all parties, the weaker as well as the more powerful. It can be little doubted that if the State of Rhode Island was separated from the Confederacy and left to itself, the insecurity of rights under the popular form of government within such narrow limits would be displayed by such reiterated oppressions of factious majorities that some power altogether independent of the people would soon be called for by the voice of the very factions whose misrule had proved the necessity of it. In the extended republic of the United States, and among the great variety of interests, parties, and sects which it embraces, a coalition of a majority of the whole society could seldom take place on any other principles than those of justice and the general good; whilst there being thus less danger to a minor from the will of a major party, there must be less pretext, also, to provide for the security of the former, by introducing into the government a will not dependent on the latter, or, in other words, a will independent of the society itself. It is no less certain than it is important, notwithstanding the contrary opinions which have been entertained, that the larger the society, provided it lie within a practical sphere, the more duly capable it will be of self-government. And happily for the REPUBLICAN CAUSE, the practicable sphere may be carried to a very great extent, by a judicious modification and mixture of the FEDERAL PRINCIPLE.

PUBLIUS.

Appendix F:
The Virginia Plan

Resolutions proposed by Mr Randolph in Convention.

May 29. 1787.

1. Resolved that the articles of Confederation ought to be so corrected & enlarged as to accomplish the objects proposed by their institution; namely. "common defence, security of liberty and general welfare."

2. Resd. Therefore that the rights of suffrage in the National Legislature ought to be proportioned to the Quotas of contribution, or to the number of free inhabitants, as the one or the other rule may seem best in different cases.

3. Resd. That the National Legislature ought to consist of two branches.

4. Resd. That the members of the first branch of the National Legislature ought to be elected by the people of the several States every   for the term of   ; to be of the age of   years at least, to receive liberal stipends by which they may be compensated for the devotion of their time to public service; to be ineligible to any office established by a particular State, or under the authority of the United States, except those peculiarly belonging to the functions of the first branch, during the term of service, and for the space of after its expiration; to be incapable of re-election for the space of   after the expiration of their term of service, and to be subject to recall.

5. Resold. That the members of the second branch of the National Legislature ought to be elected by those of the first, out of a proper number of persons nominated by the individual Legislatures, to be of the age of   years at least; to hold their offices for a term sufficient to ensure their independency, to receive liberal stipends, by which they may be compensated for the devotion of their time to public service; and to be ineligible to any office established by a particular State, or under the authority of the United States, except those peculiarly belonging to the functions of the second branch, during the term of service, and for the space of   after the expiration thereof.

6. Resolved that each branch ought to possess the right of originating Acts; that the National Legislature ought to be impowered to enjoy the Legislative Rights vested in Congress by the Confederation & moreover to legislate in all cases to which the separate States are incompetent, or in which the harmony of the United States may be interrupted by the exercise of individual Legislation; to negative all laws passed by the several States, contravening in the opinion of the National Legislature the articles of Union; and to call forth the force of the Union agst. any member of the Union failing to fulfill its duty under the articles thereof.

7. Resd. that a National Executive be instituted; to be chosen by the National Legislature for the term of   years, to receive punctually at stated times, a fixed compensation for the services rendered, in which no increase or diminution shall be made so as to affect the Magistracy, existing at the time of increase or diminution, and to be ineligible a second time; and that besides a general authority to execute the National laws, it ought to enjoy the Executive rights vested in Congress by the Confederation.

8. Resd. that the Executive and a convenient number of the National Judiciary, ought to compose a council of revision with authority to examine every act of the National Legislature before it shall operate, & every act of a particular Legislature before a Negative thereon shall be final; and that the dissent of the said Council shall amount to a rejection, unless the Act of the National Legislature be again passed, or that of a particular Legislature be again negatived by   of the members of each branch.

9. Resd. that a National Judiciary be established to consist of one or more supreme tribunals, and of inferior tribunals to be chosen by the National Legislature, to hold their offices during good behaviour; and to receive punctually at stated times fixed compensation for their services, in which no increase or diminution shall be made so as to affect the persons actually in office at the time of such increase or diminution. That the jurisdiction of the inferior tribunals shall be to hear & determine in the first instance, and of the supreme tribunal to hear and determine in the dernier resort, all piracies & felonies on the high seas, captures from an enemy; cases in which foreigners or citizens of other States applying to such jurisdictions may be interested, or which respect the collection of the National revenue; impeachments of any National officers, and questions which may involve the national peace and harmony.

10. Resolvd. that provision ought to be made for the admission of States lawfully arising within the limits of the United States, whether from a voluntary junction of Government & Territory or otherwise, with the consent of a number of voices in the National legislature less than the whole.

11. Resd. that a Republican Government & the territory of each State, except in the instance of a voluntary junction of Government & territory, ought to be guaranteed by the United States to each State.

12. Resd. that provision ought to be made for the continuance of Congress and their authorities and privileges, until a given day after the reform of the articles of Union shall be adopted, and for the completion of all their engagements.

13. Resd. that provision ought to be made for the amendment of the Articles of Union whensoever it shall seem necessary, and that the assent of the National Legislature ought not to be required thereto.

14. Resd. that the Legislative Executive & Judiciary powers within the several States ought to be bound by oath to support the articles of Union.

15. Resd. that the amendments which shall be offered to the Confederation, by the Convention ought at a proper time, or times, after the approbation of Congress to be submitted to an assembly or assemblies of Representatives, recommended by the several Legislatures to be expressly chosen by the people, to consider & decide thereon.

He concluded with an exhortation, not to suffer the present opportunity of establishing general peace, harmony, happiness and liberty in the U.S. to pass away unimproved.*

<It was then Resolved &c—&c—That the House will to-morrow resolve itself into a Committee of the whole House to consider of the State of the American Union,—and that the propositions moved by Mr. Randolph be referred to the said Committee.

*This abstract of the Speech was furnished to James Madison by Mr. Randolph.

Appendix G:
The Constitution of the United States

We the people of the United States, in order to form a more perfect union, establish justice, insure domestic tranquility, provide for the common defense, promote the general welfare, and secure the blessings of liberty to ourselves and our posterity, do ordain and establish this Constitution for the United States of America.

Article I

Section 1. All legislative powers herein granted shall be vested in a Congress of the United States, which shall consist of a Senate and House of Representatives.

Section 2. The House of Representatives shall be composed of members chosen every second year by the people of the several states, and the electors in each state shall have the qualifications requisite for electors of the most numerous branch of the state legislature.

No person shall be a Representative who shall not have attained to the age of twenty five years, and been seven years a citizen of the United States, and who shall not, when elected, be an inhabitant of that state in which he shall be chosen.

Representatives and direct taxes shall be apportioned among the several states which may be included within this union, according to their respective numbers, which shall be determined by adding to the whole number of free persons, including those bound to service for a term of years, and excluding Indians not taxed, three fifths of all other Persons. The actual Enumeration shall be made within three years after the first meeting of the Congress of the United States, and within every subsequent term of ten years, in such manner as they shall by law direct. The number of Representatives shall not exceed one for every thirty thousand, but each state shall have at least one Representative; and until such enumeration shall be made, the state of New Hampshire shall be entitled to choose three, Massachusetts eight, Rhode Island and Providence Plantations one, Connecticut five, New York six, New Jersey four, Pennsylvania eight, Delaware one, Maryland six, Virginia ten, North Carolina five, South Carolina five, and Georgia three.

When vacancies happen in the Representation from any state, the executive authority thereof shall issue writs of election to fill such vacancies.

The House of Representatives shall choose their speaker and other officers; and shall have the sole power of impeachment.

Section 3.   The Senate of the United States shall be composed of two Senators from each state, chosen by the legislature thereof, for six years; and each Senator shall have one vote.

Immediately after they shall be assembled in consequence of the first election, they shall be divided as equally as may be into three classes. The seats of the Senators of the first class shall be vacated at the expiration of the second year, of the second class at the expiration of the fourth year, and the third class at the expiration of the sixth year, so that one third may be chosen every second year; and if vacancies happen by resignation, or otherwise, during the recess of the legislature of any state, the executive thereof may make temporary appointments until the next meeting of the legislature, which shall then fill such vacancies.

No person shall be a Senator who shall not have attained to the age of thirty years, and been nine years a citizen of the United States and who shall not, when elected, be an inhabitant of that state for which he shall be chosen.

The Vice President of the United States shall be President of the Senate, but shall have no vote, unless they be equally divided.

The Senate shall choose their other officers, and also a President pro tempore, in the absence of the Vice President, or when he shall exercise the office of President of the United States.

The Senate shall have the sole power to try all impeachments. When sitting for that purpose, they shall be on oath or affirmation. When the President of the United States is tried, the Chief Justice shall preside: And no person shall be convicted without the concurrence of two thirds of the members present.

Judgment in cases of impeachment shall not extend further than to removal from office, and disqualification to hold and enjoy any office of honor, trust or profit under the United States: but the party convicted shall nevertheless be liable and subject to indictment, trial, judgment and punishment, according to law.

Section 4.   The times, places and manner of holding elections for Senators and Representatives, shall be prescribed in each state by the legislature thereof; but the Congress may at any time by law make or alter such regulations, except as to the places of choosing Senators.

The Congress shall assemble at least once in every year, and such meeting shall be on the first Monday in December, unless they shall by law appoint a different day.

Section 5.   Each House shall be the judge of the elections, returns and qualifications of its own members, and a majority of each shall constitute a quorum to do business; but a smaller number may adjourn from day to day, and may be authorized to compel the attendance of absent members, in such manner, and under such penalties as each House may provide.

Each House may determine the rules of its proceedings, punish its members for disorderly behavior, and, with the concurrence of two thirds, expel a member.

Each House shall keep a journal of its proceedings, and from time to time publish the same, excepting such parts as may in their judgment require secrecy; and the yeas and nays of the members of either House on any question shall, at the desire of one fifth of those present, be entered on the journal.

Neither House, during the session of Congress, shall, without the consent of the other, adjourn for more than three days, nor to any other place than that in which the two Houses shall be sitting.

Section 6.   The Senators and Representatives shall receive a compensation for their services, to be ascertained by law, and paid out of the treasury of the United States. They shall in all cases, except treason, felony and breach of the peace, be privileged from arrest during their attendance at the session of their respective Houses, and in going to and returning from the same; and for any speech or debate in either House, they shall not be questioned in any other place.

No Senator or Representative shall, during the time for which he was elected, be appointed to any civil office under the authority of the United States, which shall have been created, or the emoluments whereof shall have been increased during such time: and no person holding any office under the United States, shall be a member of either House during his continuance in office.

Section 7.   All bills for raising revenue shall originate in the House of Representatives; but the Senate may propose or concur with amendments as on other Bills.

Every bill which shall have passed the House of Representatives and the Senate, shall, before it become a law, be presented to the President of the United States; if he approve he shall sign it, but if not he shall return it, with his objections to that House in which it shall have originated, who shall enter the objections at large on their journal, and proceed to reconsider it. If after such reconsideration two thirds of that House shall agree to pass the bill, it shall be sent, together with the objections, to the other House, by which it shall likewise be reconsidered, and if approved by two thirds of that House, it shall become a law. But in all such cases the votes of both Houses shall be determined by yeas and nays, and the names of the persons voting for and against the bill shall be entered on the journal of each House respectively. If any bill shall not be returned by the President within ten days (Sundays excepted) after it shall have been presented to him, the same shall be a law, in like manner as if he had signed it, unless the Congress by their adjournment prevent its return, in which case it shall not be a law.

Every order, resolution, or vote to which the concurrence of the Senate and House of Representatives may be necessary (except on a question of adjournment) shall be presented to the President of the United States; and before the same shall take effect, shall be approved by him, or being disapproved by him, shall be repassed by two thirds of the Senate and House of Representatives, according to the rules and limitations prescribed in the case of a bill.

Section 8.   The Congress shall have power to lay and collect taxes, duties, imposts and excises, to pay the debts and provide for the common defense and general welfare of the United States; but all duties, imposts and excises shall be uniform throughout the United States;

To borrow money on the credit of the United States;

To regulate commerce with foreign nations, and among the several states, and with the Indian tribes;

To establish a uniform rule of naturalization, and uniform laws on the subject of bankruptcies throughout the United States;

To coin money, regulate the value thereof, and of foreign coin, and fix the standard of weights and measures;

To provide for the punishment of counterfeiting the securities and current coin of the United States;

To establish post offices and post roads;

To promote the progress of science and useful arts, by securing for limited times to authors and inventors the exclusive right to their respective writings and discoveries;

To constitute tribunals inferior to the Supreme Court;

To define and punish piracies and felonies committed on the high seas, and offenses against the law of nations;

To declare war, grant letters of marque and reprisal, and make rules concerning captures on land and water;

To raise and support armies, but no appropriation of money to that use shall be for a longer term than two years;

To provide and maintain a navy;

To make rules for the government and regulation of the land and naval forces;

To provide for calling forth the militia to execute the laws of the union, suppress insurrections and repel invasions;

To provide for organizing, arming, and disciplining, the militia, and for governing such part of them as may be employed in the service of the United States, reserving to the states respectively, the appointment of the officers, and the authority of training the militia according to the discipline prescribed by Congress;

To exercise exclusive legislation in all cases whatsoever, over such District (not exceeding ten miles square) as may, by cession of particular states, and the acceptance of Congress, become the seat of the government of the United States, and to exercise like authority over all places purchased by the consent of the legislature of the state in which the same shall be, for the erection of forts, magazines, arsenals, dockyards, and other needful buildings;—And

To make all laws which shall be necessary and proper for carrying into execution the foregoing powers, and all other powers vested by this Constitution in the government of the United States, or in any department or officer thereof.

Section 9.   The migration or importation of such persons as any of the states now existing shall think proper to admit, shall not be prohibited by the Congress prior to the year one thousand eight hundred and eight, but a tax or duty may be imposed on such importation, not exceeding ten dollars for each person.

The privilege of the writ of habeas corpus shall not be suspended, unless when in cases of rebellion or invasion the public safety may require it.

No bill of attainder or ex post facto Law shall be passed.

No capitation, or other direct, tax shall be laid, unless in proportion to the census or enumeration herein before directed to be taken.

No tax or duty shall be laid on articles exported from any state.

No preference shall be given by any regulation of commerce or revenue to the ports of one state over those of another: nor shall vessels bound to, or from, one state, be obliged to enter, clear or pay duties in another.

No money shall be drawn from the treasury, but in consequence of appropriations made by law; and a regular statement and account of receipts and expenditures of all public money shall be published from time to time.

No title of nobility shall be granted by the United States: and no person holding any office of profit or trust under them, shall, without the consent of the Congress, accept of any present, emolument, office, or title, of any kind whatever, from any king, prince, or foreign state.

Section 10. No state shall enter into any treaty, alliance, or confederation; grant letters of marque and reprisal; coin money; emit bills of credit; make anything but gold and silver coin a tender in payment of debts; pass any bill of attainder, ex post facto law, or law impairing the obligation of contracts, or grant any title of nobility.

No state shall, without the consent of the Congress, lay any imposts or duties on imports or exports, except what may be absolutely necessary for executing it's inspection laws: and the net produce of all duties and imposts, laid by any state on imports or exports, shall be for the use of the treasury of the United States; and all such laws shall be subject to the revision and control of the Congress.

No state shall, without the consent of Congress, lay any duty of tonnage, keep troops, or ships of war in time of peace, enter into any agreement or compact with another state, or with a foreign power, or engage in war, unless actually invaded, or in such imminent danger as will not admit of delay.

Article II

Section 1. The executive power shall be vested in a President of the United States of America. He shall hold his office during the term of four years, and, together with the Vice President, chosen for the same term, be elected, as follows:

Each state shall appoint, in such manner as the Legislature thereof may direct, a number of electors, equal to the whole number of Senators and Representatives to which the State may be entitled in the Congress: but no Senator or Representative, or person holding an office of trust or profit under the United States, shall be appointed an elector.

The electors shall meet in their respective states, and vote by ballot for two persons, of whom one at least shall not be an inhabitant of the same state with themselves. And they shall make a list of all the persons voted for, and of the number of votes for each; which list they shall sign and certify, and transmit sealed to the seat of the government of the United States, directed to the President of the Senate. The President of the Senate shall, in the presence of the Senate and House of Representatives, open all the certificates, and the votes shall then be counted. The person having the greatest number of votes shall be the President, if such number be a majority of the whole number of electors appointed; and if there be more than one who have such majority, and have an equal number of votes, then the House of Representatives shall immediately choose by ballot one of them for President; and if no person have a majority, then from the five highest on the list the said House shall in like manner choose the President. But in choosing the President, the votes shall be taken by States, the representation from each state having one vote; A quorum for this purpose shall consist of a member or members from two thirds of the states, and a majority of all the states shall be necessary to a choice. In every case, after the choice of the President, the person having the greatest number of votes of the electors shall be the Vice President. But if there should remain two or more who have equal votes, the Senate shall choose from them by ballot the Vice President.

The Congress may determine the time of choosing the electors, and the day on which they shall give their votes; which day shall be the same throughout the United States.

No person except a natural born citizen, or a citizen of the United States, at the time of the adoption of this Constitution, shall be eligible to the office of President; neither shall any person be eligible to that office who shall not have attained to the age of thirty five years, and been fourteen Years a resident within the United States.

In case of the removal of the President from office, or of his death, resignation, or inability to discharge the powers and duties of the said office, the same shall devolve on the Vice President, and the Congress may by law provide for the case of removal, death, resignation or inability, both of the President and Vice President, declaring what officer shall then act as President, and such officer shall act accordingly, until the disability be removed, or a President shall be elected.

The President shall, at stated times, receive for his services, a compensation, which shall neither be increased nor diminished during the period for which he shall have been elected, and he shall not receive within that period any other emolument from the United States, or any of them.

Before he enter on the execution of his office, he shall take the following oath or affirmation:—"I do solemnly swear (or affirm) that I will faithfully execute the office of President of the United States, and will to the best of my ability, preserve, protect and defend the Constitution of the United States."

Section 2.   The President shall be commander in chief of the Army and Navy of the United States, and of the militia of the several states, when called into the actual service of the United States; he may require the opinion, in writing, of the principal officer in each of the executive departments, upon any subject relating to the duties of their respective offices, and he shall have power to grant reprieves and pardons for offenses against the United States, except in cases of impeachment.

He shall have power, by and with the advice and consent of the Senate, to make treaties, provided two thirds of the Senators present concur; and he shall nominate, and by and with the advice and consent of the Senate, shall appoint ambassadors, other public ministers and consuls, judges of the Supreme Court, and all other officers of the United States, whose appointments are not herein otherwise provided for, and which shall be established by law: but the Congress may by law vest the appointment of such inferior officers, as they think proper, in the President alone, in the courts of law, or in the heads of departments.

The President shall have power to fill up all vacancies that may happen during the recess of the Senate, by granting commissions which shall expire at the end of their next session.

Section 3. He shall from time to time give to the Congress information of the state of the union, and recommend to their consideration such measures as he shall judge necessary and expedient; he may, on extraordinary occasions, convene both Houses, or either of them, and in case of disagreement between them, with respect to the time of adjournment, he may adjourn them to such time as he shall think proper; he shall receive ambassadors and other public ministers; he shall take care that the laws be faithfully executed, and shall commission all the officers of the United States.

Section 4. The President, Vice President and all civil officers of the United States, shall be removed from office on impeachment for, and conviction of, treason, bribery, or other high crimes and misdemeanors.

Article III

Section 1. The judicial power of the United States, shall be vested in one Supreme Court, and in such inferior courts as the Congress may from time to time ordain and establish. The judges, both of the supreme and inferior courts, shall hold their offices during good behaviour, and shall, at stated times, receive for their services, a compensation, which shall not be diminished during their continuance in office.

Section 2. The judicial power shall extend to all cases, in law and equity, arising under this Constitution, the laws of the United States, and treaties made, or which shall be made, under their authority;—to all cases affecting ambassadors, other public ministers and consuls;—to all cases of admiralty and maritime jurisdiction;—to controversies to which the United States shall be a party;—to controversies between two or more states;—between a state and citizens of another state;— between citizens of different states;—between citizens of the same state claiming lands under grants of different states, and between a state, or the citizens thereof, and foreign states, citizens or subjects.

In all cases affecting ambassadors, other public ministers and consuls, and those in which a state shall be party, the Supreme Court shall have original jurisdiction. In all the other cases before mentioned, the Supreme Court shall have appellate jurisdiction, both as to law and fact, with such exceptions, and under such regulations as the Congress shall make.

The trial of all crimes, except in cases of impeachment, shall be by jury; and such trial shall be held in the state where the said crimes shall have been committed; but when not committed within any state, the trial shall be at such place or places as the Congress may by law have directed.

Section 3.   Treason against the United States, shall consist only in levying war against them, or in adhering to their enemies, giving them aid and comfort. No person shall be convicted of treason unless on the testimony of two witnesses to the same overt act, or on confession in open court.

The Congress shall have power to declare the punishment of treason, but no attainder of treason shall work corruption of blood, or forfeiture except during the life of the person attainted.

Article IV

Section 1.   Full faith and credit shall be given in each state to the public acts, records, and judicial proceedings of every other state. And the Congress may by general laws prescribe the manner in which such acts, records, and proceedings shall be proved, and the effect thereof.

Section 2.   The citizens of each state shall be entitled to all privileges and immunities of citizens in the several states.

A person charged in any state with treason, felony, or other crime, who shall flee from justice, and be found in another state, shall on demand of the executive authority of the state from which he fled, be delivered up, to be removed to the state having jurisdiction of the crime.

No person held to service or labor in one state, under the laws thereof, escaping into another, shall, in consequence of any law or regulation therein, be discharged from such service or labor, but shall be delivered up on claim of the party to whom such service or labor may be due.

Section 3.   New states may be admitted by the Congress into this union; but no new states shall be formed or erected within the jurisdiction of any other state; nor any state be formed by the junction of two or more states, or parts of states, without the consent of the legislatures of the states concerned as well as of the Congress.

The Congress shall have power to dispose of and make all needful rules and regulations respecting the territory or other property belonging to the United States; and nothing in this Constitution shall be so construed as to prejudice any claims of the United States, or of any particular state.

Section 4.   The United States shall guarantee to every state in this union a republican form of government, and shall protect each of them against invasion; and on application of the legislature, or of the executive (when the legislature cannot be convened) against domestic violence.

Article V

The Congress, whenever two thirds of both houses shall deem it necessary, shall propose amendments to this Constitution, or, on the application of the legislatures of two thirds of the several states, shall call a convention for proposing amendments, which, in either case, shall be valid to all intents and purposes, as part of this Constitution, when ratified by the legislatures of three fourths of the several states, or by conventions in three fourths thereof, as the one or the other mode of ratification may be proposed by the Congress; provided that no amendment which may be made prior to the year one thousand eight hundred and eight shall in any manner affect the first and fourth clauses in the ninth section of the first article; and that no state, without its consent, shall be deprived of its equal suffrage in the Senate.

Article VI

All debts contracted and engagements entered into, before the adoption of this Constitution, shall be as valid against the United States under this Constitution, as under the Confederation.

This Constitution, and the laws of the United States which shall be made in pursuance thereof; and all treaties made, or which shall be made, under the authority of the United States, shall be the supreme law of the land; and the judges in every state shall be bound thereby, anything in the Constitution or laws of any State to the contrary notwithstanding.

The Senators and Representatives before mentioned, and the members of the several state legislatures, and all executive and judicial officers, both of the United States and of the several states, shall be bound by oath or affirmation, to support this Constitution; but no religious test shall ever be required as a qualification to any office or public trust under the United States.

Article VII

The ratification of the conventions of nine states, shall be sufficient for the establishment of this Constitution between the states so ratifying the same.

Done in convention by the unanimous consent of the states present the seventeenth day of September in the year of our Lord one thousand seven hundred and eighty seven and of the independence of the United States of America the twelfth. In witness whereof We have hereunto subscribed our Names,

G. Washington-President. and deputy from Virginia
New Hampshire: John Langdon, Nicholas Gilman
Massachusetts: Nathaniel Gorham, Rufus King
Connecticut: Wm: Saml. Johnson, Roger Sherman
New York: Alexander Hamilton
New Jersey: Wil: Livingston, David Brearly, Wm. Paterson, Jona: Dayton

*Pennsylvania: B. Franklin, Thomas Mifflin, Robt. Morris, Geo. Clymer, Thos. FitzSimons,
Jared Ingersoll, James Wilson, Gouv Morris
Delaware: Geo: Read, Gunning Bedford jun, John Dickinson, Richard Bassett, Jaco: Broom
Maryland: James McHenry, Dan of St Thos. Jenifer, Danl Carroll
Virginia: John Blair—, James Madison Jr.
North Carolina: Wm. Blount, Richd. Dobbs Spaight, Hu Williamson
South Carolina: J. Rutledge, Charles Cotesworth Pinckney, Charles Pinckney, Pierce Butler
Georgia: William Few, Abr Baldwin*

The Bill of Rights

Amendments 1–10 of the Constitution

The Conventions of a number of the States having, at the time of adopting the Constitution, expressed a desire, in order to prevent misconstruction or abuse of its powers, that further declaratory and restrictive clauses should be added, and as extending the ground of public confidence in the Government will best insure the beneficent ends of its institution; Resolved, by the Senate and House of Representatives of the United States of America, in Congress assembled, two-thirds of both Houses concurring, that the following articles be proposed to the Legislatures of the several States, as amendments to the Constitution of the United States; all or any of which articles, when ratified by three-fourths of the said Legislatures, to be valid to all intents and purposes as part of the said Constitution, namely:

Amendment I

Congress shall make no law respecting an establishment of religion, or prohibiting the free exercise thereof; or abridging the freedom of speech, or of the press; or the right of the people peaceably to assemble, and to petition the government for a redress of grievances.

Amendment II

A well regulated militia, being necessary to the security of a free state, the right of the people to keep and bear arms, shall not be infringed.

Amendment III

No soldier shall, in time of peace be quartered in any house, without the consent of the owner, nor in time of war, but in a manner to be prescribed by law.

Amendment IV

The right of the people to be secure in their persons, houses, papers, and effects, against unreasonable searches and seizures, shall not be violated, and no warrants shall issue, but upon probable cause, supported by oath or affirmation, and particularly describing the place to be searched, and the persons or things to be seized.

Amendment V

No person shall be held to answer for a capital, or otherwise infamous crime, unless on a presentment or indictment of a grand jury, except in cases arising in the land or naval forces, or in the militia, when in actual service in time of war or public danger; nor shall any person be subject for the same offense to be twice put in jeopardy of life or limb; nor shall be compelled in any criminal case to be a witness against himself, nor be deprived of life, liberty, or property, without due process of law; nor shall private property be taken for public use, without just compensation.

Amendment VI

In all criminal prosecutions, the accused shall enjoy the right to a speedy and public trial, by an impartial jury of the state and district wherein the crime shall have been committed, which district shall have been previously ascertained by law, and to be informed of the nature and cause of the accusation; to be confronted with the witnesses against him; to have compulsory process for obtaining witnesses in his favor, and to have the assistance of counsel for his defense.

Amendment VII

In suits at common law, where the value in controversy shall exceed twenty dollars, the right of trial by jury shall be preserved, and no fact tried by a jury, shall be otherwise reexamined in any court of the United States, than according to the rules of the common law.

Amendment VIII

Excessive bail shall not be required, nor excessive fines imposed, nor cruel and unusual punishments inflicted.

Amendment IX

The enumeration in the Constitution, of certain rights, shall not be construed to deny or disparage others retained by the people.

Amendment X

The powers not delegated to the United States by the Constitution, nor prohibited by it to the states, are reserved to the states respectively, or to the people.

Amendment XI

(1798)

The judicial power of the United States shall not be construed to extend to any suit in law or equity, commenced or prosecuted against one of the United States by citizens of another state, or by citizens or subjects of any foreign state.

Amendment XII

(1804)

The electors shall meet in their respective states and vote by ballot for President and Vice-President, one of whom, at least, shall not be an inhabitant of the same state with themselves; they shall name in their ballots the person voted for as President, and in distinct ballots the person voted for as Vice-President, and they shall make distinct lists of all persons voted for as President, and of all persons voted for as Vice-President, and of the number of votes for each, which lists they shall sign and certify, and transmit sealed to the seat of the government of the United States, directed to the President of the Senate;—The President of the Senate shall, in the presence of the Senate and House of Representatives, open all the certificates and the votes shall then be counted;—the person having the greatest number of votes for President, shall be the President, if such number be a majority of the whole number of electors appointed; and if no person have such majority, then from the persons having the highest numbers not exceeding three on the list of those voted for as President, the House of Representatives shall choose immediately, by ballot, the President. But in choosing the President, the votes shall be taken by states, the representation from each state having one vote; a quorum for this purpose shall consist of a member or members from two-thirds of the states, and a majority of all the states shall be necessary to a choice. And if the House of Representatives shall not choose a President whenever the right of choice shall devolve upon them, before the fourth day of March next following, then the Vice-President shall act as President, as in the case of the death or other constitutional disability of the President. The person having the greatest number of votes as Vice-President, shall be the Vice-President, if such number be a majority of the whole number of electors appointed, and if no person have a majority, then from the two highest numbers on the list, the Senate shall choose the Vice-President; a quorum for the purpose shall consist of two-thirds of the whole number of Senators, and a majority of the whole number shall be necessary to a choice. But no person constitutionally ineligible to the office of President shall be eligible to that of Vice-President of the United States.

Amendment XIII

(1865)

Section 1.   Neither slavery nor involuntary servitude, except as a punishment for crime whereof the party shall have been duly convicted, shall exist within the United States, or any place subject to their jurisdiction.

Section 2.   Congress shall have power to enforce this article by appropriate legislation.

Amendment XIV

(1868)

Section 1.　All persons born or naturalized in the United States, and subject to the jurisdiction thereof, are citizens of the United States and of the state wherein they reside. No state shall make or enforce any law which shall abridge the privileges or immunities of citizens of the United States; nor shall any state deprive any person of life, liberty, or property, without due process of law; nor deny to any person within its jurisdiction the equal protection of the laws.

Section 2.　Representatives shall be apportioned among the several states according to their respective numbers, counting the whole number of persons in each state, excluding Indians not taxed. But when the right to vote at any election for the choice of electors for President and Vice President of the United States, Representatives in Congress, the executive and judicial officers of a state, or the members of the legislature thereof, is denied to any of the male inhabitants of such state, being twenty-one years of age, and citizens of the United States, or in any way abridged, except for participation in rebellion, or other crime, the basis of representation therein shall be reduced in the proportion which the number of such male citizens shall bear to the whole number of male citizens twenty-one years of age in such state.

Section 3.　No person shall be a Senator or Representative in Congress, or elector of President and Vice President, or hold any office, civil or military, under the United States, or under any state, who, having previously taken an oath, as a member of Congress, or as an officer of the United States, or as a member of any state legislature, or as an executive or judicial officer of any state, to support the Constitution of the United States, shall have engaged in insurrection or rebellion against the same, or given aid or comfort to the enemies thereof. But Congress may by a vote of two-thirds of each House, remove such disability.

Section 4.　The validity of the public debt of the United States, authorized by law, including debts incurred for payment of pensions and bounties for services in suppressing insurrection or rebellion, shall not be questioned. But neither the United States nor any state shall assume or pay any debt or obligation incurred in aid of insurrection or rebellion against the United States, or any claim for the loss or emancipation of any slave; but all such debts, obligations and claims shall be held illegal and void.

Section 5.　The Congress shall have power to enforce, by appropriate legislation, the provisions of this article.

Amendment XV

(1870)

Section 1.　The right of citizens of the United States to vote shall not be denied or abridged by the United States or by any state on account of race, color, or previous condition of servitude.

Section 2.　The Congress shall have power to enforce this article by appropriate legislation.

Amendment XVI

(1913)

The Congress shall have power to lay and collect taxes on incomes, from whatever source derived, without apportionment among the several states, and without regard to any census of enumeration.

Amendment XVII

(1913)

The Senate of the United States shall be composed of two Senators from each state, elected by the people thereof, for six years; and each Senator shall have one vote. The electors in each state shall have the qualifications requisite for electors of the most numerous branch of the state legislatures.

When vacancies happen in the representation of any state in the Senate, the executive authority of such state shall issue writs of election to fill such vacancies: Provided, that the legislature of any state may empower the executive thereof to make temporary appointments until the people fill the vacancies by election as the legislature may direct.

This amendment shall not be so construed as to affect the election or term of any Senator chosen before it becomes valid as part of the Constitution.

Amendment XVIII

(1919)

Section 1.   After one year from the ratification of this article the manufacture, sale, or transportation of intoxicating liquors within, the importation thereof into, or the exportation thereof from the United States and all territory subject to the jurisdiction thereof for beverage purposes is hereby prohibited.

Section 2.   The Congress and the several states shall have concurrent power to enforce this article by appropriate legislation.

Section 3.   This article shall be inoperative unless it shall have been ratified as an amendment to the Constitution by the legislatures of the several states, as provided in the Constitution, within seven years from the date of the submission hereof to the states by the Congress.

Amendment XIX

(1920)

The right of citizens of the United States to vote shall not be denied or abridged by the United States or by any state on account of sex.

Congress shall have power to enforce this article by appropriate legislation.

Amendment XX

(1933)

Section 1. The terms of the President and Vice President shall end at noon on the 20th day of January, and the terms of Senators and Representatives at noon on the 3d day of January, of the years in which such terms would have ended if this article had not been ratified; and the terms of their successors shall then begin.

Section 2. The Congress shall assemble at least once in every year, and such meeting shall begin at noon on the 3d day of January, unless they shall by law appoint a different day.

Section 3. If, at the time fixed for the beginning of the term of the President, the President elect shall have died, the Vice President elect shall become President. If a President shall not have been chosen before the time fixed for the beginning of his term, or if the President elect shall have failed to qualify, then the Vice President elect shall act as President until a President shall have qualified; and the Congress may by law provide for the case wherein neither a President elect nor a Vice President elect shall have qualified, declaring who shall then act as President, or the manner in which one who is to act shall be selected, and such person shall act accordingly until a President or Vice President shall have qualified.

Section 4. The Congress may by law provide for the case of the death of any of the persons from whom the House of Representatives may choose a President whenever the right of choice shall have devolved upon them, and for the case of the death of any of the persons from whom the Senate may choose a Vice President whenever the right of choice shall have devolved upon them.

Section 5. Sections 1 and 2 shall take effect on the 15th day of October following the ratification of this article.

Section 6. This article shall be inoperative unless it shall have been ratified as an amendment to the Constitution by the legislatures of three-fourths of the several states within seven years from the date of its submission.

Amendment XXI

(1933)

Section 1. The eighteenth article of amendment to the Constitution of the United States is hereby repealed.

Section 2. The transportation or importation into any state, territory, or possession of the United States for delivery or use therein of intoxicating liquors, in violation of the laws thereof, is hereby prohibited.

Section 3.   This article shall be inoperative unless it shall have been ratified as an amendment to the Constitution by conventions in the several states, as provided in the Constitution, within seven years from the date of the submission hereof to the states by the Congress.

Amendment XXII

(1951)

Section 1.   No person shall be elected to the office of the President more than twice, and no person who has held the office of President, or acted as President, for more than two years of a term to which some other person was elected President shall be elected to the office of the President more than once. But this article shall not apply to any person holding the office of President when this article was proposed by the Congress, and shall not prevent any person who may be holding the office of President, or acting as President, during the term within which this article becomes operative from holding the office of President or acting as President during the remainder of such term.

Section 2.   This article shall be inoperative unless it shall have been ratified as an amendment to the Constitution by the legislatures of three-fourths of the several states within seven years from the date of its submission to the states by the Congress.

Amendment XXIII

(1961)

Section 1.   The District constituting the seat of government of the United States shall appoint in such manner as the Congress may direct:
     A number of electors of President and Vice President equal to the whole number of Senators and Representatives in Congress to which the District would be entitled if it were a state, but in no event more than the least populous state; they shall be in addition to those appointed by the states, but they shall be considered, for the purposes of the election of President and Vice President, to be electors appointed by a state; and they shall meet in the District and perform such duties as provided by the twelfth article of amendment.

Section 2.   The Congress shall have power to enforce this article by appropriate legislation.

Amendment XXIV

(1964)

Section 1.   The right of citizens of the United States to vote in any primary or other election for President or Vice President, for electors for President or Vice President, or for Senator or Representative in Congress, shall not be denied or abridged by the United States or any state by reason of failure to pay any poll tax or other tax.

Section 2.   The Congress shall have power to enforce this article by appropriate legislation.

Amendment XXV

(1967)

Section 1.   In case of the removal of the President from office or of his death or resignation, the Vice President shall become President.

Section 2.   Whenever there is a vacancy in the office of the Vice President, the President shall nominate a Vice President who shall take office upon confirmation by a majority vote of both Houses of Congress.

Section 3.   Whenever the President transmits to the President pro tempore of the Senate and the Speaker of the House of Representatives his written declaration that he is unable to discharge the powers and duties of his office, and until he transmits to them a written declaration to the contrary, such powers and duties shall be discharged by the Vice President as Acting President.

Section 4.   Whenever the Vice President and a majority of either the principal officers of the executive departments or of such other body as Congress may by law provide, transmit to the President pro tempore of the Senate and the Speaker of the House of Representatives their written declaration that the President is unable to discharge the powers and duties of his office, the Vice President shall immediately assume the powers and duties of the office as Acting President.

Thereafter, when the President transmits to the President pro tempore of the Senate and the Speaker of the House of Representatives his written declaration that no inability exists, he shall resume the powers and duties of his office unless the Vice President and a majority of either the principal officers of the executive department or of such other body as Congress may by law provide, transmit within four days to the President pro tempore of the Senate and the Speaker of the House of Representatives their written declaration that the President is unable to discharge the powers and duties of his office. Thereupon Congress shall decide the issue, assembling within forty-eight hours for that purpose if not in session. If the Congress, within twenty-one days after receipt of the latter written declaration, or, if Congress is not in session, within twenty-one days after Congress is required to assemble, determines by two-thirds vote of both Houses that the President is unable to discharge the powers and duties of his office, the Vice President shall continue to discharge the same as Acting President; otherwise, the President shall resume the powers and duties of his office.

Amendment XXVI

(1971)

Section 1.   The right of citizens of the United States, who are 18 years of age or older, to vote, shall not be denied or abridged by the United States or any state on account of age.

Section 2.   The Congress shall have the power to enforce this article by appropriate legislation.

Amendment XXVII

(1992)

No law varying the compensation for the services of the Senators and Representatives shall take effect until an election of Representatives shall have intervened.

Glossary

Act of Settlement of 1701   Placed the British monarchy under the power of the Parliament.

American chief executive   Known as the president. The president is directly elected by the people and is granted independent power and authority by the country's Constitution.

American Dream Restoration Act   A plank of the 1994 Republican Contract with America. It repealed the marriage tax penalty (married couples pay more in taxes than they would if they were single and had two incomes) and established a tax credit for children.

Back-benchers   Both government and opposition junior-ranking members of Parliament sit on the benches behind their respective leaders and, as such, have come to be known as back-benchers.

Bicameral legislature   A two-bodied legislature. The two chambers have historically been referred to as the upper and lower chambers or houses.

British Bill of Rights   Provided that the Parliament had authority over the monarch to raise taxes and pass laws. This bill specified that the monarch had the power neither to promulgate nor rescind a law.

British Constitution   The contemporary framework of British government has been established by a series of documents known collectively as the British Constitution. Not to be confused with the American Constitution, the so-called British Constitution is neither a single written document nor does it specify the component parts of government and the powers of each branch. It is perhaps better to think of it as a constitutional framework that has evolved over the past several hundred years and loosely directs political life in Britain.

British head of government   Refers to the prime minister.

British head of state   Refers to the monarch (king or queen).

British speaker   Chosen from the ranks of the representatives, the speaker performs an arbiter role.

Checks and balances   Occurs under a separation of powers institutional arrangement. It involves the checking and balancing of governmental power among and between the executive, legislative, and judicial branches of government.

Citizen Legislatures Act   A plank of the 1994 Republican Contract with America. It would limit the terms of both senators and representatives.

Co-habitation   This occurs under a semi-presidential system, also known as a dual-executive system, when the president is of a different party than the prime minister. In France, co-habitation first occurred from 1986 to 1988, when the Socialist President

François Mitterrand had to deal with a rightist Gaullist majority in the National Assembly, led by Prime Minister Jacques Chirac.

Common law   A source of the British constitutional framework, takes one of two forms: executive prerogative powers and the judicial interpretation of statute law.

Common Sense Legal Reforms Act   A plank of the 1994 Republican Contract with America that was designed to discourage litigation. It would limit punitive damages, institute "loser pays" rules, and limit product liability.

Convention   A source of the British Constitution. It typically embodies the terms of a resolution of a past generalized social and political crisis and, as such, carries authority.

Cross-benchers   Members of smaller parties or independent members of the British Parliament.

Democracy   May be defined, following political sociologist Joseph Schumpeter, as a political regime that meets at least the following three fundamental conditions. First, there must be broad and authentic competition among either individuals or organized political groups or political parties for all effective positions of power in the government, including the position of chief executive. Second, a high level of citizen participation, in which no major adult groups are excluded from the political process, is required. Finally, basic democratic civil and political liberties, such as the freedom of competition for political office, of assembly, of speech, and of free movement, must be guaranteed. If all three of these components are present in a political system, it may be considered to be a functioning democracy.

D'Hondt system   Invented by Victor d'Hondt of Belgium, the d'Hondt system, also referred to as the highest average system, is one of the most used versions of proportional representation. Under the rules of this system, political parties present a closed list of candidates to the voters. Voters are required to vote for one of these party lists and not for a particular candidate. Once all the votes are counted, the d'Hondt system weighs the amount of votes each party received on the basis of a formula to determine the highest average of votes cast per party. The precise calculations used to determine the allocation of legislative seats from the vote totals vary somewhat from country to country. Suffice it to say that, in general, the party with the highest average of votes cast places the most candidates from their list in the legislature, and conversely, the party with the lowest average places the fewest. Under this system it is safe to assume that those candidates at the top of each of the party's lists are elected and that those at the bottom of the lists do not receive a seat, unless the winning party has completely dominated the elections. In general, the d'Hondt method of allocating seats in a legislature tends to favor larger parties, and the countries that use it usually do not have more than three or four major parties.

Divided government   Occurs when there is an executive of a different party than the dominant party in the legislative branch.

Divine right of kings   A doctrine that held that the king's power and authority flowed to him directly and absolutely from God and that as God's custodian on earth the monarch should be given the same solemn respect and unquestioning obedience a person would offer to God.

Dual-Democratic legitimacy   Common to presidential systems. Both the executive and the legislature are elected by the people and enjoy separate bases of legitimacy.

Dual-executive or semi-presidential regime   One in which there is both a president and a prime minister.

Executive prerogative power   Technically belongs to the crown, although in practice it is utilized by the prime minister and the government.

External agreements   A number of recent international agreements that have had bearing upon the British Constitution.

Family Reinforcement Act   A plank of the 1994 Republican Contract with America. It provided tax breaks for families and the elderly, child support, and enforcement and penalties for child pornography.

Federalism   Invented by the Framers of the American Constitution, this system of inter-governmental relations is one in which powers are divided between the national and state governments. National legislatures under a federal system have more limited powers than in unitary systems because they have to contend with the legitimate authority and competing claims from state or local governments.

Filibuster   A legislative tool in the United States Senate. Senators can hold up legislation by simply talking and not relinquishing the floor so that a vote can be taken. In other words, they can simply talk a bill to death.

First-past-the-post   Also known as single-member district plurality voting system.

Fiscal Responsibility Act   A plank of the 1994 Republican Contract with America. This plank had two parts, both of which entailed amendments to the Constitution: the balanced-budget amendment and the line-item veto.

Front-benchers   The leadership of the government and of the opposition sit across from each other on the front benches in the House of Commons. As such, those in a leadership capacity are known as front-benchers.

Glorious Revolution of 1688   Resolved the religious question in Britain and constructed the monarchy on a new basis: William of Orange and his wife, Mary, owed their very position as the new British monarchs to Parliament.

Gridlock   May be defined as a stalemate in government over legislative priorities. Gridlock may function at many levels, including between the president and Congress, the president and one of the legislative houses, the Senate and the House, or between the two parties within Congress; it prevents Congress from moving on legislative programs.

Head of government   Is elected by the majority party in the legislature and is charged with effective national administration—given various labels, such as prime minister, premier, or chancellor.

Head of state   Is asked to carry out symbolic functions, such as representing the country at the Olympics or appearing in public during national holidays—known as king, emperor, or president.

House of Commons   The lower house of the British Parliament. It is a democratically elected body and controls all legislation in Parliament. At present, there are 651 members. Each member of Parliament, known as an M.P., is elected to represent a single-member constituency under a first-past-the-post electoral system. Parliamentary elections must be held no later than five years from the last ones.

House of Lords   The upper house in the British legislature. It is not a democratic body: None of its over 1,200 members have been elected to serve. As was the case in the eighteenth century, the House of Lords continues to be composed of the elite segments of British society. Today there are several ways to get into the House of Lords: The monarch may appoint you, if you have attained a prominent position in British society; you may have a birthright, if you are born into a noble family; or you may serve if you are part of the hierarchy of the Church of England. The House of Lords has very restricted powers but may play a constructive role as a debating society on the important issues of the day. It is possible for the government to appoint new members to the House of Lords as life peers.

Job Creation and Wage Enhancement Act   A plank of the 1994 Republican Contract with America. It gave incentives to small businesses, cut the capital gains tax, eliminated "unfunded mandates" (requiring states or businesses to engage in specified activities without reimbursing them).

Loyal opposition   A term from British history. It signifies that even if a political party may disagree with the policies of the majority party, it remains loyal to the crown and to the country.

Magna Carta of 1215   Predicated on the principle that Great Britain should be ruled by law, the Magna Carta placed express boundaries on the arbitrary power of the king.

Markup   In the United States Congress, "markup" sessions are when a bill is debated and amended by committee members in the Senate and in the House—members from both the majority and the minority party. Usually markup is itself open, with the press and public welcome to attend. Prior to committee consideration, subcommittees have often already completed a similar process to consider the same bill.

M.P.   A member of the British Parliament.

National Security Restoration Act   A plank of the 1994 Republican Contract with America. It prohibited foreign (UN) command of U.S. troops and the use of defense cuts to finance social programs, and it proposed developing an anti-ballistic missile system.

Parliamentary democracy   This stands in contrast to presidential democracy. Although there are several variations of this system in the world, the parliamentary system used in Great Britain is the world's most renowned form. Political scientist Arend Lijphart has referred to the British Parliamentary system as the majoritarian-confrontational system, and it is also known as the Westminster parliamentary model. This system provides for a close connection between the executive and legislative branches. Further, the British prime minister, who is the political executive, is also the head of the majority party in the House of Commons. The prime minister chooses a cabinet from members of the majority party in the legislature, and the cabinet is collectively responsible to the House of Commons. As long as the legislative majority is maintained, the prime minister can expect to have all of his or her party's legislation passed without any revisions from the opposition. The prime minister is responsible to Parliament, and must maintain the support of the governing party.

Personal Responsibility Act   A plank of the 1994 Republican Contract with America. It dealt with welfare reform, both giving more discretion to the states and providing restrictions on eligibility.

Policy window According to John Kingdon, a "policy window" opens up when politics, policy, and problems come together to create the right time for a particular piece of legislation to pass—that is, when a problem in society exists, and there is a proposal to solve that problem, and the political mood is right, legislation will be enacted. Otherwise, the legislation does not really have a chance. That is why large numbers of bills are proposed in Congress but only a very limited number ever make it to a floor vote, much less become enacted. Members of Congress are aware of the fleeting nature of these policy windows and rush to enact legislation when they feel a window has opened up.

Presidential democracy This is the system of government currently operating in the United States. It contains at least three main characteristics. First, a president must be elected by a form of direct popular election for a term of office usually ranging from four to eight years. Remember that this is a necessary but not a sufficient condition for a presidential regime. Even though a country may hold national and direct elections for president, that does not necessarily imply that the president has real power. Second, in a presidential system the chief executive may be neither appointed nor dismissed by a legislative vote—executive power derives from a popular mandate not from the legislative branch. Third, the president is in exclusive charge of the executive branch and faces no competition from senior policymakers or from cabinet officials

Presidential system A form of democratic government in which the executive branch is well-defined and partitioned from the legislative branch.

Prime minister Performs an executive function and directs the legislative branch in parliamentary systems.

Proportional representation system A voting system that disperses seats among the candidates in proportion to a candidate's party's share of the vote.

Question-time When government ministers in Great Britain, including the prime minister, are subjected to questions by members of parliament.

Representative assembly It is primarily charged with a law-making function, which we may define as the process of preparing, debating, passing, and implementing legislation. Its members consider and debate bills, which are proposals for legislative action. The discussion among legislators over bills are decided during legislative debate, which takes place on the floor of the legislature. It is known by a host of different designations, including Congress in the United States, the Parliament in Great Britain, the *Knesset* in Israel, the *Diet* in Japan, the *Dáil* in Ireland, the *Vouli* in Greece, the National Assembly in Portugal, and so on.

Rotten boroughs A corrupt system of representation in eighteenth- and nineteenth-century Britain that enabled a small group of rural electors to dominate parliamentary districts.

Senior Fairness Act A plank of the 1994 Republican Contract with America. This plank would raise the Social Security earnings limit (under which seniors who earn over a certain amount of money lose a percentage of their social security benefit) and also repeal the 1993 tax increases on Social Security benefits.

Separation of powers A political system in which the executive, legislative, and judicial powers are placed in separate institutions.

Single-member district plurality voting system There is only one winner per electoral district; a seat is allocated to the one candidate who has received the greatest number of votes.

Statute law   A basis of the British constitutional framework; it is made up of certain parliamentary acts that have defined the institutional relationship between and within the monarchy and the parliament, including the 1689 Bill of Rights and the 1911 and 1949 parliamentary acts, which centralized power in the House of Commons.

Stuart monarchs   Wanted to return Roman Catholicism to Great Britain against the wishes of the Parliament. The Stuarts hoped to follow the example of the absolute monarchs in continental Europe, particularly in France. At that time political modernization was occurring in France under the concept of the divine right of kings, which served to justify modern centralization with the traditional authority symbols of God.

Taking Back Our Streets Act   A Plank of the 1994 Republican Contract with America. It was also known as the anticrime package, which eventually was divided into several bills dealing with victim restitution, the exclusionary rule, prison construction, and law enforcement.

Tories   A political formation in eighteenth-century Britain. They were conservative and rural aristocrats, dominated Parliament in the early portion of the eighteenth century, and resisted dramatic change.

Unicameral legislature   A single-body legislature.

Unitary political system   May be defined as one in which the central government exercises authority over the regional or local governments—the national legislature faces no competing sources of power. This system in present in many countries, including Great Britain and France.

Virginia plan   Proposed at the American Constitutional Convention. It suggested the creation of a strong national government and established a bicameral legislature with representation based on population. In addition, the Virginia plan proposed that "a National Executive be instituted; to be chosen by the National Legislature." Several elements of the Virginia plan created controversy; most remember the plan for its reliance on population in determining representation. The Great Compromise (also known as the Connecticut compromise) took the bicameral legislature from the Virginia plan and gave the lower house popular representation. The compromise allowed for the upper house to have each state represented equally, as suggested by the New Jersey plan (although the New Jersey plan had proposed a unicameral, or one-house, legislature).

Vote of confidence   Under parliamentary rules, an administration is losing legislative support, there may be a formal motion for the government to face a vote of confidence. If the current government wins such a motion, it may emerge stronger than before; if it loses, it will be obliged to resign and/or call for new elections.

Westminster parliamentary model   Named for the county in which the British Parliament is located, it is the most renowned form of parliamentary government. This version of a parliamentary system is one in which the executive (prime minister) dominates the parliament, and there are no legal limitations on the actions of the legislature. This British-style parliamentary system accords legislation, and not fundamental law, sovereign status.

Whigs   A political formation in eighteenth-century Britain. They were the entrepreneurial elite, and believed in free trade.

Bibliography

Baaklini, Aldo I., and Helen Desfosses, eds. *Designs for Democratic Stability: Studies in Viable Constitutionalism.* Armonk, N.Y.: M. E. Sharpe, 1997.

Bagehot, Walter. *The English Constitution.* 1867. Reprint, London: Fontana, 1993.

Beck, Paul Allen, and Frank J. Sorauf. *Party Politics in America.* New York: HarperCollins, 1992.

Berns, Walter, ed. *After the People Vote: A Guide to the Electoral College.* Washington, D.C.: AEI Press, 1992.

Broder, David S. "Vote May Signal GOP Return as Dominant Party." *Washington Post,* 10 November 1994, sec. A, p. 1.

Cammisa, Anne Marie. *Governments as Interest Groups.* Westport, Conn.: Praeger, 1995.

_____. *Welfare Policy in American Politics.* Boulder. Colo.: Westview Press, 1997.

Campbell, Colin, Harvey Feigenbaum, Ronald Linden, and Helmut Norpoth. *Politics and Government in Europe Today.* Boston: Houghton Mifflin Company, 1995.

Cassata, Donna. "Republicans Bask in Success of Rousing Performance." *Congressional Quarterly Weekly Reports,* 8 April 1995.

Cloud, David S. "GOP, to Its Own Great Delight, Enacts House Rules Changes." *Congressional Quarterly Weekly Reports,* 7 January 1995.

_____. "House Speeds Pace on Contract." *Congressional Quarterly Weekly Reports,* 11 February 1995.

_____. "House GOP Shows a United Front In Crossing 'Contract' Divide." *Congressional Quarterly Weekly Reports,* 22 February 1995.

Conaghan, Catherine. "Loose Parties, Floating Politicians, and Institutional Stress: Presidentialism in Ecuador, 1979–1988." Paper presented at a conference held at Georgetown University in Washington, D.C., entitled "Presidential or Parliamentary Democracy: Does it Make a Difference: A Research Symposium on Stable Democracy" Organized by Juan Linz and Arturo Valenzuela, May 14–16, 1989.

Cooper, Kenneth J., and Helen Dewar. "100 Days Down, But Senate to Go for Most 'Contract' Items." *Washington Post,* sec. A, p. 6.

Constituição da República Portuguesa: As Três Versões Após 25 de Abril 1989/1982/1976. Lisbon: Porto Editora, 1990.

Corkill, David. "The Political System and the Consolidation of Democracy in Portugal." *Parliamentary Affairs* 46, No. 4 (1993): 517-532.

Curtis, Michael. *Introduction to Comparative Government.* 4th. ed. New York: Longman, 1997.

Dahl, Robert A. *Pluralist Democracy in the United States: Conflict and Consent.* Chicago: Rand McNally and Company, 1967.

_____. *Democracy in the United States: Promise and Performance.* 2d ed. Chicago: Rand McNally, 1972.

Davidson, Roger H. "The 104th Congress and Beyond." In *The 104th Congress: A Congressional Quarterly Reader,* eds. Roger H. Davidson and Walter J. Oleszek. Washington, D.C.: Congressional Quarterly Press, 1995.

Davidson, Roger H., and Walter J. Oleszek, eds. *The 104th Congress: A Congressional Quarterly Reader.* Washington, D.C.: Congressional Quarterly Press, 1995.

de Smith, S. A., and Rodney Brazier. *Constitutional and Administrative Law.* 7th ed. New York: Penguin, 1994.

Dicey, A. V. *Introduction to the Law of the Constitution.* 10th ed. London: Macmillan, 1959.

Dillon, C. Douglas. "The Challenge of Modern Government." In *Reforming American Government: The Bicentennial Papers of the Committee on the Constitutional System,* edited by Donald L. Robinson. Boulder, Colo.: Westview Press, 1985.

Dionne, E. J. *Why Americans Hate Politics.* New York: Touchstone, 1995.

Downs, Anthony. *An Economic Theory of Democracy.* New York: Harper and Row, 1957.

Epstein, Leon D. "Changing Perceptions of the British System." *Political Science Quarterly* 109, no. 3 (1994): 494.

Esberey, Joy. "What If There Were a Parliamentary System?" In *What if the American Political System Were Different?* eds. Herbert M. Levine et al. Armonk, N.Y.: M. E. Sharpe, Inc., 1992.

Freedman, Leonard. *Politics and Policy in Britain.* New York: Longman, 1996.

Frenzel, Bill. "The System is Self-Correcting." In *Back to Gridlock? Governance in the Clinton Years,* edited by James L. Sundquist. Washington: Brookings Institution, 1995.

Friedel, Frank. "The Election of 1932." In *History of American Presidential Elections, 1789–1968,* eds. Arthur M. Schlesinger and Fred L. Israel. New York: Chelsea House, 1971.

Gilbert, Charles E. "Shaping of Public Policy." In *The Revolution, the Constitution, and America's Third Century: The Bicentennial Conference on the United States Constitution.* Vol. 1, *Conference Papers.* Philadelphia: American Academy of Political and Social Science by the University of Pennsylvania Press, 1976.

Gillespie, Ed, and Bob Schellhas, eds. *Contract With America: The Bold Plan by Rep. Newt Gingrich, Rep. Dick Armey and the House Republicans to Change the Nation.* New York: Times Books, 1994.

Gitelson, Alan R., Robert L. Dudley, and Melvin J. Dubnick. *American Government.* 4th ed. Boston: Houghton Mifflin Company, 1995.

"GOP Agenda Hits Snag in Senate." *Congressional Quarterly Weekly Reports,* 4 February 1995.

"GOP Plan for a Marathon January." *Congressional Quarterly Weekly Reports,* 31 December 1994.

Graham, Lawrence S., et al. *Politics and Government: A Brief Introduction to the Politics of the United States, Great Britain, France, Germany, Russia, Eastern Europe, Japan, Mexico, and the Third World.* Chatham, N.J.: Chatham House Publishers, Inc., 1994.

Gruenwald, Juliana. "Shallow Tactics or Deep Issues: Fathoming the GOP Contract." *Congressional Quarterly Weekly Reports*, 19 November 1994.

Gugliotta, Guy. "Breakneck Pace Frazzles House." *Washington Post*, 7 March 1995, sec. p. 1.

Guinier, Lani. *The Tyranny of the Majority.* New York: Free Press, 1994.

Hook, Janet. "Republicans Step up to Power in Historic 40-Year Shift." *Congressional Quarterly Weekly Reports*, 7 January 1995.

———. "Republicans Vote in Lock Step, But Unity May Not Last Long." *Congressional Quarterly Weekly Reports*, 18 February 1995.

"House Speeds Pace on 'Contract'." *Congressional Quarterly Weekly Reports*, 11 February 1995.

Huntington, Samuel P. *Political Order in Changing Societies.* New Haven: Yale University Press, 1968.

Jennings, Ivor. *The British Constitution.* 5th ed. Cambridge: Cambridge University Press, 1966.

Jones, Charles O. *The Presidency in a Separated System.* Washington, D.C.: Brookings Institution, 1994.

Katz, Jeffrey L. "GOP Faces Unknown Terrain Without 'Contract' Map." *Congressional Quarterly Weekly Reports.* 8 April 1995.

Krauthammer, Charles. "Republican Mandate." *Washington Post*, 11 November 1994, sec. A, p. 31.

Langdon, Steve. "'Contract' Dwarfs Senate GOP Pledge." *Congressional Quarterly Weekly Reports*, 25 February 1995.

Laundy, Philip. *Parliaments in the Modern World.* Brookfield, Vt.: Gower Publications, 1989.

Leuchtenberg, William. *Franklin Roosevelt and the New Deal: 1932–1940.* New York: Harper and Row, 1963.

Levine, Herbert M. *Political Issues Debated: An Introduction to Politics.* 4th ed. Englewood Cliffs N.J.: Simon and Schuster, 1993.

Lijphart, Arend. *Democracies: Patterns of Majoritarian and Consensus Government in Twenty-one Countries.* New Haven: Yale University Press, 1984.

———, ed. *Parliamentary Versus Presidential Government.* New York: Oxford University Press, 1992.

Lijphart, Arend, and Bernard Grofman, eds. *Choosing An Electoral System: Issues and Alternatives.* New York: Praeger, 1984.

Linz, Juan J., and Arturo Valenzuela. *The Failure of Presidential Democracy: Comparative Perspectives.* Baltimore: The Johns Hopkins University Press, 1994.

Lipset, Seymour Martin. *American Exceptionalism: A Double-Edged Sword.* New York: Norton, 1996.

Lowi, Theodore. "Presidential Democracy in America: Toward the Homogenized Regime." *Political Science Quarterly* 109, no. 3, (1994): 401–438.

Madison, Jay and Alexander Hamilton. *The Federalist Papers,* ed. Clinton Rossiter. New York: New American Library, 1961.

Mahler, Gregory S. *Comparative Politics: An Institutional and Cross-National Approach.* 2d ed. Englewood Cliffs, N.J.: Prentice-Hall, 1995.

Manuel, Paul C. *The Challenges of Democratic Consolidation in Portugal, 1976–1991: Political, Economic and Military Issues.* Westport, Conn.: Praeger, 1996.

Marshall, Geoffrey. *Constitutional Theory.* Oxford: Clarendon Press, 1971.

Mayhew, David. *Divided We Govern.* New Haven: Yale University Press, 1991.

Mezey, Michael L. *Comparative Legislatures.* Durham, N.C.: Duke University Press, 1979.

Mill, John Stuart. *Considerations on Representative Government.* London: Parker, Son and Bourn, 1861.

Montesquieu, Baron de. *The Spirit of the Laws,* ed. and trans. Anne M. Cohler. New York: Cambridge University Press, 1989.

Morin, Richard. "Voters Repeat Their Simple Message About Government: Less Is Better." *Washington Post,* 13 November 1994, sec. A, p. 1.

Mowry, George E. "The Election of 1912." In *History of American Presidential Elections,* edited by Arthur M. Schlesinger and Fred L. Israel. vol. 3. New York: Chelsea House Publishers.

Norton, Philip. *The British Polity.* 3d ed. New York: Longman, 1994.

O'Connor, Karen, and Larry Sabato. *American Government: Continuity and Change.* Alternative edition Boston: Allen and Bacon, 1997.

Ornstein, Norman J., and Amy L. Schenkenberg. "The 1995 Congress: The First Hundred Days and Beyond." *Political Science Quarterly* 110, no. 2 (1995): 183–206.

Peele, Gillian. *Governing the UK.* 3d ed. Oxford: Blackwell, 1995.

Pole, J. R. *Political Representation in England and the Origins of the American Republic.* New York: St. Martin's Press, 1966.

Robinson, Donald L., ed. *Reforming American Government: The Bicentennial Papers of the Committee on the Constitutional System.* Boulder, Colo.: Westview Press, 1985.

Salant, Jonathan D. "Senate Altering Its Course in Favor of Contract." *Congressional Quarterly Weekly Reports,* 29 April 1995.

_____. "Gingrich Sounds Familiar Themes." *Congressional Quarterly Weekly Reports,* 8 April 1995.

Sartori, Giovanni. *Comparative Constitutional Engineering: An Inquiry into Structures, Incentives and Outcomes.* New York: New York University Press, 1994.

Schmitter, Philippe C., and Terry Lynn Karl. "What Democracy Is . . . and Is Not." *Journal of Democracy* 2 (Summer 1991): 75–89.

Segalman, Ralph. "The Protestant Ethic and Social Welfare." *Journal of Social Issues* 24 (1968):123–130.

Shugart, Matthew Soberg, and John M. Carey. *Presidents and Assemblies: Constitutional Design and Electoral Dynamics.* Cambridge, U.K.: Cambridge University Press, 1992.

Sundquist, James L. *Constitutional Reform and Effective Government.* rev. ed. Washington, D.C.: Brookings Institution, 1992.

_____, ed. *Beyond Gridlock? Prospects for Governance in the Clinton Years—And After.* Washington, D.C.: Brookings Institution, 1993.

_____, ed. *Back to Gridlock? Governance in the Clinton Years.* Washington: Brookings Institution, 1995.

Thompson, E. P. *The Making of the English Working Class.* New York: Pantheon Books, 1964.

Toner, Robin. "GOP Blitz of First 100 Days Now Brings Pivotal Second 100." *New York Times,* 9 April 1995, p. 18.

Weaver, R. Kent, and Bert A. Rockman. *Do Institutions Matter? Government Capabilities in the United States and Abroad.* Washington: Brookings Institution, 1993.

Wilson, Bradford P., and Peter W. Schramm, eds. *Separation of Powers and Good Government.* Lantham, Md.: Rowman and Littlefield Publishers, Inc., 1994.

Wilson, James Q. *American Government, Brief Edition.* 3d ed. Lexington, Mass.: D. C. Heath and Company, 1994.

Wilson, Woodrow. "Cabinet Government in the United States." *International Review* 7 (August 1879): 146–163.

_____. *The Politics of Woodrow Wilson,* ed. August Heckscher. New York: Harper and Brothers, 1956.

Index